D1093167

MA

Midnight Chicken

For my grandparents,
and for JMU: the Tall Man.

Midnight Chicken

(& Other Recipes Worth Living For)

Ella Risbridger

with illustrations by Elisa Cunningham

BLOOMSBURY PUBLISHING
LONDON · OXFORD · NEW YORK · NEW DELHI · SYDNEY

· · · · · · · · · · · ·· · · · · · · · · · · · · · · · · · · ·· ·

A note before you begin:
These recipes were first made in a fan oven (mine!). If you're using a
conventional oven, just raise the temperature by about 15°C – but all
ovens are different, and with most roasting and baking you'll learn as
you go along what your own particular oven is doing.

Things to Remember

This book has three main morals, and
I urge you to remember them and apply
them liberally.

1. Salt your pasta water.

2. If in doubt, butter.

3. Keep going.

There are lots of ways to start a story, but this one begins with a chicken. It was the first story I ever wrote about food, and it begins with a chicken in a cloth bag hanging on the back of a kitchen chair. It was dark outside, and I was lying on the hall floor, looking at the chicken through the door, and looking at the rust in the door hinges, and wondering if I was ever going to get up.

Perhaps, I thought, lying on the hall floor, I will just stay on the hall floor forever, and sink through the laminate, and into the concrete, and down into the earth.

But this is a hopeful story. It's the story of how I got up off the floor.

It's also the story of how to roast a chicken, and how to eat it. This is a story of eating things, which is, if you think about it, the story of being alive. More importantly, this is a story about wanting to be alive.

Eventually, the Tall Man came home, and he helped me up. 'Come on,' he said, and we went into the kitchen together, and I made this, late at night, and we ate it at midnight, with wine, and bread, and our fingers, sopping up the garlicky juices from the baking tray, sucking the bones.

So this story begins with a chicken. This is the best roast chicken you'll ever have, and I think it might just be perfect.

Midnight Chicken

For 2, with leftovers (for soup and salad and stock and sandwiches)

Chicken, mine was 1.6kg

Garlic, about 8 cloves, or as many as you can muster

Fresh chillies, 2 (or 3 if you don't have chilli salt)

Rosemary

Thyme

Mustard, the grainy sort

Pepper

Chilli salt (or sea salt)

Olive oil (perhaps)

Ginger, a nub about the size of your thumb

Honey, about a spoonful

Lemon, 1

• • • • • • ••• • •• • • •• •• • •• • •• • • •• •• •• •••• ••

Take your chicken out of its packaging. Sit it in a baking tray; let it breathe. Pre-heat the oven to 180°C.

Take half of your garlic and chop it finely, then put it in a cup. Using the kitchen scissors, chop the chillies and a few sprigs of rosemary and thyme. Put those in your cup, too. Add a hefty teaspoon of mustard, some pepper and chilli salt (just ordinary sea salt will do, if you haven't got chilli salt). You can add a little splash of olive oil too, if you like. I don't always, but sometimes I do, and then it is gold.

Peel and grate the ginger, if you have a little grater, or you can just chop it if not. It'll be okay. Add most of it to your cup with the garlic and herbs. Put the last pinch into a mug with the honey. Boil a kettle.

Take the lemon and cut it in half. Juice one half very briskly, and the other half a little less briskly. Pour most of the lemon juice into your cup of stuff. Stir.

Pour the rest of the lemon juice into the mug with the ginger and honey. Add hot water from the kettle. Stir. Drink. Steady yourself.

Go back to the chicken. Unloop the elastic string holding its little legs together, and shove four of the garlic cloves and the less-squeezed lemon half up its little bottom. Loop it up again, if you can, then rub the garlic-chilli-herbs-ginger-lemon mixture into the chicken skin; into the legs, the thighs, the wings.

Slide the chicken into the oven. Set the chicken timer (your timer might be different, but mine is shaped like a little red hen) for about 1 hour and 20 minutes, if your chicken weighs the same as mine, and your oven is temperamental in the same ways as mine. If your chicken is bigger or smaller than mine, give it about 30 minutes per 500g (there are very accurate roasting-time calculators online: I use the BBC Good Food one).

Have a glass of wine.

When the timer rings, check the chicken. I am very bad at testing when a chicken is done, but I know in theory – something about sticking a skewer into the meatiest bit of the leg and the juices running clear. If it's still pink, send it back to the oven. If not, turn the oven off and let the chicken sit for 5 minutes. Dip some bread in the juices.

Carve the chicken. Tear the meat from the bones. Drink. Eat. Feel glad.

I've begun this book with a chicken, but who knows where a story really begins? To understand the chicken, you'd have to understand what came before. It was like this: one summer, I woke and discovered that the world had become different. Or rather, I had become different. Between the world and me, something had changed. I had fallen out of love with the world. This was not the first time, but it was the worst, and I recognised it with the dull, sinking feeling of a person on a picnic looking at a cloudy horizon. A storm was coming.

I tried my best to head it off at the pass, before it could break (or before I could break). I took up yoga and Zen meditation. I gave up caffeine and bright screens. I went to work every day. But still it kept on, and I knew it was coming: the big It, the Something, the Storm.

Everything about the world was becoming overwhelming, and it was terrifying. Sounds were too loud, colours too bright, every decision a choose-your-own-adventure of potential catastrophe. People's faces moved too quickly, and their minds the same. I was dizzy and sick on crowded trains. I couldn't follow a conversation. I couldn't breathe. It was as if the whole world had been turned up, and I had been turned down: I was thinner *through*, like tracing paper, or wet newsprint. I was a ghost. I clung to things, hoping for some shape, for some pattern in me to emerge triumphant. But there was nothing, and so every day I came home from work and cried.

Summer became September. I quit my job, and cried more instead. Mostly I stayed in bed. And then, one wet day just after my twenty-first birthday, a Monday, I tried to step into the path of a number 25 bus, destination Oxford Circus.

A lot of people, cleverer and more learned than me, have written books about why people try to kill themselves. I prefer to think of the reasons I didn't.

An ambulance came and took me to the hospital, and I sat in the waiting room of the duty psychiatrist, and suddenly, for the first time in a long time, I thought of baking: of a pie. I don't remember very much about the hospital itself (the brain is clever about forgetting things it would hurt you to remember), but I remember the pie, and I remember the way I worked through each ingredient, step by step, and how, when the duty psychiatrist asked me why, I could only think of *shortcrust and soften the leeks in Irish butter until translucent and rub the butter into the flour and bind with milk*. In the end I said, *I don't know*, which is so often the only way to try and explain suicide.

And she gave me a large dose of Valium, told the Tall Man that she probably ought to keep me in for observation but that she thought I'd be better at home, and that she trusted him to keep me safe until they could make me an appointment with the emergency psychiatrist. They were talking, but I wasn't listening: instead I was thinking of pie.

And how I'd learned to make pastry with my grandmother, and how I wanted to cook again. It was like a little map: I will get through this, and I will cook something, and I will eat it, and I will be alive. I will be alive, and I will make something with my own two hands, and I will get through this. This too will pass – it has to – because there is a pie at the end. With a crisp crust and a soft yielding centre, and my first initial done in pastry on the top and brushed with golden egg, just like my grandmother used to do.

The Tall Man took me home, and that evening we made the pie I'd been thinking of: I told him, 'Like this, like this,' and he listened, and he followed. He did the chopping, and I rubbed butter into flour, and softened leeks in Irish butter, and we were I think both a little triumphant: I had not been hit by a number 25 bus going to Oxford Circus, and there were doctors on the case now, and perhaps I would stop crying all the time. And perhaps I would carry on cooking.

And I have. And it has changed my life.

This – this collection of recipes – is the story of how I learned to manage again: a kind of guidebook for falling back in love with the world, a how-to of weathering storms and finding your pattern and living, really living.

Someone once told me that she could tell a bitter cook by the bitterness in their food; and a sad one by the saltiness, from all the tears. She was a woman who could stop clocks just by thinking, but it doesn't take a witchy ancestress to tell when something is made with love, and for love. The recipes in this book have all been made and written with love. Proper love: you-are-not-alone, and let's-find-comfort-together-in-this-enormous-pan-of-paella sort of love. Practical, no-nonsense, honest love – that nevertheless makes time to hold your hand, and ask you how you are, and listen to the answer. That is what I wanted in that waiting room.

I didn't cook much as a little girl: I was a books girl, not a cook girl, and I spent most of my time lying flat along the rafters of the barn with my nose in *The Secret Garden* or *Five Children and It* or *The Railway Children*. I wasn't especially interested in cooking, and nor was my mother. My mother is many brilliant things – city lawyer, unlikely crofter, wrangler of holidays, houses, international moves, teenage girls, sheep and my father – but a devoted cook she is not. I did not learn to cook at my mother's knee. And nor did you, probably. People don't so much, now.

So I taught myself.

More accurately, the Tall Man taught me to cook, or more accurately still, he taught me that cooking was something I wanted to do. He taught me to enjoy cooking, to delight in cooking, to use cooking as a kind of framework of joy on which you could hang your day. A breakfast worth getting out of bed for. Second breakfast. Elevenses. Lunch. Afternoon tea. Dinner as glorious reward for a day done well, or consolation for a day gone badly, or just a plain old celebration of still being here, of having survived another one. Supper. A midnight feast.

I want to make this very clear, right now, at the beginning: I'm a cook, I suppose, but a slapdash, bottom-of-the-vegetable-drawer cook. A buy-first, Google-later, cover-it-in-Parmesan cook. A two-old-jugs-without-a-handle, measure-it-in-wine-glasses cook. I have, before now, grilled a loaf of bread instead of baking it. I have served dinner party guests sweet scrambled egg poured over shop-bought doughnuts. I have made parsnip soup so unbelievably, oppressively boozy it gave an instant hangover; flapjacks that needed to be soaked with bicarbonate of soda for twenty-four hours before they would even consider coming out of the tin; and a pork pie that coated everything in the kitchen with bubbling, liquid lard. This last was at two in the morning, and the Tall Man has never forgiven me for it.

I really, honestly *believe* in cooking like this. I believe in bad cooking and experimental cooking and giving-it-a-go cooking. And I believe that cooking like this is good for you, and I believe that if I can cook, you can cook. If I can cook, *anyone* can cook.

There is a German word, *kummerspeck*, that translates literally as 'grief-bacon', and metaphorically as 'comfort eating'. This book is the grief-bacon book, and grief, like bacon, can come in all shapes and sizes. No grief is too small not to warrant bacon, or something equally delicious. This is the book I wanted to read when I was sad, but it's also a book for good days: for reading sprawled out on a picnic rug under a broad umbrella, listening to the rain; for reading curled up by the radiator with a cat batting at the pages; for reading in the bath and on the bus; but, most of all, in the kitchen. I hope you get sauce and crumbs all over it; I hope you make notes on the pages and scribble bits out and spill an enormous blob of golden syrup on it, so that pages 54 and 55 are permanently glued together.

The cooking you will find here is the kind of cooking you can do a little bit drunk. It's the kind of cooking that is probably better if you've got a bottle of wine open, and a hunk of bread to dredge in the sauce. It's the kind of cooking that will forgive you if you forget about it for a little while, or if you're less than precise with your weighing and measuring. It's the kind of cooking that's there for you, when you come home pink-nosed from walking. It's the kind of cooking that makes everything feel okay. It's the kind of cooking that saved my life.

In the Kitchen

I f you have bought a cookbook before, you will have seen the endless lists of things that proper cooks want you to have before you can make their food. If you are poor, and you have a small kitchen, this makes cooking seem daunting, and difficult, and something not meant for you. This is nonsense. Cooking is for you. Just as it was for me: I began cooking when I was a student, and carried on cooking as a freelance writer, and all of it in the tiniest flat in the world.

I can't tell you how your own kitchen ought to be furnished to cook: all I can do is to tell you how mine goes. I have absolutely started from scratch, on a student budget – and, to be frank, a writer's budget doesn't go much further. I don't have any space, either. Everything in these lists is something I use, and either can be had for very little, or is worth saving up for.

You can make a perfectly delicious dinner – lots of perfectly delicious dinners – with only the things that follow. For most of the recipes in this book, you do not need anything else.

In the Cupboard, In the Drawer

These are the first things I bought, and the things I absolutely couldn't do without.

- **A big knife**, like a cleaver. Mine is from a Chinese supermarket, and I use it for dicing, slicing, chopping, partitioning and serving – if you get a big enough cleaver, and you have steady hands, you can use it to serve things like lasagne, or pie.

- **A little knife**. Just an ordinary, sharp, short-bladed kitchen knife. This is for peeling, paring, coring, skinning, and the fine details, like cutting your initials out of pastry, or shattering caramel. And opening packets that don't want to be opened.

- **A chopping board**. If you cook meat or fish, don't get a wooden one, even though they are beautiful. Get a plastic one, preferably with a chopping surface on both sides, and with a biro mark 'R' (for raw meat or fish) on one side, and 'C' (for cooked meat or fish and vegetables) on the other. Ideally, you'd have three chopping boards: one for raw meat or fish, another for cooked, and the third one for fruit and vegetables.

- **A wok**. My non-stick wok is the most useful thing in my whole kitchen, because it is so versatile: part frying pan, part saucepan. You can steam vegetables in it, and fry garlic in it, and make a bolognese sauce in it. If you need to, you can even use it to boil pasta, poach a (little) chicken, or make a caramel. If you can afford only one pan, get a wok. With a lid that fits properly.

- **A frying pan**, with a lid. Or alternatively one that fits under the wok lid. This is mostly for rice, in my kitchen (1:2 rice to stock, cover tightly, low heat, 14 minutes). But you can, of course, use it for frying eggs and other things as well (an egg fried under a lid is the best kind of fried egg – see page 59).

- **Foil**. If you can't get a wok with a lid, you need foil. If you plan to eat leftovers, you need foil. Foil is better than cling film, because you can put it in the oven: a roasting tin covered with foil does for a casserole, whereas cling film at 180°C tends to the unpleasant (of course I have done this – need you ask?).

- **A digital thermometer**. *Please* get a digital meat thermometer. I cannot stress how much I love mine. It solved all of my major anxieties about cooking meat. You don't have to judge if the juices are clear, or if your oven is the same 180°C the recipe-writer's was: you just Google the temperature the meat needs to reach, then stick your thermometer in, and if it's safe, it's safe, and you don't have to worry. (Do not, however, stick your thermometer in the washing-up bowl: I have done so three times and it's getting expensive. Just wash the prong bit as soon as you've used it.)

- **A roasting tin**. Find the right roasting tin, and it will be your friend for life. If my flat were on fire, I would take my favourite tin: old, blackened, battered, and entirely perfect for brownies, blondies, crumbles, pies, casseroles, lasagne, roast chicken, roast anything, baked anything. My tin is so ancient that the measurements are written only in inches (12 inches long, 8 inches wide, 2 inches deep) and when I say 'tin' in this book I nearly always mean a tin of this size: about 30cm by 20cm, and 5cm deep.

- **A really big spoon**. Preferably silicone or similar, so you can use it to stir things and scrape things out of your wok or roasting tin, as well as for its usual purpose of spooning. With the really big spoon and the cleaver, you're golden for serving implements.

- **Digital scales**. If you are not a confident cook, a pair of digital scales is invaluable. If you have digital scales, you can follow any recipe and, broadly speaking, it will turn out all right. Even if you are a confident cook, you'll want scales for baking. (Estimating baking is dangerous work; I know only one woman who can do it, and I suspect her of being a witch.)

- **A big bowl**. For mixing things, serving things and storing things. Technically, I suppose you could do all this in the wok, but even in this minimalist kitchen-universe, I think that might be asking a bit much.

- **Muslin cloths**. Bear with me here. I know it seems odd, but a pack of muslin squares, the sort people use to swaddle babies and mop up at feeding time, comes in really, really handy. You can use them to dry up. You can use them to wash up. You can use them to wrap food if you're out of foil, and you can use them as emergency napkins. You can use them to strain stock, to drain vegetables and tiny pasta shapes – and for big, mad, ambitious projects like making cheese (easier, in the event, than it sounds). You can cover bread dough with muslin while it proves; you can use it to make an impromptu steamer; you can even use it to mop up an infant, should it come to that. You can use muslin cloths for so many things, and I urge you to buy an enormous pack of them.

If you are just starting to cook, or you haven't cooked a lot before, this is all you really need. This, and the usual eating things: knives, forks, spoons, teaspoons, a couple of glasses, a couple of mugs, a couple of bowls and a couple of plates. You can measure with a teaspoon or tablespoon, crush with your big spoon, slice and spread with butter knives, whisk with a fork. Bowls and mugs can double as extra storage too.

Don't buy anything else until you know whether cooking is something you like to do, and something you want to do more of – and, more to the point, until you know the way you cook.

You won't know what you need in a kitchen until you've done a bit of cooking in it: I rely heavily, for instance, on a pestle and mortar, because I crush a lot of spices. Your friend might want a rolling pin, because she makes a lot of pastry or pasta by hand, but you might rejoice in being a gloriously lazy cook, and buy yours from the shops.

> *Until you know what kind of cook you are,*
> *don't rush out and buy a lot of stuff.*

I suspect, however, that if you find you enjoy cooking and do it often, you might need – or want – some or all of the things below. They will make your life easier.

- **Pestle and mortar**. This means that you can buy whole spices, which are simultaneously cheaper and nicer, and it's intensely meditative, just sitting, grinding away. Plus grinding whole spices makes the kitchen smell fantastic.

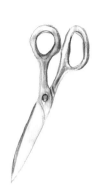

- **Scissors**. Lord love a pair of good kitchen scissors. The Tall Man swears by poultry shears: this tells you everything you need to know about the differences in the way we cook.

- **A cast-iron skillet**, like a frying pan but solid and heavy and, once you season it properly (oil; hot oven; time; Google), utterly non-stick. Like the frying pan your grandmother might have had, were your grandmother in *Little House on the Prairie*. Mine was a gift from an American friend, and I love it. I use it all the time – for omelettes, vegetables, pies and brownies – and because it can go in the oven, it is flawless.

- **A hand blender** is exceptionally useful for soups and purées, but with patience, you could also press it into service for hummus, dips, sauces and anything else you needed blending. I also use my hand blender to make oat flour, because oats are cheap, and oat flour, which I love, is not. An absolutely enormous caveat: I almost took the top joint of my index finger off with a hand blender. (The irony is not lost on me.) Hand blenders may look simple and unthreatening, but the blades are much easier to accidentally grab, and much closer to your vulnerable little fingers. It is more than a year since my finger was stitched back together, and it still aches when it rains, and sticks out at an unorthodox angle.

- **A saucepan with a well-fitting lid**. You know all the stuff you were doing in the wok? You can do some of it in this, thus saving on decanting. You can, for example (luxury of luxuries), boil pasta while you make a sauce. You can cook meals with more than two component parts. You can warm milk, and steep things, and melt butter. You can be more efficient, and therefore enjoy it all a bit more – although it does add to the washing up. (Do not be swayed by milk pans and beautiful copper sets. Buy one sensible, non-stick saucepan with a pouring spout on each side and a lid that fits – preferably a lid with little colander bits that align with the pouring spouts.)

- **A cast-iron casserole dish** that can go in the oven – mine is oval-shaped, about 30cm long and 25cm across at its widest point. Great for casseroles. Obviously. But also brilliant for bread, pot pies and other fun baking experiments.

- **Measuring spoons**. Mine were free with an Ocado shop, and although I never would have bought them, I confess I use them all the time.

- **Silicone spatula**. I hate to admit it, but this does make serving a lot easier than balancing things between a big spoon and a big cleaver. It's also a godsend for omelettes.

- **Silicone tongs**. I use these, mainly, for meat: browning chicken, turning sausages, lifting bacon out of the pan before it chars to nothing.

I have two other kinds of blender, besides the hand blender, and I use both of them regularly. They are a KitchenAid stand mixer, which was a twenty-first birthday present, and a big old food processor. You absolutely don't need these, though. I'll generally tell you what kind of blender I use for a particular recipe because that's what's easiest, but you can mostly muddle through with whatever kind you have.

In the Pantry

In my dreams, I have a pantry. My friend Caroline says that every woman has a dream pantry, even if they don't cook, because of reading historical novels. This may or may not be true; in any case, I do. It has slate shelves, my dream pantry, and jars of preserved plums. It has many sorts of jam, and many jars. A hundred kinds of flour, and things put away for the winter. It has plaits of onions, and it has Farrow & Ball walls. (In my dreams, everything is Farrow & Ball.)

As it stands, however, what I have is several small kitchen cupboards, two windowsills where things grow, and a very forgiving bookshelf for my cookbooks. This is what I keep there:

- **Olive oil**. My favourite is a fancy Palestinian kind called Equal Exchange, but for God's sake don't let's talk politics at dinner. (I'm really fond, you'll notice in the recipes, of using two kinds of fat: butter adds flavour, and oil stops the butter from burning, as well as adding its own flavour.)

- **Balsamic vinegar**. I used to think that more expensive was better, but really I think I was just being pretentious. I like balsamic better than other kinds of vinegar, and although this may be a horrifying admission in a cookery writer, it turns out I can't tell the difference between brands.

- Really good **sea salt**, like Maldon: I can't pass the salt pig without licking a finger and dipping it in. Smoked salt, chilli salt and roasted garlic salt are great too.

- **Chilli flakes**. Mine come in an enormous sack from the Bangladeshi supermarket downstairs, because Asian grocery shops tend to be a good place to get spices at a fair price, but you should be able to find these in most supermarkets.

- I have recently been convinced of the importance of **black pepper**, freshly ground with a pestle and mortar, and in enormous quantities. Otherwise, one of those little grinders is fine – just please don't use pre-ground because it tastes like old dust.

- **Dried mushrooms** are great. I tend to keep a jar of dried shiitakes for Asian cooking, and a jar of porcini for more European flavours, but my secret joy is a pot of dried mushroom powder called Shake O'Cini, which is essentially umami dust. It's wonderful.

- I have seventeen kinds of **flour**, which is excessive. Start with **plain**, and buy others as you need them.

- I have a similar range of sugars, and generally use **soft brown**.

- I love **golden syrup**.

- **Coconut milk**, for luscious soups and curries.

- **Fish sauce** is a very quick way to make something taste pleasingly umami – and with a chicken **stock pot** or **cube**, it makes a totally acceptable Thai-style broth.

- **Oats** are good for porridge (of course), and I also blitz them to make oat flour.

- I could eat Maille **mustard** with a spoon. Not even a teaspoon. An ordinary spoon.

- You can buy **breadcrumbs** in packets – Japanese **panko** are good for coating. Or you can just chuck old heels of bread into the food processor, and pulse until you have fine crumbs. I really love to do this with old rye bread: so dark it's almost sweet.

- You should probably have **tinned tomatoes**, **butter beans** and **chickpeas** (KTC brand are good, cheap and very easy to shell).

- My favourite things in the whole world are tiny **pasta stars**, and tiny pasta letters. I also keep in some kind of long pasta (linguine, spaghetti, pappardelle) and some kind of short pasta (penne, that sort of thing) for almost all pasta dishes, and **dried egg noodles** for soups, curries and stir-fries.

- **Pomegranate molasses** really is a lot of fun. And it makes raw kale edible – better than edible.

- **Risotto rice**. Carnaroli is best, the Tall Man says confidently, but you can, at a pinch, make a decent risotto with basmati rice, if you stir like billy-o and throw in absolutely lashings of cheese and a bit of cream.

- **Basmati rice**. I like brown myself.

- Don't rush out and buy a lot of extravagant **spices** straight away: if you buy them as they come up in your cooking, you'll end up with a pretty solid store of jars you actually *use*. In my house, that usually means nutmeg, chilli flakes, cloves, cardamom pods, fennel seeds, cumin seeds, coriander seeds and cinnamon sticks. I tend to keep star anise in too, mostly because it's so lovely to look at. If this seems like a lot, on the other hand, you can just buy a bag of garam masala, which has the incredible advantage of being both ready-mixed and 'authentic', and therefore never feels like cheating.

In the Ice House, Fridge & Freezer

Here's everything I'd keep in the ice house (if I had one) – and that I keep in my fridge or freezer instead:

- Buy the very best eggs you can, because goodness knows sad chickens lay sad eggs. I would rather buy no meat at all and buy brilliant eggs. I like **Burford Brown eggs**, because the yolks are like country yolks: fat and orange and silky smooth.

- Keep **pancetta** in, if you eat meat. It's good because it goes in everything, and makes everything meaty, and is miles cheaper than, you know, making the whole thing out of meat.

- I like to have **chorizo** in too, for much the same reason. It can be difficult to eat meat ethically without spending a great deal of money, but the way I get round this is by eating primarily vegetables and using meat as a flavouring. So when I cook with meat, mostly it's as stock (made from bones, see page 278) or a handful of cured meat, and chorizo is great for this, because you get a lot of bang for your buck.

- I promise you that **anchovies** are delicious, whatever you've heard – and if you like Parmesan, or salt, or umami flavours, I can teach you to like anchovies.

- Roasted **red peppers**, the kind that come packed in oil, are a very good way to get some vegetables into you if you are too fretty to leave the house.

- If you keep in **onions**, **celery** and **carrots**, you can finely dice and soften them in butter and/or oil to make a mirepoix as a flavour base for soups, pasta sauces and casseroles, and that is worth an enormous amount. Apparently, my first proper-length sentence was against celery ('No thanks, Mum, it's wood'), but I've come round in the decades since.

- When I see **vegetables** going cheap, especially anything pre-chopped, I buy them and put them in the freezer for difficult days.

I am a fan of **pre-chopped butternut squash** and **sweet potato** and **trimmed Tenderstem broccoli**.

- **Frozen peas** go well in nearly everything. Whenever the Tall Man is out I eat a mixing bowl of peas with butter and salt, just as a starter.

- **Parmesan** is my best friend. Don't ever throw away the rind; it's useful for making everything taste more umami. Be very careful with supermarket Parmesans, which seem to vary wildly in quality – look for those little white lactic acid crystals, which are the telltale sign of properly aged cheese.

- Buy **really good butter**. I mean really, really good butter, and just like in *Rooftoppers*, spread it 'with proper opinions, so you can see the toothmarks when you bite it'. (I might have misquoted that, but it's a very good book, and I am very sorry to Katherine Rundell for misquoting it here, and I hope she forgives me.)

- **Greek yoghurt** for dolloping onto crumble, making bread, or just for breakfast. Get full-fat, because otherwise what's the point? A life where I buy skimmed yoghurt is no life for me.

- **Apples** are good.

- Fresh **red chillies**, finely chopped with garlic and lemon zest, then stirred through freshly cooked pasta with a splash of olive oil make the most incredible pasta dish ever (see page 156).

- I always have a **lemon** or a **lime** on hand, or rotting gently in the bottom of the fridge. Use it anyway; it'll be okay.

- Buy **garlic**, the fattest bulbs you can find.

- Fresh **ginger** seems to keep almost forever, and you can peel it with a teaspoon (rub the back of the spoon vigorously over the skin, and it will come right away).

Blue Soup: What To Do When It All Goes Wrong

Things go wrong. They do – things go wrong for every cook, no matter how talented or dedicated, or how expensive their ingredients. When this happens to you, as it undoubtedly will, do not panic. Things can almost always be saved. That's why I've put this here, at the front. You're not alone, and this is not ruined, and the evening can be saved.

- Can you salvage it with some more fat, like butter, cream, olive oil, grated Parmesan?

- Can you salvage it with some more flavour, like lime juice, lemon juice, chilli?

- Salt and pepper – you would be amazed at how much difference these can make to a bland sort of dinner.

- Another tin of tomatoes, or a couple of chopped potatoes, will help to absorb excess salt.

- An egg yolk, whisked with a tablespoon of whatever sauce/stock you were using as a base, and then whisked slowly into the rest of it, will generally save a split sauce.

- Chuck it in the bin. Nobody you like enough to have to your house will judge you a whisker: these things happen. If you flick to the 'Storecupboard Suppers & Midnight Feasts' chapter, you'll find half a dozen recipes that will do for a dinner party, especially if you can toss a packet of prawns into the Uplifting Chilli & Lemon Spaghetti on page 156. Other options that are easy to do quickly with fairly ordinary ingredients include Goat's Cheese Puff with Salsa (see page 169); Carbonara, for Caroline (see page 151); Double Soss, Egg & Chips (see page 59); and Marital Harmony Sausage Pasta (see page 222).

- You can always go out to a café with your coat over your nightie, like at the end of *The Tiger Who Came to Tea* (one of the finest books about eating that's ever been written). Or you can order a takeaway. Nobody will care. You'll laugh a lot, and drink another bottle of wine, and it'll all be okay.

Breakfasts

I always start with a cup of tea. Writing this down it feels simultaneously absurdly English, and also not at all English, to have a proper cup of tea in the morning. Yorkshire, with a splash of milk and a teaspoon of sugar (brewed in the cup, milk and sugar and the teabag waiting for the kettle to boil), or Earl Grey with a brief twist-and-pinch of lemon. Lady Grey, Lapsang Souchong, green, red. Begin with a big mug of tea.

Or maybe you'd rather have coffee. Three spoonfuls of ground beans in the bottom of the cafetière, water just off boiling, and the bold *crema* that emerges when you press the plunger down, all glass and silver and daringly continental. I take mine black, first thing. Black, and back to bed – and perhaps that's a good rule, for the morning: however you begin, take it back to bed. I set the alarm ten minutes earlier just for this. Some people meditate; I make to-do lists in bed with a mug of something hot. Propped up against the pillows, cup in one hand, pen in the other, contemplating the day ahead: it's sort of like a battle plan.

When I was a little girl, every day I used to tell my mum: this is my Big Plan, and this is my Little Plan. I still do this, and I always begin both plans with breakfast. Partly because that way the to-do list gets off to a good start, and partly because breakfast is important. Old wives and young nutritionists are united on this one: eat breakfast, and eat breakfast well. Breakfast like a king, the old saying goes. And I do. So should you. A small space carved out at the very beginning of the day just for you – it makes everything else smoother, tidier, easier.

And something delicious, too: breakfast foods are the best foods. If I knew when I was going to die (the way witches are supposed to), I'd make my last supper a last breakfast. I am never bored of breakfast. There's so much to it, for one thing: everything from Coco Pops to bagels to eggs, spilling half-molten yellow yolk onto thick toast or a white plate. Eggs poached to go with salmon, scrambled with chives, or soft-boiled with soldiers. Fresh bread, or pikelets, with a thick pat of salted butter melting seductively into the little dimples. Oatcakes – not the dry, hard Scottish kind, but the soft, pliable Staffordshire kind, wrapped around rough, salty, melting Cheddar and fat-cut bacon.

Bacon sandwiches, with red sauce, never brown, and sausage sandwiches with brown sauce, never red. A fry-up in a greasy spoon, the indefinable and perfect taste of a cheap chipolata and a slice of Mother's Pride done in the fat. Beans, always Heinz. Fat mushrooms, done only in their own juices. Chips. Drop scones cooked straight on the hot plate of an AGA, then stacked high with maple syrup and crisp bacon, or sandwiched with butterscotch sauce and whipped cream. The cream on top of the milk, spooned off for porridge, proper porridge with brown sugar or gloriously metallic golden syrup from the shining green tin with the poor dead lion printed on it. Cafetières, and stovetop espresso pots with scalding-hot handles, and coffee served French-style in a bowl, the steam rising between your cupped hands.

Tea. Marmite. Raspberry jam. Cornflakes, Frosties, croissants. Greek yoghurt, with pale clear-gold honey drizzled over the top. Fresh orange juice, the kind so fresh it has a few stray pips. Brick Lane bagels, or better still, bagels from my friend Fiona's kitchen, eaten sitting on the floor, with the dog, Widget, begging for scraps: split straight through their glazed outside to their doughy middle and packed with soft cured salmon and chalky-white cream cheese and the blackest of black pepper. Shakshuka. Avocado, perfectly ripe. Mackerel. Kedgeree. Kippers. Quail's eggs. I love it all. I even love 'green juices'. I love, love, love breakfast.

I have pared down my favourite breakfasts to those that follow. Some are for hot days, and some are for cold days; some are for weekends, and some for weekdays; some are very quick (porridge, drop scones, smoothies) and some take a bit more energy (bagels, pikelets). None of them are complicated, because breakfast shouldn't ever be a complicated meal, but all of them will make your days – even your glum days, your grim days, your grey days – a little bit fancy, a little bit special and a little bit better.

Proper Oatcakes

Let me take you home. Or somewhere that feels like home, anyway. I'm pretty flexible, these days, on what that word 'home' means. If it's where the heart is, mine is everywhere, and I seem to have left it behind in half a dozen places by now. The older I get, the more homes I have, and this is one of the oldest: my grandparents' old pink house in Staffordshire, where the moorlands roll away green and sinuous from their kitchen window, the place where I am the most myself.

And we'll make oatcakes. Proper ones, I mean. A proper oatcake is like a pancake made with fine oatmeal; it has more flavour than regular pancakes, it's lacy-edged and stippled all over, and can be rolled up like a fat cigar full of oozing molten cheese. It's a practical food, like a Cornish pasty, for the pottery workers and their hands of clay. A working breakfast.

We used to bring them back with us from Staffordshire, packed in ice, two or even three dozen, and eke them out. The feeling of eating the last oatcake has stuck with me: a funny mix of joy and salt and homesickness, and sharp cheese, and knowing how far I was from an oatcake shop, and my grandparents, and the green-grey moorland.

There's no landscape like the Staffordshire moorlands (they aren't moors; that's important). On the edge of a national park, but not nearly so beloved, the earth dips and swoops in lazy curves that seem almost-but-not-quite like somewhere you've been before. I wasn't born there, and didn't grow up there, and yet some part of me   some mining ancestor deep in the bone – always knows: this is where the bones come from. This is a kind of home.

And oatcakes turn out to be pretty simple to make. It's really only a question of combining dry ingredients and wet, with a brief pause in the middle to activate the yeast.

I often make a stack of oatcakes the day before, keeping them in the fridge overnight and then quickly heating them up in a dry frying pan in the morning. If you don't want to eat them all at once, you can freeze your oatcakes between sheets of baking paper and re-heat them from frozen.

Here we go... ⟶

Makes about 10 oatcakes

225g rolled oats

200g strong bread flour
  (*I like a mix of wholemeal
  and white*)

1/2 tsp fine salt

450ml milk

450ml hot (not boiling) water

4g (about 1 tsp) instant yeast

1 tsp sugar

Butter or oil, for frying (if your
  frying pan isn't non-stick)

· · · · · · · · · ·ˑ · · · · · · · · · · · · ·ˑ · · · · · ·

Before you begin, blitz your oats to break them down into oatmeal:
you can do this in a blender for a count of 30 seconds, or in a bowl
using a hand blender. You're looking for a texture somewhere
between very fine breadcrumbs and wholemeal flour, if that
makes sense.

Tip the blitzed oats and the flour into a biggish bowl, then stir
in the salt.

Mix together the milk and hot water. It needs to be about blood
temperature: if it doesn't feel notably cold or hot against your
inside wrist, you're good to go. (I say don't use boiling water
because it will take longer to come down to blood heat, which
is frustrating.)

Measure the yeast and sugar into a smaller bowl, then add
1 tablespoon of the warm milk and water. Stir to dissolve –
it will smell properly yeasty – then leave it for 10 minutes to
activate the yeast. (This is what gives the oatcakes their gorgeous
bubbly texture, but don't worry if the yeast mixture doesn't go
very frothy; silky is good too.)

Add the yeast mixture, and the rest of the warm milk and water,
to the flours. Whisk until everything is incorporated into a batter.
Cover the lot with a clean tea towel, and sit it in a warm place for
an hour or so. (Mine goes under the table, by the space-heater,
covered with two big blankets.)

After the time is up, find a smallish, heavyish frying pan. Non-
stick is best, but if yours isn't just add a bit of butter or oil. Put a
plate by the hob with a piece of kitchen paper on it, and keep the
roll handy. Set the pan over a medium heat and wait until it has

come up to temperature. Hold your hand about 10cm above the pan: can you feel heat? Fab, let's go. Spoon 2 tablespoons of batter into the frying pan. Using a spatula if you need to, spread the batter over the base of the pan to coat it as thinly as possible.

Give your oatcake 2 minutes on the first side as it froths and bubbles; when it's dry on top (and so cooked through), flip it over with a spatula and give it 2 minutes on the second side. Flip it out onto the plate; set a piece of kitchen paper on top of it. Your first oatcake will probably not be perfect. Try not to worry about it. By the time you've done three or four you'll feel like a natural.

Repeat until you have no more batter left, and a stack of thin, soft, golden oatcakes.

When you're ready, heat each oatcake through in a dry frying pan, then spread with butter and Marmite, roll up, slice across and eat.

That's what I do most of the time.

Weekend Oatcakes

But for weekends? For weekends this is what I do: while the oatcake batter is resting, I grate some cheese – strong Cheddar, for preference – and slice some mushrooms. About half an hour before I start making the oatcakes, I put some slices of bacon into a 180°C oven to cook for about 15 minutes or until it's done the way I like it. I gently fry the mushrooms in a non-stick pan (I don't use butter or oil here; just the mushrooms, to really intensify the flavour), for about 15 minutes too, over a very low heat.

As each oatcake changes from batter to breakfast, I scatter over a good pinch of grated cheese, add a slice of bacon and some of the mushrooms, and then fold it in half. Using a spatula, I slide it out of the pan, and onto a baking sheet. When I have twice as many oatcakes (folded and full) as breakfasters I bake them at 180°C for about 10 minutes, until the cheese is melted and the oatcakes are almost crisp. I serve these on warm plates with a mug of tea, and I feel, always, as if I am at home – wherever I am in the world.

Drop Scones with Butterscotch Sauce

We are always swapping recipes by email, my grandmother, my mother, my sisters and I – and breakfasts, it turns out, belong to my mother and my grandmother and all the way back up.

'It isn't my recipe,' my grandmother says, when I ask her for this butterscotch sauce. 'It's from *Good Housekeeping*. 1969, I think. Or maybe 1968. But you can have it anyway.'

My grandmother's recipes are all out of magazines, and she keeps them in folders on a shelf she had specially made, in her kitchen: bookshelves aren't built right for big yellow ring-binders, she says, and she likes them neat. There's fifty years of recipes in there, from the early days of her marriage. Not much from before that. Perhaps my grandmother wasn't interested, then, in learning to cook: she lay in a cold bath in her jeans to make them tighter, and rode a red bicycle along the seafront, and had long hair.

My grandparents were married when they were both nineteen: in the photos they both have long hair, and my grandfather and his three brothers have moustaches, and flared legs on their suit trousers. My grandmother looks like my mother, and my mother looks like me. My sisters and I have never thought we looked alike, but I see it here: the long hair, the determined gaze, the steady set of the chin.

We are all far away from each other now, but it wasn't always like that: my grandparents would come down to see us, and pick us up from school on Friday afternoon, and on Sunday morning before they went back we'd all have breakfast together at the old pine table, the benches askew to accommodate my grandfather's knees. And the AGA hobs would both be propped open, with oatcakes on one, and drop scones on the other.

Drop scones are sort of like Scotch pancakes, but I like them better: little and bubbled and light as a feather, stacked with bacon (or stewed apple), and here, my grandmother's – or *Good Housekeeping*, circa 1968's – butterscotch sauce. A friend asks for American pancakes for a birthday, and I remember, and I ask my mother for the drop scone recipe. 'It isn't my recipe,' my mother emails back. 'It's from the AGA cookbook. But you can have it anyway.'

My mother's recipe (that isn't hers); my grandmother's recipe (that isn't hers): this is how it goes when you teach yourself to cook.

I have given the ingredients for the butterscotch sauce in imperial as well as in metric, because that's how I learned to make it. For me, this recipe is all about remembering, and the imperial measurements couldn't be easier to remember: 1oz butter, 1oz sugar, 1 tablespoon golden syrup.

For 4

100g self-raising flour	**For the butterscotch**
½ tsp fine salt	1oz (25g) butter
1 egg	1oz (25g) brown sugar
150ml semi-skimmed milk	1 tbsp golden syrup
20g butter	Juice of ½ lemon

Sift the flour and salt into a bowl, and mix together thoroughly. Make a well in the centre and break in the egg, then pour in half the milk, and whisk until well combined. Gently stir in the other half of the milk to make a batter.

Assuming you don't have an AGA, set a biggish frying pan over a medium heat, and melt the butter in it, swirling the pan to coat the base with melted butter.

Dollop tablespoonfuls of the batter into the pan: you will probably be able to get about four drop scones to the pan. Cook for about 2 minutes on the first side, or until you start to see bubbles forming in the surface of the batter. Flip them with a spatula and cook for 1 minute on the other side.

Meanwhile, make the butterscotch sauce. In a small, heavy-bottomed saucepan, melt the butter over a medium heat. Add the sugar and golden syrup, stirring until the sugar has dissolved, then let it boil for 1 minute. Squeeze in the lemon juice and immediately pour into a heatproof jug.

Flip the cooked drop scones onto plates and let people help themselves to the butterscotch sauce.

Fat Tuesday Pancakes

You cannot, they told me, put a recipe for ordinary pancakes
in your book. But I can, and I am, and by the time you read this,
I have. So there. I am including this recipe chiefly because I can
never remember it, and I'm tired of having to call my mother
whenever I want to make batter.

It's my book, and I'll make pancakes if I want to: proper
pancakes for Pancake Day (Shrove Tuesday, or – much better –
Mardi Gras, 'Fat Tuesday'), those beautiful lacy pancakes that
everywhere else they call crêpes, rolled up with lemon juice and
a generous shake of fine white gritty caster sugar. I'm a purist, but
I have known people eat them with jam, and my sisters (may God
forgive them) with Nutella. These are proper pancakes: I love an
American pancake in the proper place, but it's not on the day before
Lent. I am a sucker for tradition, you see, and this is one of mine.

For 4

110g plain flour	Butter or oil, for frying
Big pinch of salt	Lemon juice and caster sugar
2 eggs	(or Nutella, jam or grated
About 300ml milk, any kind	cheese), to serve

Take a large bowl, and sift in the flour from on high. I have yet to
figure out a way of properly sifting flour so that it gets airy without
covering everything in the kitchen with a fine dusting of the stuff,
but perhaps you are better organised or have less shaky hands.
I would love any tips. Stir in the salt, then make a little well in the
centre and crack the eggs into it. Whisk vigorously, so that the
edges of the flour well begin to mingle with the eggs.

Slowly add the milk (you may not need it all), whisking constantly,
until you have a smooth batter that coats the back of a spoon in
a unified sort of way. I believe this is what they call in the trade a
'dropping consistency', but I am happy to be corrected – and, God,
what a horrible expression in any case.

Set a frying pan over a high heat and add a little fat: my mother uses oil, but I'm a sucker for butter. When the fat begins to sizzle, pour a ladleful of batter into the pan and immediately turn the heat down.

Hold the pan handle and roll it, so that the batter slinks into every corner. Let the pancake solidify and bubble, which it will do very quickly, about 30 seconds. And then turn it. Or flip it, if you're skilled that way. Let it have 5 or 6 seconds on the other side – just to lightly brown. Slide your pancake out onto a plate, and get on with the next one. The first pancake always nerdles. You know what I mean by 'nerdles', even if you've never heard the word: where it gets all scrambly and tattered and refuses to flip properly. That. Think of it as a sacrifice to the pancake gods.

Have plates ready and waiting, as well as lemon wedges (or those little plastic lemons full of juice) and caster sugar. It has to be caster, I think: the fine gritty sand of it is somehow exactly right. Pancakes won't wait. And you won't want them to.

Keep on going until the batter is gone, pausing only briefly to eat your own. The last pancake will nerdle, too. That always happens. Don't worry about it.

Imperfect Pikelets

Pikelets are like crumpets, but untidy. Pikelets shouldn't be perfect or precise: in fact, with pikelets every imperfection is proof that you did it all by yourself.

I love recipes like this, reading them and making them. There's something brilliant about a recipe that doesn't ask too much of you; a recipe, in fact, where getting it exactly right would be exactly wrong; a recipe you can fiddle with, and tend to when you remember. The bicarb here gives both a slight sour tang, and a gentle rise; it's not in all pikelet recipes, but I really like it.

If you're on your own, I suggest you make the full quantity anyway. The cooked pikelets will be fine in an airtight container for a few days, and you can toast them in a regular toaster without any hassle. I confess I have never been able to keep pikelets in the house without eating them for longer than about four days, so I don't know how well they keep past that...

For 4

175g plain flour

1 x 7g sachet instant yeast

½ tsp caster sugar

½ tsp fine salt

½ tsp bicarbonate of soda

150ml milk

150ml hot water

Oil, for frying (if your frying pan isn't non-stick)

Butter and jam, Marmite or strong Cheddar, to serve

• • • • • • ••• • •• • • ••• •• • •• • •' • •• •• •• • •••• ••• ••

So. Breakfast.

You get up, and put the kettle on for tea. While the kettle's boiling, you measure everything out: dry ingredients into a big bowl, and milk into a jug. When the kettle boils, pour 150ml hot water into the jug with the milk (and the rest into the teapot). Stir to a sort of baby's bath temperature, so it feels pleasant on the back of your hand, neither too cold nor too hot – and when it gets there (no hotter, please), pour it into the bowl with the dry ingredients.

Now whisk like billy-o. Keep whisking: 3–4 minutes of whisking with your whole strength. Come on, you'll get an hour to rest in a minute... This puts the holes in the pikelet, which sounds like an

old-fashioned idiom for breaking something ('By Jove, that's put the holes in the pikelet!') but isn't: the bubbles of air you're beating into the mixture become the holes when you griddle it.

Cover the bowl with a clean tea towel, and take your tea back to bed.

After an hour or so (it'll stand a little bit longer, so don't worry if you're at a good bit of your book, or otherwise occupied), come back and check the mixture. It should be bubbly and frothy, and about half as big again as when you left it. Stick your largest frying pan over a medium heat, adding a drizzle of oil if your pan's not non-stick.

Get someone else to put butter and jam on the table, or butter and Marmite, or thin potato-peeler strips of cheese.

Take a tablespoonful of your batter and dollop it into the hot pan. Repeat a couple more times, depending on the size of your pan; leave some space in-between for the pikelets to spread out. Cook for about 90 seconds, then flip over with a spatula and give them another 60 seconds.

Use said spatula to lift your pikelets out onto a plate. Drape immediately with cheese, or a hunk of best butter as thick as a thumb.

Fiona's Bagels

I met a girl at a party, and she gave me a pirate pop-gun, and a recipe for bagels, and then she was deported. All of this is true.

This is her bagel recipe: she lives in Paris now, with her husband (to whom the pop-gun belonged), and a kitten called Smitten, and a lemon tree, and we make bread together on Skype, flour drifting joyfully across the camera, so that from Paris, it looks as if London is in the midst of a blizzard. And vice versa.

She learned this recipe, she told me, from a café in California, and she brought it to London, where she gave it to me. And now I am giving it to you.

I thought bagels were much more complicated than this. They aren't. I can never get over how easy these are, and how recognisably bagel-y they are even when you get them a bit wrong. They are tender yet properly chewy, and just begging to be piled high with cream cheese and smoked salmon.

There's also some really solid kneading to be done here, which is the best cure for a troubled heart: hands in the dough, window wide, something jaunty on the radio.

Makes 12 bagels

400ml lukewarm water	2 tsp fine salt
1 x 7g sachet instant yeast	1 egg, lightly beaten
1¹/₂ tbsp dark brown sugar, pounded to get the lumps out	Sesame or poppy seeds, for scattering, if you like
600–750g strong white bread flour	

Measure out your lukewarm water, and check its temperature the same way you would a baby's bath, by touching a drop to the inside of your wrist – it should feel pleasant, neither too cold nor too hot. Take a good big bowl, and beat together the yeast, warm water and sugar. Let it rest for a minute or two while you weigh out 600g of your flour. Tip the flour into the bowl and sprinkle over the salt.

And now: mix it all together (I told you it was simple). Get your hands in, and mix, and knead, and pummel it right out for 15 minutes or so. The dough should be really stiff and tough:

pinchable, formable, pull-apart-able; and it should smell like bread. If the dough seems too sticky, you can add some more flour.

Anyway, once you have a good stiff dough, let it rest for 10 minutes while you put things away and wash up spoons, or whatever.

Find a good knife, and cut the dough into twelve roughly equal pieces: I do this by halving the dough, halving each half, and then cutting each of those halves into three. (I write this because I am frequently baffled by having to tell by eye how much is one-twelfth.)

Take one of the twelve, and roll it between your palms to make a long, smooth sausage. Repeat, obviously.

Next pinch the sausages into hoops, overlapping and twisting the ends together. You want the ends to stick firmly together, or your bagels will all go to hell when you try to boil them later; if you need to, dip the ends in water to make them stick.

Sit your dozen bagels on a lightly greased baking sheet, and cover with a damp-ish tea towel, then leave them alone for a good hour at least to rise. When they have doubled in size, pre-heat the oven to 200°C.

Find the tongs. Get your biggest pan, fill it with water, and bring it to the boil. And when it's boiling big, roiling bubbles, take the tea towel off the bagels, pick up each bagel with the tongs and drop into the boiling water. Fiona's recipe says to do them all at once, but I am not competent enough for that yet. So I go one at a time, lifting each bagel out as it floats to the surface, after about 20 seconds, more or less, and popping it back on the baking sheet.

When the full dozen have been boiled, brush them with beaten egg and scatter with seeds, if you want. (I am a sucker for a sesame seed bagel, but feel free to use poppy seeds or any other seeds that you think might work.) Bake for 10–15 minutes until they are golden-brown and lovely.

I would, probably, split one open immediately and spread it generously with salted butter, and eat it standing up by the oven, because that's the whole joy of being a cook, and a grown-up. And I would call Fiona and tell her: 'I made your bagels again, and they were wonderful.' Because they would be. They always are, you see.

Lazy Sunday Pastries

I am, as I've said, reasonably lazy. I like long mornings punctuated by drawn-out brunches, and I like sunlight playing through the window onto white bedsheets; I like my warm house, and I dislike getting dressed and going outside; I dislike queuing, and digging for my debit card and hoping it won't be declined; and, above all, I dislike having to talk to strangers before I've had my breakfast.

All of this leads me to make things like these pastries, because baking is less hassle than showering, and finding my shoes, and hoping I've got some money.

Also, people are terribly impressed by it, and I live for praise. Ten minutes' work, most of which can be done on the sofa, and then a passing Tall Man or any unexpected breakfast guests can sing you to the skies for being an excellent hostess.

It's just this: puff pastry, bought pre-rolled and frozen, with chocolate or butter, jam or Nutella, folded into little origami shapes. This is barely a recipe. I know. You do have to become the sort of person who puts ready-made puff pastry into their weekly shop, but that, again, is easier than becoming the sort of person who makes their own puff pastry. I am an enthusiastic cook. I cook for a living. Yet I can never be bothered to make puff pastry. Not even rough pough (ruff puff?). There is nothing wrong with shop-bought puff pastry, and there's something a lot wrong with having to put shoes on and venture out, just to have pastries for brunch.

Makes about 8 pastries

1 x 320g packet of pre-rolled chilled puff pastry

16 squares of dark chocolate (or butter and/or apricot jam, or Nutella)

1 egg, lightly beaten (optional)

· · · · · · · · · · · · · ·· · · · · · · · · · · ·· · · · · · · →

⟶ You take the puff pastry out of the freezer the night before and leave it in the fridge to defrost.

In the morning, you unroll it – or roll it out if it's not pre-rolled (between two sheets of baking paper, for ease) – and cut along the (imaginary) dotted lines shown in the picture below.

Then you put the chocolate here, like this (the dark bits in the picture). You can also spread it with butter, or butter and apricot jam, or Nutella.

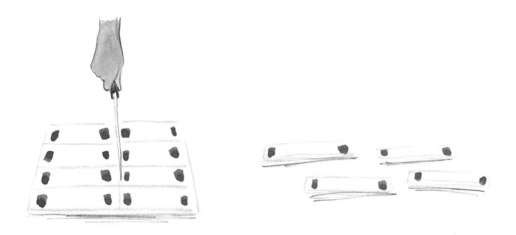

And you fold the pastry up around the filling, like this, like you're making a sort of scroll, or the curlicues on wrought-iron gates.

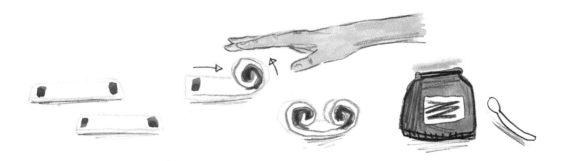

Then you put the pastries on a baking sheet. If you're feeling fancy, you brush them with beaten egg (but not if you're not) and you bake them at 180°C for 15 minutes or until they're risen and golden.

And then you offer a little platter of miniature pastries to your people, and everybody tells you how wonderful you are, and you have done nothing but be gloriously lazy and make pastries on the sofa. Serve these pastries with very hot coffee made in one of those natty little Italian espresso pots. Having wanted such an espresso pot for years, I recently acquired one, and it is an endless joy to me. I recommend, if you can, fulfilling small dreams like this as often as possible.

Improper Burnt Butter Berry Crumble Muffins

For a long time I made these muffins for other people, but refused to eat them myself. It was a kind of misguided patriotism: these are not proper English muffins, and I resented them so deeply for it. They aren't really American muffins, either: they aren't really even breakfast muffins. They are only breakfast muffins in the sense that they contain breakfast-y ingredients – oats, eggs, honey, butter, berries, yoghurt – but they don't have that health-conscious, not-really-muffin muffin vibe that I loathe.

These are nothing at all like those muffins, and also nothing at all like shop muffins, which is to say that they taste neither of virtue nor of plastic wrapping; however, scarred by my early experiences with both kinds, I scorned them. I only made them because I liked the way the batter rose in the oven, and the ritual of it, and because the Tall Man liked them, but I would watch him eat them and sulkily turn to my own porridge, thinking, *Tchah, keep your stupid muffins.*

And then, happily for me – and also for you, reading this – I relented: they are delicious. They are best eaten hot and fresh, and they are so good: soft and sweet and slightly sour, with little pockets of hot pink or navy blue where the berries have burst and stained the crumb; also firm and tender and tug-apart-able, which is so important in a good muffin. These travel well, too, which is at least part of the reason I started making them in the first place: I am disorganised and chaotic, and I thought these would be good for eating breakfast on the Tube and out walking and in the back of cabs. Of course, they mostly get eaten long before this happens, but the idea is fundamentally solid: I will rephrase, and say instead that if you have the self-control, they travel beautifully.

You'll need a muffin tin and some paper muffin cases, but you can get both in the supermarket. ⟶

Makes 8 big muffins

125g wholemeal flour

90g rolled oats

1½ tsp bicarbonate of soda

50g salted butter

120g runny honey

75g Greek yoghurt

1 tsp vanilla extract

1 egg, plus 1 egg yolk

150g berries (*I like half raspberries and half blueberries*)

For the crumble topping

60g rolled oats

40g dark brown sugar

60g cold butter

Pre-heat the oven to 180°C and put eight muffin cases in your muffin tin.

First, make the crumble topping. Put the oats and sugar into a bowl. Take the butter, cut it into dice, and then rub it into the oats and sugar to make rough, nubbly clumps.

Now put your flour, oats and bicarb into a big bowl, or the bowl of your stand mixer.

Find a saucepan, sit it on your scales and weigh out the butter. Set the pan over a very low heat and let the butter melt: no, go further than that, let it burn. You'll know when it's starting because it will go from gold to nutty brown, and the scent will be lovely – and when it does, quickly fetch your honey.

Carefully lift the saucepan off the heat onto the scales again and pour the honey straight into the pan, very slowly and keeping an eye on the weight, so as not to overshoot (although it doesn't matter if you're a bit out; of course, you could weigh the honey separately, but I loathe washing up, and honey is a pain). Return the saucepan to the heat, still on very low, just to warm the honey through, giving it a stir every now and then.

Tip your yoghurt and vanilla extract into another bowl, then lightly beat in the egg and the extra yolk with a fork. (The easiest way to get the egg yolk out of the egg is to crack it in half, then pass the yolk back and forth between the two halves of the shell, letting the white run down and away. Egg shell will also cut cleanly through egg white if you need it to: it is the best, best way to fish out any stray bits of shell.)

Tip the yoghurt mixture straight into the bowl with the dry ingredients. Take the butter-honey off the heat and add that too. Beat until you have a smooth batter: about 3 minutes with a stand mixer on the lowest setting, or about 5 minutes with a wooden spoon and some vigorous arm work. Then add your berries, reserving eight or so to put on the tops of the muffins later. Stir them in very lightly (it doesn't matter if some berries split; nevertheless, you don't want all of them to do so).

Dollop the mixture into your muffin cases, dividing it evenly between them as best you can. Scatter over the crumble topping and balance a berry precariously on top of each one.

Into the oven they go, for about 25 minutes; test them by sticking a skewer into the centre, and if it comes out clean, they are done. Lift onto a cooling rack (they will sweat if you leave them in the tin), and leave to cool. Or eat warm. Either way: delicious.

Glumday Porridge

I think, sometimes, that porridge is the perfect breakfast. Hearty, deep, rich and silky might be a horrible combination in a man, but it's what lends porridge its magic: that, and the fact you can tweak it to suit almost any kind of day. (The ratio is always 1:3 oats to liquid, if you're going to do some experiments.)

I used to eat porridge cold when I was small, which seems to me now about the most horrible way to wake up I could imagine. (I also used to have my milk warmed for nineteen seconds precisely in the microwave, which seems almost equally disgusting.) I was a funny little kid, and while I can't claim to have grown out of the peculiar entirely, I have at least grown up to appreciate proper porridge on a winter's morning. Especially glum winter's mornings; those mornings where you, yourself, feel like a pile of cold porridge in eighty-denier tights. For those mornings, proper porridge is an essential antidote. It sits with you, warming you gently from the inside. Everything else might be dreadful, and difficult, but you ate your porridge, and all the little oats are calmly and quietly rebuilding your energy levels.

You can have your porridge with gold-top milk and brown sugar, so the brown sugar settles into a lovely crisp skin on the top. You can have it with coconut milk and ginger. You can have it with water and salt, like a Scot. You can have it with almond milk and berries, like a vegan. You can have it like a little lord, with banana or raisins, and cream simmered slowly with cinnamon. You can have it with tinned peaches, or a handful of coconut flakes. You can have it – oh, holiest of holies – with golden syrup. There is almost nothing in this crazy wide world that I love more than golden syrup. It has to be Tate & Lyle, of course; I don't even know if there are other brands. The green and gold of the tin, with the lion half-eaten by bees, and the wildness of meeting the Old Testament face-to-face over breakfast.

Proper porridge, gold-top milk (you can still get this, you know, in some supermarkets), golden syrup. What else could you want for a glum morning?

For 2

$1/2$ mug porridge oats	1 tbsp golden syrup
$1/4$ mug walnuts (optional)	Small pinch of flaky sea salt
$1^1/2$ mugs ice-cold milk, any kind (*but I think full-fat is nicest in winter*)	

. . . .

Start by toasting the oats. This is much simpler than it sounds, and it really does make a difference: you just chuck the oats into a dry saucepan over a medium heat. Stir them with a wooden spoon for about 3 minutes – or until they turn very slightly darker, and start to smell wonderfully nutty and earthy.

Then turn the heat right down and let the pan cool for a minute, stirring the oats all the while. Add the walnuts here, bashed up with the end of a rolling pin, if you want some extra protein.

Add three-quarters of the milk, and stir constantly for 10 minutes, this time using the 'wrong' end of the spoon. The idea is to mimic a thing called a spurtle, which is what you are supposed to stir porridge with. I am a stickler for tradition.

Cover the porridge. Heat off. Let it sit for 5 minutes. Fetch a bowl and a spoon, and lever the lid off the golden syrup tin.

Dollop out porridge.

Drizzle porridge with syrup, twirling the spoon. Lick the spoon.

Scatter porridge with a tiny bit of sea salt.

Pour over the last of the ice-cold milk.

The Tall Man's Maple, Banana, Bacon & Coconut Porridge

This sounds terrible, but is delicious, and sort of makes sense when you think about it. A tablespoon of desiccated coconut in with the oats (which doesn't add flavour so much as creaminess), sliced banana on top, and sometimes – why not? – a sprinkling of some crumbled very, very crispy bacon. A drizzle of maple syrup to finish off. (Golden syrup doesn't work nearly as well here, so do make the effort for maple, if you can.)

Jam for Out of Doors Jam Sandwiches

This very quick, very easy, softly set jam is good on porridge (see page 54), on toast, and even folded into the little pastries on page 47, but it's best (in my opinion) in a doorstop sandwich: the kind you could make when you were barely tall enough to reach the kitchen counter, before you let yourself out into the bright, clear light of an August morning; the sort of morning where you just know already that the sun will be hot, and the sky high and blue, and the day will go on forever.

I had the kind of childhood which is supposed not to exist any more, but I think probably does. It was the kind of childhood where everything felt like a small adventure, where we ran in a pack: a bare-legged, brown-legged, nettle-stung, bee-stung, bitten and burned pack. We got into trouble; we built treehouses and dens and rafts that sank; we sailed, and when the sailing boat sprung a leak, had to be towed back to shore. We put the baby on the banisters to see how fast she would slide. The baby was fine. Nobody minded, because nobody knew.

We ran in a pack, and the oldest of us was twelve, or something like it. Older than twelve seemed ancient. We ran through fields of tall wheat and cycled for miles. We carried lemonade and jam sandwiches and rock cakes; we ate apples from the trees; we sucked the honey from nettle flowers. We chewed straw, like old farmers do. We ate everything we could get our hands on. The oldest boy once ate a spoonful of mustard powder on a dare, and I really thought he was going to die of it. We were little scavengers: I think that's why they sent us out to play.

That's how I remember it, anyway. And still, when the sun slants under the curtains early, and the air is full of electricity and adventure, I feel a kind of calling: to make myself a jam sandwich – two doorstops of white bread, a slab of salted butter, a fistful of strawberries boiled up and dolloped in – and to go off in search of adventure. I never do, of course. I have bills to pay, and promises to keep, and I am old. Ancient, by my younger self's own standards.

But I have never forgotten that thrill, and I know that adventures are still out there. Adventures remain; wheat fields remain; the stars remain. Somewhere outside the city, it goes on. It must. They say this kind of thing doesn't happen any more, and perhaps they are right, but I hope they aren't. It would break my heart. And so I will go, next time.

Makes about 375g

500g mixed, frozen berries (sometimes labelled Smoothie Mix)	Pinch of salt
200g soft brown sugar	Finely grated zest and juice of ½ lemon

. . .   . ˙ ˙   . . .   . ˙.   . . .   . . .

This is so very simple: put all the ingredients into a heavy-bottomed saucepan. Bring to the boil over a medium heat, then turn down to a simmer and cook for 20–30 minutes. Stir your jam every so often, so it doesn't stick to the bottom of the pan. It mostly sorts itself out, but you want to keep an eye on it and use the back of your spoon to break up any clumps of fruit that don't seem to be taking the hint. It will rise and froth and bubble like something living: it's incredibly pretty.

Meanwhile, find yourself some bread and butter, and either sterilise your jar (see below), or fill it with hot water and leave it to stand for a few moments. (This stops the hot jam from cracking the jar.)

When the jam is recognisably jammy ('The jam's jammed!', as Ezra the cook says in the lovely Elizabeth Goudge book *The Runaways*), carefully pour it into your clean warm jar. Secure the lid and leave to cool.

Immediately fill the saucepan with cold water and leave it in the sink: jam really does jam, and washing up is incredibly boring. Besides, we've got places to be. Slice your bread thickly. Spread it with butter. Spoon over some warm jam, then sandwich together. Wrap in a napkin, shove in a pocket and go.

A Note on Jars

This jam is a quick, not-quite jam. It won't keep for much longer than a week in the fridge, so I don't usually bother with sterilising the jar. However, if you're making this for kids, elderly people or anyone who is immuno-compromised, here's how it's done. You'll need a glass jar with a good seal, such as Kilner. Simply bung it in the dishwasher on a hot cycle. Or wash it thoroughly in hot soapy water and rinse well, then take the rubber ring off, stand the jar and its lid upside down on a clean baking sheet and dry in a 170°C oven for 15 minutes.

In Defence of Avocado on Toast

I was raised on a book by John Burningham called *Avocado Baby*. It's about a baby who lives only on avocado, and is much maligned for it. Reader, I was – I am – that baby. I would eat avocado for every meal if you let me: zizzed up with lime and chilli and plenty of salt and really good olive oil, drizzled with balsamic vinegar, sliced into salads, baked into brownies. For a long time avocados were very 1980s, and then they were cool, and then they were passé again. I don't care, and nor should you. Avocados are wonderful.

Take a **perfectly ripe avocado**. (Squeeze gently to see if it's ready: it should just give under your fingers; and if not, set it on the windowsill in the sun.) Mash your avocado in a bowl. Stir through a teaspoon of **chilli flakes**, a grind of **black pepper**, a teaspoon of **flaky sea salt** and the juice of a bright, sharp **lime**, and then heap onto **Marmite toast** – and that's it. I love it.

Avocado toast is what I eat on days when I need to get things done. Maybe I'm channelling the Avocado Baby himself: I eat it and I feel better and more capable of dealing with the world. And that's why it's in this book: everyone needs a meal that makes them feel very capable which is also very easy to do (once you know how). It took me a little while to work out the perfect balance of pepper, salt, chilli and lime above, so you might as well know it right away.

(This is also very good with an egg on top. I have never been able to master poached eggs at home – not with vinegar or whirlpools, or even those little silicone contraptions – and so I usually do soft-boiled. There is a very good technique for soft-boiling eggs on pages 62–3, and even if you think you know, I urge you to look at it, because it changed my life. Or at least the part of my life concerned with eggs.)

Double Soss, Egg & Chips

There is no better Double Soss, Egg and Chips than the Double Soss, Egg and Chips you can get in our local greasy spoon, with the windows steamed up and the smell of decades of frying drifting through from the back kitchen.

However, you can't always count on having a greasy spoon nearby when you need one – and so it is worth writing down, even if only briefly, how to make the perfect sausage, egg and chips at home. Because sometimes, that is all you need.

Chips: On page 189 of this book you will find a recipe for Goose Grease Roast Potatoes. Peel your potatoes (Maris Piper, for preference); cut them in half, and then into batons, and then turn to that recipe, following the steps exactly.

Sausages: The absolute best you can get, reasonably fatty, fried *very* slowly and gently for 40 minutes over the lowest-possible heat.

Eggs: The secret to a good fried egg is to get a non-stick frying pan nice and hot. Add a tiny bit of butter, let it foam up, then crack the egg into it. Splash $^1/_2$ teaspoon of water into the pan, and cover immediately, either with a lid that fits snugly or foil, and cook for 3–3$^1/_2$ minutes. You're after perfect set whites, and golden, drippy yolks. Sprinkle cracked black pepper over the taut yolk.

Scrambled Eggs on Toast

In her book *Home Cooking*, Laurie Colwin says scrambled eggs are harder than people believe, and she's right, but only if you don't know the secrets, which are these:

Eggs	Bread
Butter	Salt and pepper

. . . .

Break the eggs into a receptacle and whisk.

Add bit of sea salt, but don't put pepper into the eggs; it makes them look grubby.

Don't bother adding cream or milk; it only dilutes the egginess, and makes them pallid.

Non-stick pan over a medium heat. Bit of butter, not too much. Let it melt, and swirl it about the pan.

Put your bread in the toaster at this point, and get a plate, knife and fork and things ready, because scrambled eggs won't wait.

Tip the eggs into the pan, and let them almost set, then use a spatula to kind of half-stir, half-fold, gently bringing them over and under each other. Don't over-stir.

Instead of over-stirring, butter your toast.

The eggs will keep cooking once you turn the heat off, so turn off the heat a fraction before they seem done. Spoon your scrambled eggs onto the toast and grind over some pepper.

Bingo.

Viennese Eggs

I know a lot of people who make this for breakfast, and no two of them call it the same thing: eggy cuppy, cuppy eggy, eggs in a cup, eggs mashed in a cup, mishmash eggs, coddled eggs, becky eggs, and the rather arch 'smashed eggs'. Although I have never been to Vienna, for me these will always be Viennese eggs, because my Polish stepmother called them *jajko po wiedeńsku*, 'Viennese eggs' – and she taught me to make them.

Buttered and salted and studded with slivers of sharp green onion, these eggs are what she would give me for breakfast when I was a little girl: I would sit at the long table looking out at next door's chickens while she warmed the butter, diced the spring onions and bacon, and toasted two fat slices of proper heavy-duty black bread. And boiled the eggs. I thought she must be a witch to know the exact moment when the eggs would be just right: the whites set, the yolk glossy, drippy and golden.

I did not have the easiest relationship with my stepmum, mostly because I did not have the easiest relationship with my father. But, making these eggs now, I find a great deal of comfort in remembering those small moments and realising that, in every difficult time, there can be moments of real joy, of real safety. Of real love. ⟶

For 1

2 eggs

2 slices of the best bread
(*of course, I want you to
have this with the Wicked
Stepmother Black Bread on
page 75, but any sort of dark
bread would be good here*)

Handful of ice cubes

Knob of butter

2 spring onions

1 smallish stem of cherry
tomatoes

Marmite (optional)

Flaky sea salt

Black pepper

• •• • • • • • • • • • • • • • • •• • • • •• • • ••• • •• • •• •• •

Put a pan of water on to boil, and while it's getting there, find
yourself an accurate timer (you will have one on your phone,
I expect).

When the water is properly boiling, with big fat bubbles breaking
on the surface, gently lower the eggs in with a spoon, and
immediately set your timer for 1 minute.

First minute: The eggs are boiling rapidly in a lid-off pan,
over a medium heat.

You are cutting the bread for the toast while they do this.

The absolute second the timer goes off, you turn off the heat,
clamp the lid on the pan, and re-set your timer for 6 minutes.

Second and third minutes: The eggs are cooking in the lid-on
pan, with no heat under it at all.

The bread must go in the toaster right away, and you also need to
fill a reasonably sized bowl with iced water and spread a sheet of
newspaper over the kitchen counter (to catch the egg shells later).

Fourth minute: The eggs continue to cook in the lid-on pan, still
with no heat under it.

Put a little pat of butter – I like salted – into the cup or glass
you want to eat your eggs out of. Pop it in the microwave for
30 seconds or so, until the butter has melted. (If you don't have
a microwave, wash your cup or glass in very hot water to warm it,
then melt the butter in a small saucepan and carefully pour it in.)

Fifth and sixth minutes: Ditto.

Rinse your spring onions and pat them dry, then put them straight into the buttery warm cup or glass, and chop them finely using scissors. (You could use a knife and a board here, but it will mean more washing up.)

Seventh minute: The eggs are almost done, and will be ready to come out at the end of this minute. Prepare your plate.

The toast should be popping up about now. Grab it. Butter it. Put it on the plate, along with the cherry tomatoes. (I like Marmite on my toast here, too, but I am aware that Marmite – of all things – is not everyone's cup of tea.)

At the exact stroke of the timer, lunge in with your slotted spoon and grab the eggs.

Eighth minute: The eggs go straight into the bowl of iced water. Immediately. This stops them cooking.

One at a time, pick each egg out of the iced water and bash on the kitchen counter (over the newspaper) to crack the shell. There's a fine membrane under the shell of a fresh egg, all translucent and silky: you want to get hold of that, and pe-e-e-el it and the shell off as quickly and fluidly as you can; the fewer motions you can do it in, the better. Drop the shelled soft-boiled egg into your cup or glass, then quickly repeat with the other egg. Stir with a fork, beating the eggs with the butter and spring onions.

Ninth minute: The eggs are in the cup or glass. And breakfast is ready.

Find sunbeam in which to sit. Heap eggs on toast. Scatter with sea salt flakes. As always, pepper lavishly.

Soup & Bread

On the third-worst night of my life, I made soup. Or, I suppose more accurately, I heated up some soup. The worst and second-worst nights now are mostly a blur – the mind has this neat protective trick, sometimes, of forgetting – but the third-worst night of my life is crystal clear. And I can tell you, without a shadow of a doubt, that on that third-worst night it was Heinz Cream of Tomato that saved me.

It had been a very hard day, for complicated reasons, and I was crying. I hadn't eaten properly for days, and I had barely been home, either. I was sick of syrupy double-shot coffees instead of supper, and I was crying on the kitchen floor: the kind of crying where you suspect you might actually die of it.

Somehow I managed to dig out half a tablet of Valium from the debris of the medicine cabinet – and then, miracle of miracles, a tin of Heinz Cream of Tomato from the chaos of the kitchen cupboard. And I took the Valium, and heated up the soup, gently, over a low flame, and poured it into a mug, and took it to bed with a hunk of stale bread, toasted and laden with butter. I held the mug of soup in my two hands, and watched the steam rise from the surface as I breathed, and sipped it slowly, dipping in the toast and not minding when the butter dripped golden onto the sheets. It was two in the morning, and I was eating soup in bed, and I felt better.

And this, more or less, is how I always feel about soup and bread. Soup from a tin, soup on the stove, shop-bought bread, bakery bread, home-made bread: soup makes me feel better for reasons I cannot quite articulate, and buttered toast is the greatest of foods. The smells of bread baking and soup simmering might be the most evocative, reassuring and altogether lovely of all smells. No haute cuisine ever worked half so well for sorrow as a deep bowl of pumpkin soup and proper bread with proper butter.

It's not terribly fashionable any more to like bread. It's sort of lucky that I've never managed to be fashionable, because I've always loved bread: I love it wholeheartedly and overwhelmingly. Sometimes I think there is no meal – no matter how thoughtful or beautiful or delicious – that I wouldn't swap for Marmite toast, or the end bit of a loaf fresh out of the oven.

Bread is one of the only things I remember my mum making when I was little. She made milk bread: it rose on the back of the AGA, and we were allowed to shape the loaves with little hands;

to use a butter knife to slash the doughy top; and to crack an egg to brush over to form a glossy, golden crust. I loved bread day. I still love bread day.

I felt like a proper grown-up the first time I made bread for myself in my own home, like I had passed some kind of invisible test. I had taken flour and water and salt and yeast, and by some kind of magic we could now have toast and sausage sandwiches and fried bread. It's domestic magic, and I've always been a sucker for alchemy.

I should say here that I always weigh my liquids for bread making, rather than measuring them out; it's more accurate, and if you can set the bowl directly on digital scales, it also saves on washing up.

If you're very new to bread-making, start with the Maslen bread: it is infinitely adaptable, easy as anything, and a joy. The milk bread is easy too. The challah is a bit harder, and the black bread is a tiny bit harder still. But all of them are, fundamentally, easy breads: breads to live with, bread to live by.

Maslen Bread

This is the easiest bread in the world.

I call this Maslen bread, partly because my maternal family name is Maslen, and partly because the blend of flours is based on medieval maslin flour. Both words apparently come from the old French word *miscelin*, meaning mixture, which I love. I love the idea of coming from a family that's all mixed up, and I love the way the mixture of flours in this bread gives it such a complex, subtle flavour.

Traditionally, maslin flour is a combination of wheat and rye, but I tend to use wheat, rye, oats and spelt. I have to tell you, gathering those four flours is the most complicated thing about the whole business. I weigh out all the ingredients into one bowl, so there is minimal washing up, and minimal fuss.

As I say, this is a very simple bread, and very fast. It requires no kneading and no proving. Only flour, a little salt, a little sugar, buttermilk and bicarbonate of soda. A hot oven and a cast-iron casserole. Half an hour. Little things, morning things: the sun coming through the window in that light that is almost the colour of a ripe peach, and the dust motes dancing in it, and under your hands the dough binding together. And then there is bread for breakfast, hollow-sounding as you rap the hot floured base of your freshly baked loaf with your knuckles.

I like to make this bread once a week, on Saturday morning, for toast, and the ritual of it pleases me: I feel established. One of us gets up to make the tea, and lights the oven, and opens the kitchen window, and we drink tea in bed. Then the Tall Man goes out for the papers and bacon, while I blitz the oats into flour and pinch the salt flakes into fine grains.

Makes 1 loaf

200g rolled oats,
   plus 1 tbsp extra
100g spelt flour
100g rye flour
50g wholemeal flour

1 tsp bicarbonate of soda
1 tsp soft brown sugar
$1/2$ tsp fine salt
350ml buttermilk

Put your cast-iron casserole in the oven – we're looking for a Le Creuset-type casserole here, with a lid that can go in the oven. Turn your oven to 220°C, and pre-heat both the oven and the casserole with its lid on. You're making a mini-oven, essentially: it traps the steam released from the dough as it bakes, which keeps the crust crisp and firm. (I don't know the science behind it; only that it works.)

While the oven pre-heats, make your oat flour. Weigh out your oats (except that extra tablespoon) into a big bowl and use a hand blender to grind them into flour, pressing the blade down into the rolled oats. This is absurdly satisfying. Add your other flours. Stir, vigorously, until combined. Add the bicarbonate of soda, sugar and salt. Stir again.

When the oven and your casserole are at temperature, add your buttermilk to the bowl of flours. (You may remember making a volcano with bicarbonate of soda when you were small: that's what we are doing here, more or less.) Anyway, working fast, bring everything together to make a dough – you have to work fast, because the bicarb and the buttermilk are reacting together, which is what makes the bread rise, the way the volcano did.

Make the dough into a sort of round, flattish loaf. Carefully lift your hot casserole out of the oven and dust the inside liberally with a handful of flour, then pop your loaf inside. Scatter with the extra tablespoon of oats, put the lid back on, then put the whole thing in the oven and bake for 25–35 minutes.

You'll know it's done because it will smell like bread, and the loaf will sound hollow on the bottom when you (carefully) up-end it and rap it with your knuckles. Remove from the oven and let the cooked loaf sit in the casserole for 5 minutes more, then turn it out onto a cooling rack. Or eat it hot: I always do. I always mean to let it cool, but instead I find myself tearing hunks from the split crust, piling it with slabs of salted butter, good cheese and the kind of thick-cut bacon you find only if you go looking for it.

Making Buttermilk & Making Do

If you don't have buttermilk, you can use the same amount of full-fat yoghurt, or you can sour normal milk with a squeeze of lemon: just add a tablespoon of lemon juice to 350ml of milk and stir.

AGA Mama's Milk Bread

Unless you have lived in a house with an AGA you cannot possibly understand what is so good about them. They are ludicrous, old-fashioned and inefficient, but in my childhood it was the greatest technological advance since the last Bronze Age man first made iron. Before the AGA we had a tall, thin Rayburn, which fitzed and putzed and kept the six inches of air directly around it warm, but nothing else. I had five blankets on my bed, and three electric heaters by it, and frost on the inside of my windows – and then the AGA, mighty, purring and Prussian blue, came into our lives like divine intervention.

The AGA heated the whole place: it made ancient radiators creak into life, and it hummed all night long – the beating, pulsing heart of the house. We draped clothes over the front to dry, and bread rose on the back, and you could put thick slices straight onto the big hotplates to make toast. There is nothing in this whole wide world as good and delicious and wholesome as AGA toast, and I miss it every day. We kept a sofa in the kitchen and I viewed any attempt to get me off this sofa as a personal attack: I loved it there. It had soaked up so much dripped butter, and absorbed into the cushions so many toast crumbs, that it smelled distinctly of breakfast, and even now, when I think of somewhere I feel safe, I think of the kitchen sofa at Dairy Farm. It was always warm by the AGA, and sitting in front of it was where I did my homework, and wrote horrible poems, and kneaded the bread on bread day, working out my teenage angst into the soft, sweet dough of this milk bread.

My mum didn't much like cooking, but she liked – and likes – good bread. And my childhood was full of bread rising. This bread is the one we had every week. My sisters refused to drink milk, and I think that's why we had this milk-enriched bread so often, slathered with egg to make it golden, and good for toasting. This is not a difficult bread to make. I tried hard to improve my mother's recipe but I couldn't: this bread is, I think, pretty unimprovable, especially for the ungifted baker. ⟶

Makes 2 little loaves (1 for now, and 1 for the freezer)

500g milk	1 tsp fine salt
25g butter, plus extra for greasing	1 x 7g sachet instant yeast
	1 egg
700g strong white bread flour, plus extra for dusting	Flaky sea salt, for scattering

. . . .

If you have digital scales, weigh the milk and butter together in a saucepan. (If not, measure out 500ml of milk and add it to the weighed butter in the pan.)

Set the saucepan on the stove over the lowest-possible heat, and stir very gently. You want the butter to slowly melt into the milk: enjoy the gold slinking into the white; spring-like, glossy, the colour of crocuses. Don't let the milk get hotter than blood heat – it should feel comfortable on your fingertips the whole time. When the butter has melted, take the pan off the heat.

Weigh out your flour into a large bowl, or the bowl of a stand mixer, then scatter in the salt and yeast. Stir everything together so you can't see either the salt or the yeast.

Now you need to combine the wet ingredients with the dry, using either a stand mixer or your hands: you're trying to get a smooth, slightly sticky dough – which, after kneading, will become a smooth, stretchy dough. You may not need all the milk and butter, so you'll want to add it carefully. The amount you need can vary based on where you are, and how wet it is that day, and things like that, so to get *really good bread*, go slowly and keep an eye on it. This feels daunting. It isn't. All it means is: if the dough has come together smoothly, without shaggy edges of loose flour, you've added enough.

I'm going to give the stand mixer instructions first, because they are very simple. Fit the dough hook to your mixer and, with the motor running on about the second setting, very slowly tip the milk and butter into the flour, salt and yeast. After 6–7 minutes of electric 'kneading', you should have a smooth dough.

If you're working the dough by hand, you just have to get stuck in. Slowly add the milk and butter – no, slower than that – and work it for at least 10 minutes. Hands in, folding the dough over and over itself, bringing your hands together, and then apart, pushing it, pummelling it: really go for it. Once the dough starts to come together, tip it out onto a clean, flour-dusted work surface and keep pummelling until you have a supple, pillowy ball of dough.

Butter the bowl the dough has been in (if you're using a stand mixer, pick the dough up in one hand, butter the bowl with the other and drop the dough back in), and butter some cling film. Pop the dough back in, stretch the buttered cling film taut over the top, then put a tea towel over that and set the bowl somewhere warm: the airing cupboard, a chair by the radiator, the windowsill in high summer. (The AGA lady leaves hers by the AGA, of course.) Leave it for about an hour, or until doubled in size, and while it's doing that, grease two 450g (1lb) loaf tins with butter.

Punch the dough down once, swiftly, to 'knock it back', then lift it out of the bowl and onto a flour-dusted work surface. Cut the dough in half, and shape each half into a loaf. Put the loaves into the tins, seam side down, cover loosely with the buttered cling film and return them to their warm place to rise for another hour, or until doubled in size again.

As the loaves start to peek over the tops of their tins, set your oven to 200°C. Beat the egg in a small bowl and brush the loaves with the beaten egg. Scatter with a little flaky salt, cover again and leave until fully risen. You know what you want your loaves to look like: like that – high, graceful.

Slash the top of each loaf with a sharp knife, just once, and quickly slide your loaves into the hot oven. After 25 minutes, take the loaves from the oven, and carefully turn them upside down, tipping them from their tins. They should have a golden crust on top, be firm on the sides, and sound hollow when you rap the bottom with your knuckles. Return the loaves to the oven, without their tins, and bake for 5 minutes more, so they're golden all over.

Find the salted butter. Find the bread knife. Take the loaves from the oven once more, and cut yourself a hot slice of new bread. Butter thickly. Isn't that something else?

Wicked Stepmother Black Bread

My stepmother called us her Cinderellas. We called her the Wicked Stepmother.

She wasn't wicked, as it happens. Nobody ever made us pick beans out of the ashes. We liked our stepmother, and I think she liked us: nonetheless, we called her the Wicked Stepmother, and she called us Cinderellas, and that was that. We all knew our stories too well to try anything different.

This is not her recipe, though I wish it was. She made black bread every week, and her loaves were heavy with nuts and seeds, dense loaves leavened with something mysterious in a little jar that came from Poland in my stepmother's mother's hand luggage. It had been handed down for generations, she told me. I know now it must have been a kind of sourdough starter. Back then, it seemed like magic.

My relationship with my father was always difficult, and one hot summer's day I left his house for the last time. I was eighteen, and I ran away to London, to sleep on the sofa of the boy who would later become the Tall Man. Even then, you see, I knew that he was a safe place.

I took my red ankle boots, with the button; I took my laptop; I took my leather jacket (which had been my father's), and I gave it to a cold man asleep in a Paris subway, as a kind of exorcism. But I could not take everything. I left things: a box of plastic horses, a plum velvet hat with a fine net veil, a sage green coat with a princess collar. My stepmother.

I miss my hat, and I miss my sage green coat. And I miss her. I wish I could ask her for her recipe for her bread; I can't. You can't jump in the same river twice, and you can't cross a bridge you've already burned.

So, instead, I pulled this together from half a dozen recipes. It's especially indebted to those of Dan Lepard, Diana Henry, Deb Perelman and Anne Shooter.

This bread is wonderful with beetroot soup and gravlax, perhaps because of its Eastern European roots – but it's best toasted, with salted butter and Marmite. It's dense and fluffy at the same time, richly flavoured, complex and all the things you want bread to be. It tastes like bread from a proper bakery, and I am amazed, every time I make it, that I did it. $\longrightarrow$

Makes 1 loaf

50g salted butter	250g rye flour
50g black treacle	2$^1/_2$ tsp instant yeast
2 tsp instant coffee	2 tsp each of caraway and
2 tsp cocoa powder (*not* drinking chocolate)	fennel seeds, plus extra for sprinkling
3 tsp soft brown sugar	300ml hot water
2 tbsp cider vinegar	150g carrots, about
400g strong white bread flour	5 skinny ones

. . . .

Measure out – a small saucepan on digital scales is best here – your butter and treacle, then add the coffee, cocoa, sugar and vinegar: set the pan over a low heat. Stick the kettle on, and while it boils, weigh your flours into a big bowl and add the yeast and seeds.

Measure 300ml of hot water from the kettle, and stir it into the butter and treacle mixture, which should be melting together nicely. Let it bubble gently for a minute or so, then remove from the heat and leave to cool while you get on with grating the carrots. It takes more time than you'd expect, grating carrots: try to use it as meditation, or stick something on the telly. Either way.

When the treacle and butter mixture is lukewarm (carefully test it with a finger: you want it to be blood temperature), make a well in the centre of your dry ingredients, and pour in about half of the butter and treacle. Add the grated carrots and stir well. Once it's all combined, you can begin to knead, adding just enough liquid to bring everything together into a sticky dough. I do this all in a stand mixer with the dough hook fitted, and it works just fine. If the dough seems *too* sticky, add a little more flour to bring the dough to a supple ball (a 'rusty mud colour, flecked with carrot', as Diana Henry writes about hers, and she notes – completely correctly – that the smell is the most wonderful thing on earth). It already smells like a bakery in some foreign city, or a foreign corner of your own city. It is delightful. Knead for 5–6 minutes in a mixer or about 10 minutes by hand, working the flour into the dough with each pummel and turn.

When the dough is a smooth ball, transfer it to an oiled bowl (if using a stand mixer, you can just tip out the dough, rinse and then oil the bowl, and put the dough back in again), and cover with oiled cling film. Set the bowl in a warm place, and leave for an hour, or until doubled in size. I put mine on a chair by the radiator, covered with a clean tea towel, and then drape a big towel over the whole lot, to make a sort of tent for it. An airing cupboard would be better, if you have one.

While that's happening, go and do the washing up, and line a baking sheet with baking paper.

When the dough has doubled in size, knock it down: punch the air out of it once, briefly, then shape it into a round loaf, with the seam at the bottom. Set it on your baking sheet, cover it again with the oiled cling film, and the tea towel, and the big towel, and leave it to prove again for an hour. Don't prove it for much more than that hour, though. (I over-prove this constantly, because I forget I'm doing it, and it makes everything much harder, so aim for as close to an hour as you can.)

Pre-heat the oven to 220°C and find a pastry brush. After the hour is up, brush your loaf with water, scatter with the extra seeds, and slash the top in an X-shape – the deeper the cut, the airier your loaf will be.

If you have one, fill a roasting tin with boiling water, and slip it onto the lower shelf of your oven: this creates steam, and so makes for a high, crisp crust. Bake your loaf for 20 minutes, then turn the oven down to 180°C and bake for a further 30 minutes.

When the time is up, slide the bread out of the oven and, using oven gloves to protect your hands, flip it so it stands on its end and rests against your oven-gloved palm: rap the bottom with the bare knuckles of your other hand. A hollow-sounding loaf is a done loaf. If not, brush it with water and return it to the oven for another 10 minutes. Check again: rap with your knuckles; if not done, brush with water and bake for 5 more minutes; repeat until the page is full and the bread is ready.

Let the loaf cool slightly on a wire rack before slicing.

How to Grieve with Challah Bread

My grandfather let me eat apple pie for breakfast. Once we asked him could we have ice cream before breakfast, and he said if we could find any, we were welcome to it. We went to the outside freezer and found two boxes of Cornettos. He let us eat them all. Perhaps this means that he was a man of his word. I hope so. He was my father's father. He was a teacher, and some kind of occasional preacher. He came from a village called something like Jacksondale, which I cannot find on a map.

My grandfather was a storyteller who used to pull invisible stories out of his sleeve, wrapped in his handkerchief: he would shake the handkerchief and stoop down and say, 'Ah, I remember this one!' He told good stories, and I remember them as well as if I had seen them myself.

He was kind to us when he saw us, but he did not see us often – and when he died, I had not seen him in a long time. That made it harder, perhaps. I was in my early twenties, and I had not known many deaths, and this death seemed to me to be stranger than most: someone I knew, and had known, and did not know. A person whose death left no hole in my present, but whose dying made clear a breach with the past: someone I missed not for me, but for who I used to be. How do you grieve for someone you no longer know?

Me, I grieved with bread. Bread is the staff (stuff?) of grief because it is the staff of life. Tiny microscopic life-forms, breathing and bubbling and growing under your hands: it lives. Life goes on.

The rules of grief were written somewhere I couldn't see, but the rules of bread-making were clear. I didn't know how to grieve, but I knew how to make bread. A six-strand challah braid: knead in anger, rise in grief, plait to find a pattern in it all. I needed, I think, to keep my hands busy. I have never found a better remedy for this kind of sorrow than plaiting bread; I come back to this particular recipe whenever I am feeling fidgety or bewildered, because it's just complex enough to keep your mind and hands occupied.

After my grandfather died I made so many of these loaves I had to give them away: visitors, strangers, neighbours. I think I was trying, in a subconscious way, to build a kind of tribe. There is something about sharing bread that appeals to almost everybody: perhaps it is hardwired in us, written into the bone. Break bread with me, and share my strange and uneasy grief, and be my people when my people are gone.

And, in any case, people love these loaves: they are beautiful and intricate and look far more complex than they are. People are impressed by them, and people are impressed by bread generally, because they think making it is much harder than it is.

Makes 1 loaf

1 x 7g sachet instant yeast

250ml lukewarm water

40g golden caster sugar

625g strong white bread flour

2 tsp fine salt

3 eggs

4 tbsp neutral-flavoured oil, such as groundnut

Flaky sea salt and poppy seeds, for sprinkling, if you like

•. .. . . • • . . ..- . ... . • •. • .. ..

Begin with the yeast: you're bringing it to life, essentially. Pour your lukewarm water into a small bowl and sprinkle over the yeast, plus a pinch of the sugar. Stir until dissolved, and then leave for 5–10 minutes until a frothy thick layer starts to form.

Put the flour, salt and the rest of the sugar into a big bowl, or the bowl of a stand mixer with the dough hook fitted. Stir together, letting the flour lift and fall to capture plenty of air. Breathe.

Hollow out a little well in the centre of the flour. Crack two of the eggs into it. Separate the third egg. (You can separate the egg like this: crack the shell in half, catch the yolk in one half and let the white fall. Move the yolk to the other half-shell and let the white fall. Repeat.) Save the white to brush over your loaf later. Add the yolk to the well with the other eggs, followed by the oil, and stir to form a kind of loose batter, sometimes called (rather grimly) a 'slurry'. Tip your frothing yeast over this slurry, and stir again, mixing everything together to form a shaggy, tough-to-stir dough.

You can, at this point, set your stand mixer on to your shaggy dough: 'knead' with the dough hook for 6–8 minutes. Or turn it out onto a floured board, and knead into it all of your fury. Push your knuckles in, fold it around your fingers; 10 minutes at least, until it's supple and smooth and forms an easy ball. You'll know when you get there. ⟶

→ Set the dough to rise in an oiled bowl (you can just oil the bowl you made it in): cover with a clean tea towel and leave in a warm place for about an hour, or until doubled in size.

Take your risen dough, and weigh it. Divide this number by six to get the weight of each of your strands. Pull the dough into six balls of about the right weight (you will be better at this than you think), then roll each ball into a long, thin strand. The length and thickness of these strands will determine the shape of your loaf: shorter, fatter ones for an everyday loaf, longer and thinner for a ring-shaped loaf – a celebration loaf, I think they call it.

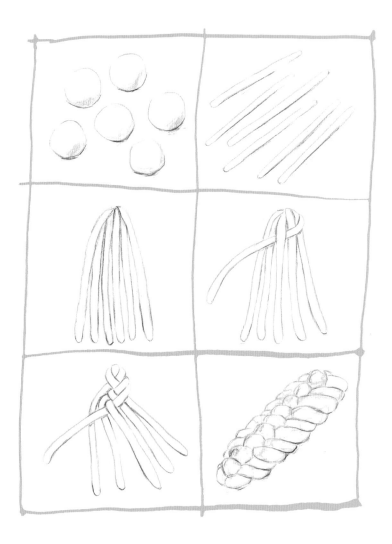

Lay out your six strands of dough, and pinch them all together at the top. Plait them, like this: pick up the right-most strand and take it over two strands, then under one, and over two again, so it becomes the furthest-left strand. Repeat, starting with the right-most strand each time, until the strands are all plaited together. This is not nearly so hard as it sounds, and you will be able to do it. But you will have to focus on the bread, which is good: when you are thinking about bread you are not thinking about knowing, or remembering, or feelings. Only bread, and braids.

If you have made a shorter, fatter loaf, squidge the strands together at the end, and then sort of cup the bread between your palms, pushing it together to make it higher, fatter and more loaf-like.

If you have made a longer, thinner loaf, you'll need to make it into a circle. Just lift it. Don't worry, the loaf is well made, and it won't break. Bend it around into a circle, and join the ends together, weaving the end of the braid into the beginning. Haphazard braiding is okay here.

Lift your plaited loaf onto a baking sheet lined with baking parchment, then return it to its warm place for another hour, until it is risen and puffy. Pre-heat your oven to 175°C. Brush the pillowy plait with egg white – you can mix your egg white with a teaspoon of water if you don't think it will go far enough. Scatter the bread with sea salt and poppy seeds, if you like.

Bake for 30 minutes, turning it in your oven at the halfway mark. The loaf is done when it is deep golden-brown, and a thermometer inserted right in the centre reads 88°C. If you have no thermometer, it is done when it sounds hollow when you rap the bottom with your knuckles.
(And in this it is also like grief, especially a grief you don't understand: hollow, heavy.)

Turn out your challah loaf onto a cooling rack, by the window. Eat as soon as it stops steaming; or wrap in a tea towel, and go knocking on your neighbour's door. I am sad, and I would like to be less alone: share my bread with me.

Pea Green Miso Soup

Sometimes I think there is no weather I love more than fog. Don't quote me on that – I love thunderstorms and snow and the first glorious sunny day of spring too. But today, with mist clinging tenderly to every facet of the buildings, lapping against the lampposts, hiding the skyscrapers of Canary Wharf, on days like these I almost expect to see Sherlock Holmes coming down the street. My London and his London, in the fog, are not so different after all. A real 'pea souper' they used to say, didn't they?

I go down to the market and buy vegetables by the armful. Peas from the farm. Mooli, chillies and coriander from the street stall, along with spring onions, green peppers and Thai limes, dark and knobbly and incredibly aromatic. I pinch them to check the ripeness, and my fingertips are suddenly slicked with sharp, floral oil: I am always surprised that the scent can permeate the thick rough skin. All the way home through the fog it clings to me, densely, something strange and foreign and beautiful under the low grey-yellow sky. And then I make soup – pea soup, of course.

This couldn't be easier, but you will need a blender or food processor to blitz everything together. It tastes completely like what you would buy for lunch if you were cold and trying to be healthy and wandering the city in your lunch break, looking for something to warm you and cheer yourself up. But better, because you made it yourself.

For 4

Bunch of coriander

5 spring onions

15–25g ginger, depending on how gingery you want your soup to be

3 garlic cloves

Splash of olive oil

1 lime

1 tsp white peppercorns

1 tsp Szechuan peppercorns

650ml boiling water

2 tbsp miso paste

500g frozen peas

• • • • • • ••• • •• • ••• •• • •• •• • • •• •• •• • •••• •••• ••

Get out your blender or food processor. Remember to put in the blade bit; I forget to do this about half the time, and it's a pain.

Rinse your coriander under the tap, picking out any brown leaves, then chop it roughly with a pair of scissors straight into the blender, keeping a small handful for garnishing the soup later. You can chop your spring onions with kitchen scissors too, and it saves on the washing up. Into the blender with them as well, again keeping a little for later. Peel the ginger with the blunt side of the scissors, rubbing it vigorously – the skin will just come right away. Roughly chop the ginger and put that in the blender, along with the garlic cloves, peeled but not chopped.

Blitz, drizzling a splash of olive oil through the hole in the top to help things along, and then slowly squeezing in the juice of the lime. Limes can be tricky – mine only yielded about a tablespoon of juice (pathetic) – so go easy and stop the blender every so often to have a taste.

Grind the white and Szechuan peppercorns with a pestle and mortar, set a pinch aside for later and tip the rest into the blender. Don't be tempted to add any salt, as the miso will make the soup salty enough. Blitz on high for 2–3 minutes, scraping down the sides as needed; the finer you get this paste now, the smoother your final soup will be.

Scrape out the paste into a saucepan, and set it on a low heat, stirring gently. Put the kettle on, and when it comes to the boil, measure the 650ml of water straight into the saucepan. Add the miso and stir like mad, then simmer for 10–12 minutes, stirring regularly to stop it sticking.

Turn the heat back up so the soup comes to a rolling boil, then add the peas and simmer for a couple of minutes, but no more: peas overcook so easily.

Take the soup off the heat and either tip it back into the blender and blitz again, or use a hand blender in the pan until the soup is reasonably smooth. I like mine with a bit of texture: it feels to me somehow more hearty, more satisfying.

Ladle into bowls and scatter with the reserved coriander, spring onions and pepper.

Smoky Beetroot & Pistachio Soup

I don't know if you've ever built a bonfire, a proper one.

In the village where I grew up, they had a particular way of doing it: a tunnel made of pallets led to the centre of the bonfire, where a miniature bonfire was built of firelighters, newspaper and dry tinder. On the night, some brave child would tiptoe into the tunnel with a lit match, do a last check for hibernating hedgehogs, then drop the match and beat a hasty retreat. I am sure this isn't how it happened every year, and probably isn't how it happens now, but it's how I remember it: I remember thinking it was the cleverest and bravest way to light a fire that I'd ever seen.

When I think of the bonfires of my childhood (proper Bonfire Night bonfires, I mean, not garden bonfires) I think of the ones that were lit in the field halfway between our village and the next. This field had a vast depression in the centre of it, as if a giant had thumped his fist down on the soft earth. For some of the year, this hollow was filled with rainwater. But on Guy Fawkes Night it was where we built the bonfire, and the earth would be dark with ashes for months afterwards, and there would be scorched circles on the grass where the fireworks had been, and the smoke would linger for days on the road between the villages.

One evening, sitting on the windowsill of the Tiny Flat, breathing in the November air, I needed suddenly to recreate that smoky bonfire atmosphere, and my cold hands wanted soup. Beetroot, of course, for the earth, and pistachios, partly for the nutty way autumn tastes, but mostly (I'll admit) for their bright, beautiful green against the deep ruby of the soup.

Some days in November, even the city has that tinge of woodsmoke on the air. That deep, beautiful scent of earth and smoke, like raking through ashes. I haven't had a bonfire in years, but this soup feels the same. Sweet, and earthy, and rich, and so, so pretty: I'm not much of a fusser for presentation usually, but this soup is exactly the right shade of ruby-pink, and the pistachios exactly the right shade of startling green, and the Parmesan just a small scattering of white, like late morning frost, or something else less fanciful. ⟶

For 4 dinner servings, or 6 lunch ones

4 beetroots	500ml boiling water
2 red onions	250ml milk
4 garlic cloves	1 tbsp black peppercorns
4 tbsp shelled unsalted pistachios	Dash of cream (optional)
	Little chunk of Parmesan
1 tbsp olive oil	Salt and black pepper
10g (about a handful) dried mushrooms (*I like chanterelles*)	

Pre-heat the oven to 180°C.

Unearth your beetroots, either from the bottom of the fridge or from the ground, and give them a good scrubbing under the cold tap. I always leave the skin on for this soup, both for its nutrients, and for sloth: peeling beetroots is a messy business, and it all gets whizzed up in the blender anyway. Still, if you prefer to peel, peel here, and you'll get an even smoother soup.

Peel your onions and cut them into quarters, then put them and your whole beetroots in an ovenproof dish or tin with a lid: I use my old favourite baking tray, with another baking tray (actually the base of the grill pan, with the grill part taken out) over it for a lid. Scatter over half of the pistachios, and a very, very generous grind of black pepper. Drizzle with the olive oil, cover and bung in the oven to roast.

While that's happening, put your mushrooms into a heatproof bowl, pour over the boiling water and leave to soak.

After the beetroots and onions have been roasting for $1^{1}/_{2}$ hours, check to see if they're ready: they should be erring on burnt, but not in a bad way; if they aren't, whisk the lid off, and stick them back in for another 10 minutes. Ignoring any actually burnt-to-buggery bits, tip the whole lot straight into the blender and blend on high for 4–5 minutes. You're looking to get this as smooth as possible.

Very slowly, introduce the mushroom-soaking water into the still-running blender. You can add the soaked mushrooms too, if you want, but I tend not to: they can be a bit rubbery, and it's the liquor I really love. While the mushroom liquor and the beetroots are making themselves acquainted (about 2 minutes), warm the milk in a small saucepan, and introduce that to the blender too. Slowly, slowly, slowly; all at once and it will burst out of the blender, if yours is anything like mine.

When the soup is smooth, tip it into a saucepan set over a low heat and *rinse the blender immediately*; beetroot sticks like mad. While the soup is gently heating, coarsely crush the peppercorns and the rest of the pistachios with a pestle and mortar.

Taste the soup now, and season with salt: you'll need less than if you add it any earlier. Ladle into bowls, and swirl (if you like) with a tiny dash of cream. For restaurant-style pretty, spoon the cream into the centre, and swirl it with the wrong end of a spoon. Scatter the pistachio-pepper mixture in a line straight down the middle of the bowl, bisecting the pretty cream pattern, and grate over a very fine dusting of Parmesan. Notice how completely beautiful it is. Serve, and sit with the dark burn of November earth, and the musty taste of late autumn, and the fierce bite of the pepper, and feel warmed, as if you were sitting by a bonfire in the field with the flames rising in front of you, and your best friends beside you, and the whole world waiting for you.

Tipsy Amaretto Squash Soup

There's this restaurant just down the street from where we live, and they make these little puffed balls of pasta stuffed with sweet, subtle pumpkin and cream, and drizzled with amaretto: I have almost never eaten anything so lovely. I'm not sure what the dish is called, or even if it has a proper name, but it's perfect. This soup is like that, sort of. I love it best with some of the labneh on page 116 swirled through it, like a dream, or a cloud, and with crushed amaretti biscuits, black pepper and toasted almonds scattered on top.

It's incredibly simple, because it all virtually takes care of itself. It's the kind of cooking that occupies a Saturday afternoon like nothing else – a gentle, low-level faff that occupies the hands and mind, Radio 4 burbling away in the background, a glass of white wine in one hand, and your stirring spoon in the other, humming to yourself as you move about the kitchen. And the result is the kind of Saturday supper that makes the heart rejoice. I'm not much of a one for going out, and my perfect Saturday looks, I think, like this: an afternoon pottering in the kitchen, and an evening curled up on the sofa, with the sharp smell of autumn drifting up from the dark street through the open window, the sweet smell of squash rising from a sturdy clay bowl, and a battered copy of something tried and tested and true, *Treasure Island*, say, or *Jane Eyre*.

The Italian chefs at the restaurant, cooking to mamma's recipe (this may be a stereotype, but in this case, is absolutely true, they tell me), don't need to fancy anything up. I have never yet been able to coax the kind of golden-carriage subtleties out of the pumpkin the way they do there, so I add things. Not much, but enough: a kick of spice, a handful of crushed amaretti biscuits to echo the amaretto liqueur, some strained yoghurt flecked with parsley and just a little glossy gold olive oil. This soup is the colour of autumn leaves, and it tastes like autumn too, and like the harvest. $\longrightarrow$

For 4

1 butternut squash, about 1kg (or 2 x 500g bags pre-chopped)

2 tbsp amaretto

1½ tbsp olive oil

½ nutmeg

6 shallots

4 garlic cloves

1 celery stalk

1 tsp butter

500ml chicken or vegetable stock (or a stock pot/ cube diluted with 500ml boiling water)

2 tsp flaked almonds

4 tsp labneh (see page 116), yoghurt or cream

4 amaretti biscuits

1 tbsp finely chopped parsley

Black pepper

. ' .. . .

Pre-heat your oven to 200°C. Find a roasting tin, ideally one you can set on the hob, to save on the washing up.

If you're using a whole squash, a) you're brilliant, dedicated and much more capable than me, and b) use a big knife to peel it, because a peeler won't take off enough of the white pithy stuff just under the skin. You want it to be that nice orangey colour, not muted – you'll see what I mean once you start peeling. De-seed it; chop the squash into chunks (biggish is fine) and put in the tin. Drizzle with the amaretto and 1 tablespoon of the olive oil, then grind over lots of black pepper and finely grate in the nutmeg. Turn it all about with your hands, so that everything is nicely coated. Either ask a friend with clean hands to take the tin from you and put it in the hot oven, or you can go and wash your hands and do it – but it's easier with a friend.

The squash will take about 35–45 minutes to roast, depending on how small you chopped it. This gives you plenty of time to finely chop the shallots, garlic and celery.

After 35 minutes, fetch your squash from the oven and pierce it with a fork; it should be soft and tender. If not, don't worry: just give it another 10 minutes, then check it again.

When the squash is cooked, sit the tin with everything in it over a low heat. (If you don't have a roasting tin that will go on the hob, you can transfer the lot to a heavy-based saucepan for this bit.) Add the butter and the rest of the olive oil (the oil stops the butter from scorching), along with the shallots, garlic and celery. Cook, giving it a stir now and then, for about 20 minutes or until everything is soft. Turn off the heat.

Have your stock made up in a jug at the side, still hot. Take your hand blender, and blitz everything in the tin. Very slowly, drizzle in the stock – this stops it from splashing or going lumpy – and keep blitzing until smooth. Taste for salt and add some if you think it needs it, and perhaps another quick grating of nutmeg and a twist of pepper. Turn the heat back on (lowest-possible) and let the soup simmer gently, while you toast the flaked almonds in a dry frying pan over a medium heat, shaking the pan until they turn a deep gold.

Ladle into bowls and swirl through the labneh, yoghurt or cream. Scatter over the almonds and the crushed amaretti, and the parsley, for a pop of green, then serve. Curl up; enjoy.

Perfect Roast Tomato & Garlic Soup

When I am tired I turn to tomato soup: I always have. It used to be Heinz, Cream of, and then I made this. And now, more often than not, I send the Tall Man out for a punnet of fresh tomatoes and make this instead. Everything else you will already have in. Salt, pepper, olive oil, balsamic vinegar, garlic. The dregs of a jar of pesto, if you're feeling fancy. Hot water and a hand blender. That's all. There's no cream or butter in this soup, but you would be forgiven for thinking there was: it's some kind of alchemy.

Tomatoes from the supermarket can taste of nothing, so instead of eating them raw, I roast them, driving off the water and shrinking them down to little jewels, wrinkled and dark. This way they taste as they should, or at least something like it: proper, rich tomato flavour, in the flesh as well as the seeds. (I am suspicious of any recipe that calls for the discarding of tomato seeds – don't they know they're the best part?)

This is my end-of-my-tether recipe, my Monday-night stock-in-trade, my failsafe. It requires a minimum of effort and tastes like heaven. I love it, and I think you will too.

For 2 generous servings

8 big tomatoes	Splash of balsamic vinegar
8 fat garlic cloves	600ml boiling water
About 2 tbsp olive oil	Salt and black pepper
1 generous tsp pesto (optional)	

Pre-heat your oven to 180°C.

Take your tomatoes and slice them into quarters, or eighths if you can be bothered; I rarely can. Scatter the papery garlic cloves, still in their skins, into a roasting tin, followed by the tomatoes. Dress the lot with a tablespoon of the olive oil – whisked with the pesto, if you have it (I like to make this soup to use up the end of the jar, screwing the lid on and shake, shake, shaking). Season well with salt and a good grind of black pepper, then roast for 35 minutes.

Next comes the tricky bit: take the garlic out of the roasting tin, but leave the tomatoes. When the garlic cloves are cool enough to handle, gently squeeze each one between your thumb and forefinger, and shuck them, the way a snake sheds her skin – they should be soft and golden and yielding. Discard the skins, and put the soft roasted garlic into a smallish mug or bowl. (I have an enamel cup I use for everything: blue and white, just like the mugs of my camping-holiday childhood.) Tilt the baking tray so you can spoon out the sweet olive oil from around the tomatoes and add it to the garlic.

Re-dress the tomatoes with another splash of olive oil and a little splash of balsamic vinegar. Return to the oven for 20–30 minutes until they're very soft and slightly charred.

While the tomatoes are in the oven, use a hand blender to zizz the garlic into a smooth, nutty-smelling garlicky paste. Try to resist spooning it onto bread, and put the kettle on.

Take the roast tomatoes from the oven and put them into a heatproof jug. Splash a little more olive oil and balsamic vinegar into the roasting tin, then pour in 600ml of boiling water. Stir vigorously, scraping up the sticky, delicious tracings from the tin.

Blitz the tomatoes with the hand blender, then add the garlic and blitz again. Slowly, slowly, add the juices from the roasting tin, blitzing each time, until the soup is smooth. Grind over a generous amount of black pepper to taste. Eat from a mug, with buttered toast.

Picnics & Pack Ups

Food tastes better outside, or so I've heard: Claudia Roden said it, and I trust her; and the Famous Five said it too, and I trust them. Nobody – *nobody* – knows more about picnics than the Famous Five. You know the drill: a wild yomp across the moors, and a gingham-lined wicker basket full of ginger beer and hard-boiled eggs with a twist of salt, and sausages cooked fat to bursting over a campfire, and seedy cake. Lashings of it all.

And food does taste better outside; half the reason I don't make seedy cake or eat hard-boiled eggs much is because they don't hold up in here against the way they taste out there. This is partly because food tastes better without distractions – without cutlery, and manners, and worrying what the person over there thinks of your garlic. And partly it's because if you've made the effort to get outside, you're going to have more of an appetite. It sounds obvious, and it is: food tastes better when you're hungry. And we have mostly forgotten how to be hungry.

The Famous Five – and almost all of Enid Blyton's work – comes with a constant background hum of post-war peckishness; a constant feeling of wishing for a little bit more, and wishing you didn't have to count out or quibble or worry. The universal sign of love in an Enid Blyton book is giving away sticky buns or a loaf of bread or a jar of jam like you've never heard of coupons: you can tell a nice farmer's wife from a secret smuggleress by how little she worries about the sugar ration.

It feels like a kind of longing for abundance, and for freedom. A longing to be allowed to go where we like, to eat where we like, what we like and how we like – and to eat it with our hands. It's a longing that never really seems to leave me. In offices, and tower blocks, and grey buildings in the city centre, the minute the sky peeks blue and bright through the double glazing, I start dreaming of gingham cloths and blue-rimmed white enamel; of tender little samosa-like parcels, filo on the outside, spiced lamb or bright peas on the inside; good bread or crackers, ready to heap with red pepper hummus and green harissa hummus; lazy tangles of quick-pickled onions, done in a matter of hours with a splash of vinegar, sugar and spices; an enormous wedge of pork pie, studded with boiled eggs, the golden yolks still a little soft and yielding to the knife. A Thermos of something boozy and hot, with the wind tugging at your hair, and the chill of it on your fingers.

It is so easy to eat distractedly: to have one hand on your phone, or one eye on your emails, or half a mind on what fork to use next. It is so easy to eat without thinking about what you are eating, or how you are eating it. But if you strip away the tablecloths and the cutlery and the manners, you strip away everything that might come between you and the feeling of being really, vividly, absolutely alive: fingers in the chicken carcass, grease and salt on the lips, grass against bare legs. And you can do this, really, anywhere. You don't need to be in an Enid Blyton book to step outside, to make something lovely to eat, and to take it somewhere green or wild. Wherever you are, and whatever you are doing, you probably have a minute – ten minutes, even – to step outside and breathe in and out. You can have a picnic wherever you are.

I didn't know this when I was working in an office; I spent months eating pre-packaged sandwiches at my desk, and wishing I was dead. It would be unfair to blame all of this on the sandwiches, but what *is* true is that as soon as I found a green place in the city, I felt better. I had sort of forgotten that wild places are everywhere; I had sort of forgotten, I think, to look for little wild things that might have made me feel like I belonged. I didn't really know about the small and tender loveliness of daffodils pushing up through the earth in a city park, the secret sweetness of unexpected moss on an Underground platform, the breathless, irrepressible joie de vivre of butterfly-studded buddleia pressing through a hoarding.

The world is so hard, and life is so short: you must make things lovely where you can. You have to make mundane things like packed lunches into something glorious and important and worth having. You have to make ordinary days worth having, is the thing – and investing a bit of time in what you eat and where you eat it (which is really investing a bit of time in looking after yourself) is one of the easiest ways to do it.

Everything in this chapter will pack well, and carry well, and is very easy to eat with your fingers, or with the help of a hunk of good bread.

Some Practical Notes on Picnics & Pack Ups

A pack up is just a little picnic. The sooner you realise this, the nicer your lunches will be: the tyranny of school lunchboxes or a meal deal is that you sort of forget the infinite variations you could be eating for lunch. Invest in a good lunchbox that seals shut, and you can have just about anything. As the wonderful Alice Waters once wrote, 'plain or fancy, just about anything portable' goes.

This is how I plan my picnics: one thing from each category makes a really splendid spread. And most make brilliant pack-up ingredients too.

Something to dip into

- Wildly Easy Hummus (see page 114)
- Would I Lie to You Labneh (see page 116)
- Exceptionally Easy, Fast Green Harissa (see page 205)
- Tapenade (my favourite – usually from a shop)

Something to dip with

- Good bread
- Danish Crackers (see page 121)
- Posh crisps (you can make these by slicing potatoes very, very thinly with a mandoline or cheese slicer thingy and roasting them in sizzlingly hot oil for 35 minutes at 180°C; of course I never really bother, but it's nice to know that one could)

Something green and crunchy

- I don't like taking dressed salads on picnics, because they wilt. Instead I pack a bag of salad leaves and some Decent Dressing (see page 164) in a separate tub.
- Carrot, cucumber, fennel and celery, sliced into little batons and wrapped in damp kitchen paper to keep them crisp, and perhaps some cherry tomatoes or little radishes too.
- Nice Little Nibbly Things (see page 173) or Quick Pink Pickled Onions (see page 113) packed in a sealed Tupperware container.

Something savoury and substantial

- Meaty things, like Trashy Ginger Beer Chicken (see page 102) or Rare Roast Beef for Two (see page 183). If your picnic party is large enough (or you're hungry enough), you could even make The Tall Man's Pâté (see page 118) or Midnight Chicken (see page 8).
- Otherwise, just pack up some cured meats: prosciutto, salami and chorizo (the cured kind); or chorizo sausages (the raw kind), slowly cooked in a frying pan, then quickly wrapped up in foil and a tea towel to keep the heat in.
- All of these things make a really decent sandwich, with some good bread and condiments. Also try A Proper Ham Sandwich (see page 128), thinly sliced roast beef with horseradish and salted butter on How to Grieve with Challah Bread (see page 78), or goat's cheese and figs on Wicked Stepmother Black Bread (see page 75). It's probably worth saying here that, if you possibly can, aim to make up the sandwiches once you're there: stops them going soggy.
- If not sandwiches, go for pastry, like Danny the Champion of the Pie (see page 104), Pigeon Pickle Pies (see page 110), Inelegant Samosas (see page 132), or Goat's Cheese Puff (see page 169) without the salsa.

Something sweet

You need things that hold their shape, and don't need much in the way of careful handling:

- Paris Cookies (see page 263)
- Whiskey & Rye Blondies (see page 254)
- Reading in the Rafters Parkin (see page 252)

Some decent cheese and a big bag of apples

Pocket Potatoes

The young Laurie Lee went off to school with a baked potato in his pocket. I have adopted the habit when travelling to somewhere tricky ever since learning this, and have discovered that a potato in the pocket is a genuine source of comfort and joy, even if you're not 'three feet tall and fatly wrapped in scarves'.

They are not difficult to do well, although you could be forgiven for thinking the opposite, given how often they are terrible: a microwave jacket potato is (usually) a sad imitation of the real thing, and should be given a wide berth. Purists would probably insist on baking potatoes in the embers of a fire, but I think an oven is fine: the crucial thing is that they should be baked so that the jackets go crisp, and the insides go properly fluffy. You want the skins rubbed vigorously with oil, scattered liberally with flaky sea salt, and pricked with a fork; you want the oven at 180°C, and you want to bake them for close to two hours – long enough that you can split them open with minimal pressure (no need for a proper knife) and slip in a fat pat of golden butter.

For winter picnics, baked potatoes keep hot for an absurdly long time, especially if bundled up in tin foil.

Take the butter with you in a little tub, and a pepper grinder, and a twist of salt, and don't split the potato until you absolutely have to. There is almost nothing nicer than the puff of domestic-smelling steam that rises from a newly split, well-baked jacket potato. Wonderful and completely satisfying, and they can be topped with just about any topping that will go in a Tupperware.

Lid Potatoes

If you are eating at home, the best thing you can possibly do is make like Milly-Molly-Mandy's Muvver, and go for some lid potatoes: she 'nearly cut the tops off them, but not quite. Then she scooped all the potato out of the skins and mashed it up with a little salt and a little pepper and a lot of butter. And then she pushed it back into the two potato skins, and shut the tops like little lids.' And then, obviously, you can include a bit of cheese and put them back in the oven to melt it. So, so good.

Trashy Ginger Beer Chicken

The heart wants what the heart wants, and sometimes what my heart wants is this: sticky, trashy, salty-sweet chicken drumsticks, eaten with the hands, covering everything they touch with their gloriously unpretentious sauce. This is miracle chicken, and it tastes as if you couldn't possibly have made it from scratch. It tastes like you got it from some food truck, or some old man barbecuing on an American street corner, or somewhere else dirty and delicious and real.

This is for all the people who find themselves drawn to dubiously cheap burgers and late-night kebab shops; those who dive into the kind of curry house where everything is the deep red of batch-cooked tomato, and the kind of Chinese restaurant where everything is smattered with day-glo orange. This is proper grubby food, only made with ingredients that (whisper it) aren't really terribly bad for you. This tastes like it ought to be a guilty pleasure, if I believed in those (I don't); it tastes like an absolute scandal.

Serve this with a very crisp green salad dressed, if at all, with just bright lemon and flaky sea salt. Maybe a bit of bread to dredge the plates. Nothing else, except hundreds of napkins. Paper napkins. Paper plates. Don't try and gussy this up. This is what it is: the kind of chicken that makes you want to lick the plate.

For 4

60ml ginger beer

30ml light soy sauce

2 tsp chilli flakes

$^1/_2$ tbsp miso paste

100g fresh ginger

6 garlic cloves

1kg chicken thighs or drumsticks (drumsticks are easier to eat, thighs have better flavour)

1 tbsp sesame seeds (optional)

Flaky sea salt (optional)

In your biggest bowl, whisk together the ginger beer, soy sauce, chilli flakes and miso paste. Peel the ginger (rubbing it vigorously with the back of a teaspoon should do it) and grate it finely, straight into the bowl; do the same with the garlic (don't rub it with the back of the spoon, though). The gnarly end bits from the grating can go in too. Stir everything together.

Chuck the chicken into the bowl, and stir well, turning the chicken over and over in the marinade to make sure it's properly coated. Cover and leave in the fridge for about an hour, maybe a couple if you can. I do this mostly as a weeknight dinner and usually only have an hour, or even half an hour, to let it marinate: that's okay too.

About an hour before you want to eat, pre-heat your oven to 200°C.

Pack the marinated chicken into a roasting tin, skin side down, and pour over a tablespoon of the marinade – I like to get plenty of the grated ginger and garlic in there as well.

Put the chicken in the oven and cook it for about 45 minutes in total. After 10 minutes, pour over another tablespoon of the marinade. After another 10 minutes, do the same, turning the chicken over, so it's skin side up. Tongs are useful here. Sprinkle over a tablespoon of sesame seeds, if liked (my favourite cookery book directive), and perhaps a few flakes of sea salt. Be careful, though, because of the saltiness of the soy sauce and the miso. Cook the chicken for a final 25 minutes. Don't be tempted to baste the chicken with any more marinade after this, as it has been in contact with raw chicken and so needs at least 20 minutes in a hot oven.

Either use a meat thermometer to check if the chicken is cooked (which is what I always do, because I'm an anxious person) or pierce the thickest bit with a skewer – if the juices that bubble up are clear (not pink), you're good to go.

Danny the Champion of the Pie

All good stories have a moral, even if you have to dig a bit to find it. Here are the morals of this story.

First: that it is in nobody's best interests to begin to make a complicated pie at quarter to eleven at night.

Second: that hot pork jelly will (if it can) go everywhere.

Third: that hot pork jelly, a gas hob, two a.m. and an impossible dream of a marvellous pie are a terrible recipe for a happy relationship.

Fourth: that no pie you make will ever live up to the description of the perfect pie you read when you were seven, and it was the start of the summer holidays, and you were upside-down three-quarters of the way up the pear tree in the back field.

Fifth: that the truth of morals one through four doesn't mean it isn't worth trying anyway.

You will remember this fictional pie, I think. You will probably remember the illustration, and almost-but-not-quite-precisely, the description itself: 'I began to unwrap the waxed paper from around the doctor's present, and when I had finished, I saw before me the most enormous and beautiful pie in the world. It was covered all over, top, sides, and bottom, with rich golden pastry. I took a knife from beside the sink and cut out a wedge. I started to eat it in my fingers, standing up. It was a cold meat pie. The meat was pink and tender with no fat or gristle in it, and there were hard-boiled eggs buried like treasures in several different places. The taste was absolutely fabulous. When I had finished the first slice I cut another and ate that, too. God bless Doctor Spencer, I thought.'

This is the pie from *Danny the Champion of the World*. This is the pie that Doctor Spencer gives to Danny the morning after he has bravely driven to the woods, alone, at night (a little boy!) to rescue his poacher dad from the mantrap dug by the gamekeepers. This is a pie to celebrate an adventure; a pie to celebrate a parent who is – let's not forget – sparky. I can't read that last page without crying. I have a complicated relationship with parents, and with sparky, but I remember so very, very vividly the feeling of triumph that this pie tasted of. *Danny the Champion of the World* is a triumphant book, above all. It's a book about things going wrong, and things going right, and clever people and difficult situations, and a book about being vulnerable. The scene (taken almost ⟶

$\longrightarrow$ wholesale, I think, from *Boy*, and therefore life) where Danny is beaten by his teacher is one of the most heart-hurty in the world. It isn't fair. It isn't just. Life isn't, sometimes, but if you're very lucky you'll have a dad who can put things right. I do, as it happens. I have a dad who puts things right (I have a dad who puts things wrong, too, but that's another story), and when everything is wrong it seems apt to make a pie about fixing things.

A pie to eat the morning after then. And, since this pie needs to be left for approximately twelve hours to be at its best, the morning after is the very best time to eat it. Unless of course it is the early hours of the morning by the time you finish making it, in which case you will have to wait until lunchtime to work out if it's any good or not. It almost certainly will be, and if it's not, you can begin again. You're a clever person. You're a sparky person. You can try again, and it will be better, and your relationship will not be ruined by a two a.m. row about pig fat on the gas hob. And in any case, you'll find that hot pork jelly comes off a gas hob with copious applications of Dettol and elbow grease.

It is probably worth a trip to your butcher for the diced pork shoulder, pork jelly and good sausages, because that will make everything easier. You will also need a 20cm springform cake tin and a baster or small funnel.

For 6 generous servings

For the pastry

110g butter

90g lard

About 550g plain flour

2 tsp sea salt

3 large eggs

For the pig bit

About 6 sage leaves

Leaves from a sprig of thyme

Leaves from a sprig of rosemary

2 tsp mixed peppercorns

1kg boneless pork shoulder, cut into 5mm dice (*you will need to either ask the butcher to do this, or have a very sharp knife and lots of patience*)

250g diced pancetta

3 fat Cumberland sausages, about 250g in total

6 eggs

Handful of ice

1 bay leaf

About 250g pork jelly

We'll begin, at almost eleven o'clock at night, with the pastry. Weigh out and dice your butter and lard. Put them into a saucepan set over a low heat and pour in 200ml of water, then heat them *very* slowly.

Meanwhile, weigh your flour into a large bowl and add the salt. Make a well in the centre, crack in two of the eggs and 'cut' them in; that is to say, bring your knife through the eggs and into the flour. Repeat, repeat. Slowly add the melted fat and water, and keep cutting and mixing with your knife to make a rough dough. This goes against everything you know about pastry, but it works here. Don't ask me how. You may need to add a little more flour. I did. It's fine.

A small trick: once all the melted fat and water is in the bowl, immediately rinse and fill the saucepan with cold water, then return it to a high heat. This simultaneously prevents the fat from coating the pan, and means you'll have a pan of water already bubbling away when you come to boil the eggs to go inside the pie.

Form the pastry into a solid, if sticky, dough. Wrap it in cling film and leave it in the fridge to chill while you get on with making the pig bit of the pie. Put your herbs into a mug, and snip them finely with scissors, then grind the peppercorns using a pestle and mortar and mix with the herbs. Tip the pork shoulder and pancetta into a large bowl. Take the fat sausages and squeeze the insides from their skins into the bowl: this is bizarrely satisfying. Mix briefly, then add the herb and pepper mixture and stir vigorously.

Take your eggs and, one by one, lower them into the pan of boiling water. Set a timer for 1 minute. This is the Egg Trick, and it's marvellous – prevents green-rimmed yolks entirely. When the minute has passed, cover the pan, turn the heat off completely, and re-set the timer for 5 minutes. When their time is up, take the eggs out of the pan and plunge them into iced water. This stops them cooking further in their shells, and also allows you to have iced water in the kitchen, like a lord.

Pre-heat your oven to 180°C and lightly grease your 20cm springform cake tin. $\longrightarrow$

─➤ Take your pastry from the fridge. Separate off a third of it for the pie lid, and roll out the rest into a 40cm circle, approximately 5mm thick; if in doubt, err on the side of thickness. (Mine was too thin, which is why, as you will learn later, the pork jelly went everywhere.) Roll the remaining third of the pastry into a circle about 25cm across.

Gently but firmly, press the larger circle of pastry into the tin. You want a decent overhang, in order to crimp the lid on later. Spoon about two-fifths of the meat mixture into the pastry casing and spread out evenly, pressing it down lightly.

Spread out a sheet of foil or newspaper, or a tea towel, and peel your boiled eggs. The eggs will be flimsy. This makes them trickier to peel, but exponentially more delicious. Place the eggs, pointy ends facing inwards, in the tin on top of the meat. Carefully spoon over the rest of the meat mixture; press the bay leaf into the centre, then lay over the pastry lid and crimp the edges shut. I use the sharp end of a knife to get a neat thin crimp, but my grandmother always used her thumbs. Your call.

Use the tip of your knife to poke a substantial hole through the top crust. Pop your pie into the oven (marvelling a little). You now have 1^1/$_2$ hours to play with. You may not, however, sleep. I suggest having an enormous row with the person you love best about the practicalities of making pie at one in the morning, or reading a good book. Again, your call.

Set a timer for 30 minutes; when it goes off, turn the oven down to 160°C, and re-set the timer for 45 minutes. Continue with row/good book.

When the time is up, beat the remaining egg in a small bowl and take the pie out of the oven. Carefully release the springform (but don't remove it) and brush the top and sides of the pie with beaten egg, pushing your brush down between the released springform and the pastry. Set the timer for 15 minutes.

You should, by this point, have finished either the row or a chapter of your book, leaving you the next 15 minutes free to tackle the pork jelly. Gently warm it up in a small saucepan to melt it and prepare a baster, if you have one. (I did not have one, so I used a piping bag instead. This was not a good plan, per se.)

Carefully take the pie out of the oven and leave it to cool, still in its tin, for 5 minutes. Now for the tricky bit. Inject your pie with the melted pork jelly like you are Doctor House doing one of those horrible biro-to-the-throat manoeuvres; that is how precise and swift you have to be. (If you don't have a baster, you can pour in the pork jelly through a small funnel.) However, it is worth noting here that I ended up drizzling lukewarm pig fat across myself, the Tiny Flat and the Tall Man, and still ended up with a smart-looking pie and a happy home life.

It is now two a.m. You may well be so exhausted you could collapse, but doesn't that pie smell glorious? Set it on a cooling rack, cover with an enormous bowl or something, put it in the fridge and go to bed. Sleep well. Do not wake up early. Your pie will not be ready before lunchtime in any case. I tried to eat mine for breakfast, and it was awful. Truly awful. Soggy, unsettling.

Later that day, grimly, self-pityingly, post-fight, I cut myself a masochistic slice of horrible, humble pie. It was wonderful. Crisp. Pink. Golden. The pig fat had crisped itself into gorgeously piggy pastry. There is a sixth moral in this somewhere, but I am too busy eating pie to look for it. It's probably something about triumph. Unlikely triumph, like a small boy driving a mile and a half in the dark to haul his dad out of a mantrap. Unlikely. Glorious. Pie.

Pigeon Pickle Pies

I cannot lie to you: these pies are a moderate faff. But, oh God, they are worth it. They are small and dainty, yet substantial, and they work just as well on a romantic dinner date as they do on a picnic, and any filling left over makes the most delightful sandwiches you've ever had in your life. More often than I care to admit I have given up on the pastry shell and fed people bowls of this filling, with baguette, for a dinner party. Pickles on the side. But as pies they are perfect, the platonic ideal of a pie. Apart from anything else, they are so pretty: pink and green and precise, and if you could prise their pastry lids off, you'd see the patterns inside. The deep, woody, bloody richness of the pigeon; the melty way of the port and the cream and the Dijon mustard; the sour pickles; and the crisp flaky pastry with the letters on top, cut precisely with your sharpest knife, spelling out the name of each predestined pie-owner.

You don't need to make the letters on the top, but I like to: I think because my grandmother always wrote our names in pastry on top of pies, and also because when I was small my name was still too unfashionable for me to buy any of those sheets of stickers with my name on in gift shops, and since then I have always written my name all over everything. I suggest you do, though, because it's oddly delightful, and people are thoroughly charmed by it. 'For me?' they say, incredulously, and you get to nod proudly and be praised, and they get to feel special and adored. They should feel adored that you've made them a pie anyway, but the human mind is a funny thing and somehow people are made happier by the little letters on top than the rest of it put together.

The Tall Man is the kind of man who goes about with a pie and a bottle of ginger wine in his coat pocket: I think this is an awful lot of the reason that I fell in love with him. So I first made these pies for him. We had planned an adventure, but I was too mad to leave the house that day, so we stayed in, and ate the pies by candlelight on our sitting-room floor.

Makes 2 small pies

4 shallots

6 garlic cloves

A dozen little dill pickles
 (sometimes sold as
 cornichons)

200g Parmesan

Butter and olive oil, for frying
 and greasing

500g pigeon breasts

50ml port (a small port glass)

1 tbsp Dijon mustard,
 or more to taste

About 2 tbsp double cream
 (*you might like a bit more
 or less*)

375g chilled shortcrust pastry
 (*I use bought, but if you want
 to make your own, there's a
 recipe on page 250*)

1 egg, lightly beaten

Flaky sea salt and black pepper

· · · · · · · · · · · · · ·· ··

Take the shallots, and the garlic, and slice them into loops (the
shallots), and tiny, fine shreds (the garlic). Divide your dill pickles
into two even piles: slice one pile into long strips, and dice the
other. Grate the Parmesan. Sip your drink and sit for a while,
admiring the pale shell-pink of the shallots, and the way the garlic
cloves are tinged almost purple at the ends. Maybe eat a stray
cornichon. It gets a tiny bit hectic for a minute here, so enjoy this
moment of calm.

Once you're feeling ready, hop up and set your frying pan over a
medium-high heat. Add a knob of butter. Have a chopping board
and your sharpest knife ready. Put your pigeon breasts into the
pan and sear for 2–3 minutes on each side for rare, 3–4 minutes
for medium-rare: you want them to have a decent seal on the
outside, but still be quite rare on the inside. Once they're done,
flip them out onto the chopping board and let them rest for a few
minutes before slicing each one lengthwise (against the grain)
into four strips. They'll be a gorgeous, pinky-purple jewel colour
and pretty bloody, but that's okay as they'll get cooked some more
in the pie later.

Leave your sliced pigeon on the side, and go back to your pigeon-y
pan. Set it over a low heat and add another knob of butter and a
splash of olive oil. Add your shallots, garlic and diced pickles. Give
them 20 minutes or so, stirring gently, until the shallots are sweet
and tangly and disintegrating a little. $\longrightarrow$

⟶ Now pre-heat the oven to 180°C, and liberally grease two small flan tins with butter.

Add your port to the pan, and stir, letting it simmer and reduce to a syrup. Stir in your mustard, along with any blood that's seeped from the sliced pigeon. Stir, stir. Add the cream and grated Parmesan, season with salt and pepper, and let the sauce thicken for a few minutes, then remove from the heat.

Take your pastry out of the fridge, and roll it out thinly between two sheets of baking paper – this will stop it sticking to the bench and the rolling pin. Cut the pastry into quarters. Press the rim of a flan tin into two of the quarters, using it like a cutter: these will be your pie lids. Cover them with cling film for now.

Use the remaining two quarters to line the tins. Press the pastry down lightly with your fingers, pushing it into the fluted sides of the tin and patching up any tears by pinching them together. Slice off any excess pastry, then slip one of the sheets of baking paper you used for rolling the pastry into each tin. Fill with baking beans, if you have them, or uncooked rice if you don't, and blind bake for 15 minutes.

Meanwhile, cut out the initial letters of your name, and your dinner pal's name, from the pastry off-cuts.

Bring the pastry cases out of the oven. Empty out the beans, and the paper, and begin: one layer of sauce, one layer of bright pink pigeon, one layer of pickle strips. Repeat until everything is used up.

Top your pies with their lids, using your thumb and fingers to pinch the edges together where the base meets the lid and make a sort of pleated pattern. Brush with beaten egg (I use an old paintbrush, but a pastry brush really would be better) and gently press on the initial letters. Brush again with beaten egg and scatter with salt flakes, then bake for 15 minutes, or until the pastry is golden and bright.

Serve with a crisp green salad and a glass of red, if you are eating at home; if you're taking them on a picnic, let the pies cool on a rack, and then pack into Tupperware, with scrunched-up baking paper to protect the edges and the top.

Quick Pink Pickled Onions

This is the absolute easiest way to make pickled onions, and will work with whatever quantities of aromatics you have to hand. These are nothing like pickled onions one gets in pubs: they are glorious, sharp, bright pink slivers. They are also very quick to make, and if you make them in a nice clip-top Kilner jar, make beautiful presents. You can also just take the jar straight out with you, and dollop them into sandwiches.

Makes 1 medium jar

1 garlic clove

2 sprigs of thyme

2 red onions

200ml cider vinegar (or white wine or rice vinegar)

1 tbsp golden caster sugar

2 tsp salt

7 black peppercorns

7 coriander seeds

7 allspice berries

To sterilise your jar, bung it in the dishwasher and run it through a hot cycle. Or wash it thoroughly in hot soapy water and rinse well, then take the rubber ring off, stand the jar and its lid upside down on a clean baking sheet and dry in a 170°C oven for 15 minutes.

Peel the garlic clove, and cut it in half. Drop it, and the thyme sprigs, into the bottom of your jar. Peel and slice your onions: I like to cut them into half-moons, then press out the layers with my fingers, because I think they are prettiest that way; dump them into a sieve set over the sink. Put the kettle on to boil.

Tip everything else into a stainless-steel saucepan, set over a low heat and slowly bring to a simmer. Meanwhile, pour boiling water from the kettle over the onions and leave to drip-dry (feel free to shake the sieve vigorously). Pack the dripped-dry onions into the jar, then pour over the infused vinegar.

Allow to cool, then refrigerate, preferably for at least a couple of hours – the longer you leave them, the pinker they will be. Once they're pickled, they'll keep in the fridge for a few weeks, I'm told, but they never seem to last that long in our house.

Wildly Easy Hummus

One Christmas, the Tall Man gave me Yotam Ottolenghi and Sami Tamimi's *Jerusalem*, and in it they call hummus the 'most explosive of subjects'. I imagine the Israelis and the Palestinians would be equally horrified by the things I've done to their national dish/es, but this really is both very good and wildly easy. It isn't especially quick – you have to shell the chickpeas for perfectly smooth hummus – but it's meditative. Once the hummus has been blitzed to silky-smoothness, it's scattered with za'atar (you should be able to find this in most big supermarkets), which I learned to love at school in Dubai, and it's also sharply lemony, because I am a lemon fiend. It makes me happy. I hope it makes you happy too. Don't forget the pitta bread, for toasting and scooping.

For 6

1 x 400g tin of chickpeas

4 fat garlic cloves

2 big lemons

4 tbsp tahini

2 tbsp olive oil (maybe more, keep the bottle by you)

2 tsp flaky sea salt

2 tbsp za'atar or 1 tsp paprika

· · · · · · · · ·· · · · · · · · · · ·· · · ·· · ·· · · · · ·· ·· ·· · ·· · · · ·· · ·

Drain the chickpeas into a bowl, cover with cold, clean water and leave to soak for 15 minutes. I know, I promised you easy hummus. But this is how to make your tinned chickpeas taste a little bit less tinned, a little bit less... cat-food-y.

While you wait, chop the garlic very finely, grate a little of the zest from your lemons (you need about a teaspoon) then squeeze the juice out of them, and maybe watch a bit of *Chicken Run*.

Drain the chickpeas, then return them to the bowl. In the Tiny Flat we have this concept, born of ultimate laziness, known as a 'chable': it's a chair-table. Of course it is. Set yourself up with the bowl of chickpeas in your lap, your blender jug on a chable, and a bin alongside. Take a chickpea between finger and thumb, and squeeze lightly: the skin, a pleasing little shrug of a thing, will slip off. Drop the shelled chickpeas into the blender and the skins into the bin. Like separating beans from ashes, once you get going, there is a Zennish quality to the process.

When the chickpeas are all shelled and in your blender, blitz them to fine crumbs. With the motor running, gradually add the tahini, followed by the lemon zest and juice, and then the garlic. Keeping the motor running, add a little cold water, then a little of the olive oil and some of the salt. Stop and have a taste. The hummus will probably seem too thick, so with the motor running again, keep on adding cold water, olive oil and salt and tasting until it seems like the sort of hummus you like. (I would have kept blending mine, but the blender started to smoke, so I stopped.) When the hummus is done, or the blender threatens to give up the ghost, spoon into a bowl and cover. Chill for as long as you can bear it – at least half an hour, I think.

Drizzle with olive oil and scatter with za'atar or paprika. Pittas, toasted, warm. Yellow roses. Lemons. Laziness. Love.

Variations on a Hummus Theme

Red Pepper Hummus, which I make either with 4 red peppers, sliced into quarters, de-seeded, drizzled with olive oil and then roasted at 160°C for 25 minutes, or a handful of pre-roasted red peppers from a jar. I like smoked paprika in this one, and some chilli salt: about a teaspoon of each, into the blender with the peppers and the hummus, and zizzed until smooth.

Green Harissa Hummus is a tiny bit more complicated, but not by much: you need a bunch of coriander (the most useful guide to size I can give you here you is that the stems, held together, should be about the size of a twenty-pence piece), rinsed and roughly chopped; some lime juice (about half a lime's worth); and a generous tablespoon of either bought green harissa or your own home-made (see page 205). Whizz together the hummus as normal, and when it's broken down into a rough paste, add the coriander, lime juice and green harissa and blend until smooth.

Would I Lie to You Labneh

I did not believe for a long time that making a quick, cheat-y cheese could be this easy, but it is: use it wherever you might use cream cheese, or even feta or curd cheese. I promise you this is as simple and good as it sounds, and I would never lie to you about cheese.

It's delicious, soft and salty, and it is sharp enough to take as much flavour as you care to throw at it. You don't need anything much to make this: some muslin – which is useful for everything anyway (straining, mopping up, and of course labneh-making) – and a place to hang your muslin-wrapped labneh as it drains. I hang mine off the top of my stand mixer, with a dish where the bowl should sit, to catch the whey, but I know people who just hang it from their kitchen tap (and then there's no need for a whey-catching bowl).

Makes 1 little round cheese

20g coriander

20g curly parsley

2 spring onions

4 tbsp full-fat Greek yoghurt

2 tsp lemon juice (a bit less than 1/2 lemon)

1 tsp fine salt

Piece of muslin about 30cm square

Black pepper

Olive oil, for drizzling

· · · · · · · · · ·· ·· · · · · · · · · · · · ·· ·· · · · ·

Take your herbs and the spring onions, and shred them as finely as possible; add a good grind of black pepper.

In a bowl, vigorously mix your yoghurt with the lemon juice, most of the peppery herbs, and the salt. Spoon into the centre of the muslin, gathering up the edges of the muslin and holding them closed just above the yoghurt. Tie firmly, either with an off-cut strip of muslin or some string. Use the tail ends of your tying material to knot the whole thing around the top of your stand mixer, or whatever else you're going to hang it from. Set a bowl beneath it, and go away for some 8–10 hours, depending on the thickness of the yoghurt you started with: you'll be able to tell it's ready when it stops dripping. You can leave it for longer, if you like – even overnight, if you have enough space to hang it in the fridge. Once your labneh is made, it will keep in the fridge for a few days.

To serve, unwrap the labneh (it will sit beautifully, like a whole set cheese, a real proper cheese) and carefully tip it out into a ramekin, then drizzle with nice olive oil. Unless you're taking it on a picnic, in which case cover the dish tightly with cling film and drizzle the olive oil on when you get there (those tiny plastic bottles of oil you sometimes get with shop-bought fresh pasta are absolutely perfect for this).

The Tall Man's Pâté

In my life I have had several moments of total clarity. Not revelations, necessarily, but times and places where I have, fleetingly, felt that everything in the world was more real than usual, and that everything was brighter and truer and clearer than ever before.

I spool through them, these moments lit with gold, whenever I am sad: sailing into a harbour in Greece, about fifteen years ago, and seeing a woman shake out a white cloth from a balcony on a house on top of the hill; a grey street near Euston, when I was seventeen, and where I was standing the day I realised I was in love with the Tall Man; a picnic, when the Tall Man and I were newly together, and lying sprawled on a hillside, cutting thick wedges of pâté, and balancing them precariously on doorstops of home-made soda bread, and spreading the whole with bolshy yellow mustard. I have a particular weakness for mustard-yellow, and I love it best in the context of that little yellow tin. It feels like a leftover from an earlier and simpler time, and when I see it on the supermarket shelves I rejoice for it. It's a lovely thing.

This is that pâté, exactly as the Tall Man makes it, and I watch him make it now and marvel: I marvel at the unlikely deftness of his hands dicing the livers small, and at the fact of his being. I marvel at the way the meat fits exactly into the little enamel dish. I marvel at the quick precision of his onion chopping. I try, now, to marvel at everything, and it is not hard: I believe very truly that my illness has made me better at looking, and at taking nothing for granted. The world is made up of golden moments such as these, and anything can be transformed into a golden moment if you look with the right and eager eyes. The scrubby, grim little kitchen of a Tiny Flat in the East End can be an absolute paradise, and everything in it tinged with glory, because for this minute we are alive, and looking, and that is as much as anyone can ask for.

I like this pâté recipe because it's quick, easy to tweak and you can do the whole thing with one ring on the hob, plus a food processor. We normally make it with chicken livers and a fairly low weight of pork, but if you're going for something a bit punchier (goat liver is delicious and incredibly cheap – ask a halal butcher), you might want to up the proportion of pork to keep the flavour nice and mellow.

For 4

1 small onion or 2 banana shallots	Butter, for frying
2 garlic cloves	4 cloves
30 black or white peppercorns, or a mixture	1 tbsp brown sugar
	2 capfuls of brandy
175–250g fatty pork: streaky bacon, pancetta or pork belly	2–3 tbsp double cream
	Salt
500g liver (such as chicken or lamb's)	

. · . · . · . · . · . · . · . . · . · . · . · . · . · . · . · . . ·

Do all your prep first, so you don't have to keep washing your hands and finding clean chopping boards. Chop the onion and garlic incredibly finely, keeping them separate. Grind the peppercorns using a pestle and mortar (we like about 50/50 black and white peppercorns, but whatever you've got will do).

If your pork isn't already diced, cut it into 1cm cubes. Finally, trim the liver of fat, tubes, blood and anything else that doesn't look tasty, then chop into pieces about the size of a walnut – for chicken livers, that'll be about two per lobe.

Melt a little butter in a frying pan and add the pork. Fry it on a fairly low heat for 10 minutes or so, giving the fat plenty of time to render and pool invitingly in the pan, then pop in a bigger slice of butter and your onion. This will smell outrageous. Once the onion is softening nicely – don't let it caramelise, or you'll have brown flecks in your pâté – pop in the garlic. Fry for a few more minutes, then add the ground peppercorns, the crumbled heads of the cloves (pinch them between your fingers) and anything else that takes your fancy (fennel seeds go really nicely with gamier livers). Sprinkle in a couple of big pinches of salt, the sugar and the brandy, then stir it all up and keep frying for a minute or two.

Trying reasonably hard not to burn yourself, scoop everything out of the frying pan and into the food processor (having made sure the blade is already in...). ⟶

$\longrightarrow$ Pop a bit more butter into the same pan and add the liver. Give it about 2 minutes per side to get nicely coloured, but watch out – well-cooked liver will tend towards graininess once you've zizzed it, so aim for medium-rare. Don't be afraid to lean in every minute or so and chop one in half, like a haruspex inspecting the entrails: once the liver is deep pink in the middle and has lost its raw-meat sheen, you're good to go (the livers will cook a little more as they're blended). Tip them into the food processor, not forgetting to scrape in the pan juices.

This next bit's up to you, really – you can keep blending until you have something approaching a smooth parfait, or do the bare minimum for a chunkier, farmhouse-type pâté. I tend to blend for 5–10 seconds, then scrape down the sides, add a dribble of cream to help it come together, and salt to taste, and repeat until I'm happy, which is usually after three or four blasts of 5–10 seconds.

Once you're happy with the taste and texture of your pâté, let it cool in the food processor for 15 minutes or so and then pack it into a bowl. If you're feeling fancy, you can line the bowl with cling film, so your pâté can later be turned out onto a plate, like a meaty molehill. I'm told some people top their pâtés with clarified butter so they keep better, but I tend to eat them too quickly for this to be worthwhile. That said, letting it rest in the fridge overnight will really improve the flavour.

If not picnicking, serve the pâté thickly spread on hot toast, letting crumbs fall down your jumper. If picnicking, cover your bowl of pâté with cling film, grab a baguette and away you go.

Danish Crackers

This is my mother's recipe for crackers – from her wonderful Danish friend, Cristina – and she gave it to me. It makes excellent, firm, seedy little crackers, and I like them very much. They are very simple: everything is measured in a measuring jug, rather than being weighed, so you don't even need scales.

These are just right for piling high with The Tall Man's Pâté (see page 118), Would I Lie to You Labneh (see page 116) or smoked salmon; or for dredging, slowly and deliberately, through hummus (see page 114), Miso Ginger Aubergine (see page 200), or – my mother's favourite, and mine – a good deli jar of black olive tapenade, the kind that stains your fingers purple.

Makes about 30 crackers

100ml plain flour	100ml roasted pumpkin seeds
100ml rolled oats	1 tsp baking powder
100ml sesame seeds	2 tsp salt
100ml flax seeds	1–1^{1}/$_{4}$ tsp olive oil
100ml sunflower seeds	Flaky sea salt

• • • • ' • • • • • • • • • • •' • • • • ' • • ' • •' • • • • • •

Pre-heat the oven to 200°C and find a measuring jug. Measure out the flour, oats and seeds. Add the baking powder and salt. Tip the contents of the jug into a biggish bowl, and stir; measure 200ml of water, and stir it in, along with a teaspoon of the olive oil. Everything should incorporate beautifully, but if it doesn't, feel free to add a pinch more flour (go easy), a dash more oil or a tiny splash more water. The texture should be like thick porridge.

Dig out two baking trays and cut out three sheets of baking paper the same size as your baking trays. Cut the dough in half and, working with one half at a time, sandwich the dough between two sheets of baking paper, and roll it out on a smooth surface. Roll until the dough is as thin as you can get it; carefully manoeuvre it onto a baking tray, then peel away the top sheet of paper. Scatter with sea salt flakes. Repeat with the other half of the dough.

Slide the trays into the oven to bake for 20 minutes or until the crackers are golden. Leave to cool, then break into shards. See? Simple. And good for you too.

Chilli Challah Salad

I made this for the first time a fortnight after my paternal grandfather died. I'd been baking a lot of the challah bread on page 78, as a sort of mad coping mechanism, and then, after the unsettled grief subsided, I found myself with a houseful of rapidly staling bread and a deep urge to eat something other than toast.

There is a moral here, maybe: there will always be a time when you want more than toast; there will always come a time when you remember that life had something else in it besides crying. Woman cannot live by toast alone – and although it might feel, at some points in your life, as though the effort to make anything else might kill you, that will not last. There will be another feeling. You will wake up one morning and remember other things: the ripe sharp-sweet burst of a good tomato; the kick of a chilli; the salty, meaty bite of an anchovy. Nutrients. Vitamins. Colours.

This is what I made, when I felt like that: a kind of panzanella, or bread salad. This is why it's so good for picnics: the longer it sits, the better it is, and the more profoundly the salt-sharp-sweetness will penetrate into and transform the stale bread. You could, of course, make this with any kind of stale white bread, or in fact any bread, but I made it first with challah, and I like it best with challah.

For 4

1 punnet (about 200g) cherry tomatoes
2 big red chillies
$^1/_2$ cucumber
1 red onion
250g challah bread
Olive oil
1 garlic clove
1 tsp Dijon mustard

1 tbsp balsamic vinegar
2 anchovies
$^1/_2$ lemon
Chilli flakes, to taste (optional)
Half a dozen Kalamata olives
A fistful of torn-up basil leaves
Flaky sea salt and black pepper
Soft goat's cheese, to serve

• • • • • • ••• • •• • ••• •• • •• • •• • •• •• •• •••••• •• ••

Pre-heat your oven to 180°C and find a large baking sheet.

Set a colander over the big bowl you're going to make the salad in. Roughly chop your tomatoes, chillies, cucumber and onion. Put them in the colander, and salt liberally. Mix well, then leave for about 10 minutes. The juices from the vegetables will drain into the bowl beneath, forming the basis of your salad dressing.

Dice your bread, scatter it over the baking sheet and drizzle with oil. Shove it in the oven and cook for 15 minutes, until crisp and golden.

Take your garlic clove, and grate it into a mug or small bowl. Stir in the mustard and vinegar. Add the anchovies. Mush. Stir. Mush. Stir. Add a teaspoon each of salt and pepper. Stir. Squeeze in the juice of the lemon half too. Now, drizzle in a tablespoon of olive oil, whisking the whole time, so the dressing emulsifies. Slowly add the juices from the salted vegetables to the dressing, still whisking the whole time, to form a lovely thin dressing. Taste to see if it's got enough of a kick for you; if not, add some chilli flakes.

Tip the beautifully toasted challah bread into the big bowl and add the chopped vegetables from the colander, along with the olives and basil. Gently mix with your hands. Drizzle over the dressing. Hands in again, to gently toss everything together. Leave the salad to settle for at least half an hour, to let the flavours mingle.

Serve with some soft, soft goat's cheese, maybe even goat's curd.

Fig, Fennel, Freekeh & Cauliflower

(...and Coriander, Parsley and Parmesan, but the title was too long for the space above)

This is another picnicky dish that benefits from a while in a Tupperware container to let the flavours develop, although I regularly eat it warm for dinner too. It's beautiful: the wide, flat curls of brittle umami Parmesan and the sweet pinky-purple insides of the figs set against the bronzy-gold of freekeh and well-roasted cauliflower, the green of parsley and coriander, and the aniseedy yellow-green of fennel. Also, this is the quickest way I know to eat a whole cauliflower without thinking about it.

Freekeh is a kind of green wheat – I always buy it pre-cooked, for ease and speed. I believe it's quite good for you, but it's also very delicious: nutty and hearty and wholesome, and it's just crying out for a spicy, salty-sweet dressing like this one. If you can't get freekeh (most supermarkets sell it now, but not all of them), you can swap in lentils, such as puy or beluga. I think it would also be lovely with little white beans, or any kind of solid hearty grain; I'd probably stay away from couscous, which might be a bit small, but giant couscous would be fine.

For 2

1 lemon

4 garlic cloves

1 tbsp cumin seeds

1 tbsp fennel seeds

1 tbsp balsamic vinegar

2 tbsp extra virgin olive oil

1 cauliflower

1 fennel bulb

12 cherry tomatoes

4 figs

50g Parmesan

Handful of coriander leaves

Handful of flat-leaf parsley leaves

250g cooked freekeh

Salt and black pepper

Pre-heat your oven to 180°C.

Zest and juice your lemon and grate your garlic into a large bowl. Add the cumin and fennel seeds, vinegar and olive oil, and whisk together.

Roughly chop your cauliflower into little florets and roughly dice the fennel. Add to the bowl and toss everything together, then shake the lot into a roasting tin. Press in the cherry tomatoes, whole (they will basically disintegrate, adding their characteristic sweetness to the dressing) and season with salt and pepper. Roast for 35 minutes, or until the cauliflower is tender, bronzed and a little bit crisp.

While the vegetables are roasting, quarter your figs, and shave your Parmesan into fine, flat slivers: run the blade of the knife down the side of the cheese, so that it comes away in wide, brittle curls. Chop the coriander and parsley. Set to one side.

Take your roast vegetables out of the oven, tip in your freekeh and shake the tin vigorously. Return to the oven for 5 minutes, then remove and stir through the herbs.

If serving immediately, decant into a pretty bowl, shake the Parmesan over the top and stud with figs; if for a picnic, allow to cool to room temperature (so it doesn't sweat) before packing into a Tupperware container and arranging the Parmesan and figs across the top.

When in Rome Burrata Salad

This is the fanciest salad you're ever going to eat, and it's really just a showcase for burrata, a kind of mozzarella filled with mozzarella scraps and cream. Here, it sits, beautifully heavy, balanced precariously atop a salad of sun-yellow plums and bitter rocket, scattered with pepper and drizzled with golden olive oil, before bursting gloriously over the whole.

I first made this in Rome, where I had gone on a whim to meet a stranger off the internet. I had been having a bad day, and a stranger said: I love your writing. You seem like you're having a bad day. I've got a spare bedroom in Rome. Come and stay.

I found flights for pennies. They were horrible flights, of course, but there they were. This Friday. So I booked them. And I went.

The stranger was called Astrid, and her apartment was perched high on a hill (one, I later worked out, of the Seven Hills) on a cobbled street in Trastevere: a little corner mostly ignored by tourists, populated by butchers and bakers, and sprawling markets plump with greens and plums and tomatoes of all shapes and sizes and colours. I had never seen so many colours of tomato before: striped, subtle, gaudy; scarlet, green and gold. I was so entranced by the tomato stand, and by the butcher's shop, and by the cheese shops that I forgot, really, to look at Rome at all. My Rome was all food: you can keep your Colosseums, only leave me the markets and the cheese man's grandmother, with whom I struck up a brief, wordless but devoted, friendship. Astrid would go about her business, running errands here and there, and I would come home laden with packets of *fantasie di salumi* (all kinds of off-cuts and ends) from the supermarket meat counter, and baskets of vegetables, and perfect burrata. Far too much food, of course. But delicious. We had a little terrace, of that particular European kind where your only view is of the sky and other people's terraces, and we dragged the table out there and ate this.

If you want to take this on a picnic, I really suggest taking a knife with you and making it at your chosen spot: buy a paper bag of plums, and another of tomatoes, not forgetting a plump burrata, and arrange it all once you're there. I have done this often, and it's wonderfully Famous Five, roughly slicing tomatoes and plums with a penknife, and laying it all out on an enamel plate, and dipping in hunks of crusty bread.

For 2

1 x 200g bag rocket leaves

6 yellow plums

12 yellow cherry tomatoes

½ lemon

1 burrata

Your very best olive oil,
   for drizzling

Black pepper

· · ·· · ·· · · · · · · ·· · ·· · · · · · ·· · ·· · · · ··

Lay out the rocket on a large and lovely plate.

Take the golden plums and slice them as neatly as you can,
then fan them around the plate, leaving a fringe of rocket on
the outside and a circle of rocket in the centre.

Take the little yellow cherry tomatoes, quarter them, and fill the
inner circle of rocket with them.

Squeeze over the juice from your lemon half.

Take the burrata from its tub and sit it on top of the tomatoes.
Drizzle with the very, very best olive oil you can get your hands on.
Grind black pepper over it like you've never ground before.

Serve with an absolute ton of good bread, and cold white wine,
and sit in the sun and bask.

A Proper Ham Sandwich

I know. A recipe for a ham sandwich. Bear with me. This ham sandwich is so very good it seemed worth sharing. It's still essentially nursery food; but nursery food or not, some days nothing but a proper ham sandwich will do. All told, this will take you fifteen minutes to prepare, plus approximately three hours of simmering. It's good for picnics, packed lunches and blustery evenings in mid-autumn – and with the last one, you can use the stock from the ham hocks to make a gorgeous and comfortingly wintry pea soup for the next day.

For 2

1 ham hock (uncured if you can get it, cured if you can't)

1 large onion

2 carrots

Handful of fresh herbs
(*I use rosemary; everyone else seems to use parsley*)

1 bay leaf

4 garlic cloves

2–4 thick slices from an excellent loaf of dark bread, like Wicked Stepmother Black Bread (see page 75)

Very best salted butter

Grainy French mustard

1 large Bramley cooking apple

You start by blanching the hock, to get rid of any impurities. And you absolutely must do this. I thought for a long time it was just something people said to do, and then one day I skipped it, and the smell was obnoxious. So, put your hock in an enormous pan, cover with cold water, and bring to the boil. Let it simmer for about a minute, then drain off the liquid, rinse the ham under the cold tap, and put it back in the pan. Add the onion, quartered roughly, the carrots, ditto, and the herbs and bay leaf. The garlic cloves can go in whole, but peeled. Cover the lot with cold water and a lid, and sit it on a gentle heat at the back of the stove. Let it simmer slowly for 3 hours. (You could, if you wanted, use this time to make some bread...)

After 3 hours, lift out your hock – I find a spaghetti spoon and a fork quite useful for this – and set it down on a large chopping board or plate. Don't throw away the cooking liquid: you'll want this hammy stock to make pea soup (see page 82; just replace the water with ham stock for exceptionally good soup), or for reducing to a jelly for pork pies (see page 104). Strain the bits out, let it cool, and then keep it in the fridge (a few days) or freezer (a few months) until wanted.

Pre-heat the oven to 220°C. Using a sharp knife, strip the remaining fat and skin from the pink, pink meat; you'll think it can't possibly be that pink, but it really is. Lay the fat and skin onto a baking sheet, sprinkle with salt and a little oil, and put it in the oven for 30 minutes to crisp up – the crisper, the better, when it comes to crackling for sandwiches.

When the hock is cool enough to handle, shred the meat using a fork and your fingers – it should come away from the bone in lovely chunks. You will not be able to resist eating a bit. It will be entirely glorious.

Cut two oversized slices of dark bread. Butter lavishly; add a little grainy mustard. Slice your Bramley apple as paper-thinly as you can, almost translucent. Set several slices of apple over the butter and mustard. Heap with shreds of ham hock and shards of crackling. For picnic purposes, top with another slice of bread and wrap in foil.

Summon your hungry companion. Gesture wordlessly at the shredded ham, the sliced apple, the golden butter, the mustard, the dark bread.

Eat. Rejoice.

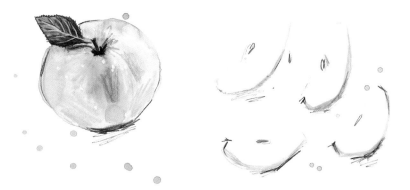

The Tall Man's Cheese Scones

The Tall Man is a better baker than me. Baking is all about rules, and I am very bad at rules; I love to cook because it's all about intuition and invention, about looking deep into the stew and trying to predict what it might want or need. This is not the Tall Man's way, which is why this is his generously shared recipe for scones, not mine. They are perfect scones: they rise beautifully, and split beautifully; you can spread them with butter or chutney or more cheese. I like them with Marmite. And I like them on their own. They are high and light and solid, all at once. They are cheesy, but not overpoweringly so (we tend to go with about 2:1 Cheddar to Parmesan, but anything hard enough to grate will do). The cayenne kick, which I was initially reluctant about, is absolutely crucial.

These scones are the kind of thing you can eat warm with melting butter on drizzly afternoons with half an eye on a game of Scrabble; or pack up and take out for a wet walk if you need an escape, and they keep well enough that you could even make a batch in advance and take them camping for the weekend.

Makes 10 scones

340g self-raising flour	70g salted butter, cubed
2 tsp baking powder	70g cheese, grated
1$^{1}/_{2}$ tsp cayenne pepper, or more to taste	About 220ml milk
	Flaky sea salt

Scones are very easy to make – all the danger and risk comes right at the end, when most people seem to either overbake them or ruin them on the plate, by cutting instead of tearing them. First, pre-heat your oven to 210°C and find your biggest bowl.

Sift together the flour, baking powder and 1$^{1}/_{2}$ teaspoons of cayenne pepper – or more, if you prefer your scones to have a body slam rather than a kick. (If you're waiting for someone to come round so you can assemble scones on cue, pause here and just weigh everything else out, ready to go.)

Rub in the butter, using just your fingertips and trying to be as light as possible, until your mixture looks a bit like breadcrumbs. Stir in your cheese and then pour in your milk.

Cut the milk into the dough with the back of a knife, resisting the urge to stir – any overworking now will make you look a right prong in 15 minutes' time. You might need a bit more milk, but within a minute or so you'll have a soft, pliable but not too sticky dough. Well done.

On a floured surface, roll out your dough to a thickness of around 2cm. Choose a cutter (no novelty shapes, please) or an appropriately sized glass; I ruined my favourite cutter by using it to make perfectly round fried eggs, so I use a slightly wonky one with scalloped edges. Cut out as many scones as possible, rolling the leftover scraps of dough up like a Chelsea bun or, if all else fails, squashing them into a lump. I usually get about ten scones out of this mixture.

Space out your scones on a floured baking sheet, sprinkle with flaky sea salt or a bit more cheese, then pop them in the centre of the oven for 11 minutes or so. A well-baked scone will sound distinctly hollow when tapped on the bottom.

There's no need to let your scones cool – in fact, they're better still warm from the oven – but tread carefully, because this is where people go wrong. Cutting a fresh scone will make its wonderful springy interior coalesce into a grim, doughy slab – all you need to do is make the tiniest crease along one side with a knife, and then ease the scone open. Load it with chutney and/or more cheese.

If you're not planning to eat all your scones right away, pop them on a cooling rack and then into something airtight.

Sweet Scones

For sweet scones, simply replace all the cheese (and the salt flakes) with caster sugar, and omit the cayenne. Load your freshly baked scones with jam and *then* clotted cream...

Inelegant Samosas

There's a line about love in a Laurie Lee essay: 'Love still has the intimations of immortality to it, if we're willing to pay it tribute... [it is also the delight] in being content now and then to lie by one's sleeping love, and to shield her eyes from the sun.' I would add to this, I think, a mystery novel (something properly ghoulish and precise on human nature, like Ruth Rendell), and a bottle of fiery ginger beer; perhaps also a small dog soundly asleep; and a samosa in the hand that isn't shielding the eyes of the sleeping love: that's a little moment of perfect happiness right there, which is all I want from immortality.

These are not proper samosas, but crisp little parcels that mimic them: filo pastry, folded into triangles, packed around punchy spiced chickpeas, with either butternut squash or minced lamb, depending. The secret to sealing them is to fold the pastry, then add the filling afterwards. I learned this from a wonderful woman named Lally, who is from Sri Lanka, and was so appalled at my poor folding that she gave me a samosa lesson.

Makes 12 samosas

About 75g butter, for brushing
  (don't bother measuring!)

2 x 270g packets of filo pastry
  (12 sheets)

For the filling

1¹/₂ tsp cumin seeds

1 tsp coriander seeds

2 cloves

1¹/₂ tsp black peppercorns

1¹/₂ tsp ground turmeric

¹/₂ tsp cayenne pepper

¹/₂ tsp mustard seeds
  (black or yellow)

1 red onion

3 garlic cloves

1 x 400g tin of chickpeas

330g butternut squash
  (*about half a one, although*
  I often just use a 250g bag of
  pre-chopped squash instead)
  or 250g minced lamb

Oil, for frying (*any is fine –*
  I tend to use rapeseed)

Salt and black pepper

· · · · · · · · · · · · · · · · · · · · · · · · · · · · · · · · ·.

For the filling, set a decent-sized frying pan on a low heat, and add your cumin and coriander seeds. Pinch the heads off your cloves, crush them between your finger and thumb, and add them too. You're going to dry-fry the spices in the pan for about 4 minutes, stirring and turning the seeds over and over themselves in the hot pan, so they don't burn. The cumin seeds should turn almost reddish, a kind of tobacco colour, and will smell wonderful.

As soon as they're done, tip the spices into the pestle and mortar. Add the peppercorns and bash away until they are finely ground, then stir in the turmeric, cayenne and mustard seeds (these are nice left whole as a little crunch, a little kick).

Finely chop your onion, and your garlic. Put your frying pan back on a low heat and add the onion and garlic, a splash of oil (just a tiny bit, to coat) and all the spices from the mortar. Stir like mad, until it's all intermingled, then cook slowly for about 10 minutes, stirring often – you want the onions to have a little bit of bite left.

Open your tin of chickpeas, drain and rinse well. Chuck them in too, and cook for 10 minutes more.

While this is happening, peel and dice your butternut squash (if you're not using pre-chopped). ⟶

⟶ When the 10 minutes is up, add the butternut squash or minced lamb to the pan: your butternut squash will want a big splash of water and a lid sticking on it, so it can cook for about 20 minutes or until tender; your mince will want stirring often and cooking for about 15 minutes until well browned. Taste it. Salt. Taste a bit more. What does it need? Pepper? More salt? Season to taste, then remove from the heat.

Pre-heat your oven to 180°C.

Melt the butter, either in the microwave or a small saucepan. Open your packets of filo. Yes, it is meant to be that thin. It's papery, but strong – don't worry, you're not going to break it.

Lay out a sheet of filo on a flat surface: there'll be two short sides and two long sides. Brush lightly with melted butter, and fold it: first into thirds (along the imaginary dotted lines in the picture above), and then into triangles. My dad used to fold crisp packets into triangles in the pub, and this really is just like that, if you've ever done the same. Like this:

When you've got a neat triangle, with a little bit left over, open the triangle out into a pocket, and stuff it. Brush the edge with water (using your finger) and fold the last flap closed. Pinch to seal.

You'll soon get into a kind of rhythm: the first one will be inept, the second merely clumsy, but by number three you'll feel like you've really *got* this, and you'll pleat and fold and brush with butter like you've been doing it all your life. I haven't, and my samosas are inelegant enough to prove it – but, alone in my kitchen, I get to pretend that I made them at my mother's knee.

Tuck in any stray ends, brush with more melted butter and set on a baking tray lined with baking paper. When you've got your dozen, stick them in the oven and cook for 30 minutes until crisp and golden.

Leave your samosas to cool on a rack, then wrap up in foil for your picnic. Or, of course, serve hot on a big platter with some lovely chutney and the kale salad on page 201.

Storecupboard Suppers
& Midnight Feasts

T his, more than any other chapter in this book, is cooking for the tired. Cooking for the home-late and the stayed-up-late; cooking for the sleepy, the knackered, the shattered and the insomniacs; cooking for lovers looking for something post-coital for the early hours; cooking for Caroline and me at two in the morning when there's nobody else around and I can't stop (won't stop?) crying. Cooking for when you're feeling too sad, or too scared, or too small to leave the house. Cooking for when you're in a hurry, and there's no time to shop properly; cooking for right now. Cooking for when you just don't have it in you to do something complicated: Monday-to-Friday cooking, or middle-of-the-night cooking. Everything here is easy and reasonably quick to make, with minimal washing up involved.

Most things in this chapter are made primarily from the pantry, fridge and freezer ingredients listed in the introduction, with a few fresh ingredients, but not many. Obviously, you won't always have everything for everything, but you'll probably have everything for something, and if you don't you can swap it for something else. You'll be able to get most of the extra bits at a mini-supermarket or corner shop on your way home. There is nothing in this chapter that requires a Big Shop.

And here is the most important thing: everything in this chapter is completely delicious. You would not be embarrassed to serve any of these things at a dinner party, or on a date, or after a date; nothing in this chapter feels stingy or parsimonious or scrabbled from the fridge in a fit of panic. There are hearty soups and a couple of ways with rice, plenty of pasta options, comforting potato pancakes and cauliflower cheese, and a dressing to glitz up the most unmentionable of fridge-bottom veg.

You will find something to make here, whatever your mood and whatever the weather. There are recipes for winter and for summer, but mostly for grey days – the kind of glum day when you find yourself equally torn between wanting something nice to cheer you up, but not wanting to go outside to get it. This is the best of both worlds.

Emergency Risotto

The best thing about me, as a person, is that I absolutely always have the things to make risotto. You need some rice. You need some flavourful liquid: wine, stock, mushroom liquor, or a stock pot or cube dissolved in boiling water. Butter, oil, or some other kind of fat. Vegetables of some kind. Maybe a little meat. Maybe a little cheese. A spoon, a frying pan, some patience. Some time. That's all. If you have those things, you can have a risotto.

I have made risotto in times of personal and political crisis, and in times of great and overwhelming joy. I can make risotto when I'm depressed and cheerful and furious, but however I'm feeling when I start, I always feel better at the end of it. I have made risotto bleakly, sobbingly sober, and gleefully hammered, and both times it was a solid, reliable, grain-based joy. (And there is nothing like taking a pan full of hot risotto back to bed with you, although I must confess the scorch mark on the duvet cover never quite came out.)

The recipe below is for walnut, pancetta and kale risotto, but feel free to improvise. When I make it for my little goddaughter, Leila, I make it with prawns and chorizo, like a kind of faux-paella; she calls it 'gold rice'. And when I make risotto for dinner parties, I make it with leeks and taleggio. As far as the rice goes, though, it's best to use proper risotto rice (arborio or carnaroli), because it simply cooks better and more easily – but at a pinch you could use pudding rice, or even basmati, if you have the patience to stir a while longer.

For 4

6 garlic cloves

2 onions

400g kale

Handful of walnuts

200g diced pancetta

Butter or olive oil, for frying

400g carnaroli or arborio rice

About 600ml chicken stock (or 1 chicken stock pot/ cube dissolved in 600ml boiling water)

About 300ml white wine

About 60g Parmesan

Dash of lemon juice (optional)

Salt and black pepper

⟶ Start with your garlic: chop it as finely as you can manage, and then a little finer (please don't be tempted to grate it – grated garlic can go funny in risotto). Finely chop your onions too. Wash and shred the kale: I do this by putting it in a colander, rinsing vigorously, and then going at it with the kitchen scissors. Squeeze the walnuts in your fists to break them up a bit.

Now take your biggest frying pan – a deep one is ideal. Fry the pancetta in the dry pan over a medium-low heat, stirring occasionally, until it renders its fat and starts to turn golden. Throw the garlic and onions into the pancetta fat and cook for about 10 minutes; keep an eye on it – you might need to add a bit of oil or butter.

If using home-made stock, bring it to the boil in a small saucepan; if using a stock pot or cube, put the kettle on.

When the onions are translucent, and everything smells good, add the rice and plenty of black pepper. Stir the dry rice through the soft onions, then pour over just enough stock to cover (this always makes me think of walking on a flooded field: the way the water puddles up through the grains as you pour it over, the way the surface seems to shine). Stir occasionally; let the rice absorb the stock. Add the wine. Wait. Stir. Add some more stock. It will stick if you don't keep stirring it, but it almost certainly won't matter too much. Wait. Stir. Taste. Add stock. You can carry on like this for quite some time. The Tall Man notes that making risotto is a very meditative thing, and it is.

After 20 minutes, you can start to taste – before that, the rice will be unpleasantly chalky. I'm with Marcella Hazan on this, and like my rice soft all the way through. Grate in the Parmesan and taste again – you may need salt, or a little lemon juice to cut the fat.

When the rice is done to your taste, or just a little moment before, throw in the kale. A last splash of white wine, if you like; I do like, because I like a slight boozy tang. Lid on for 5 minutes. Stir. Throw in the broken-up walnuts. Stir. Spoon into bowls. Add a last grind of black pepper, and a brief twist of lemon juice. Sofa. Blanket. Slump. Eat.

A Risotto for All Seasons

For autumn I make my risotto with mushrooms, saffron and egg yolk. Raggedy golden girolles are my favourites, and I sauté them alone in a non-stick pan to intensify their flavour, and stir the saffron (in a little milk) through the rice. I then serve the risotto in white bowls, pressing the back of a spoon into each mound of steaming rice before cracking in a raw golden yolk, for each diner to stir through, like a kind of risotto carbonara.

On a winter's night, I make risotto with diced cooked beetroot and butternut squash, and grated hard goat's cheese.

For late spring I make it with pea shoots, frozen peas, young Parmesan and shredded ham hock.

I don't tend to make risotto in summer, except when I am home alone, and then I make it with whatever is left in the fridge: an old lump of stone-hard Parmesan, a couple of old onions (cutting off the bad bits), a wilted stalk of celery and some stock made from a stock pot or cube. Perhaps the finely grated zest of half a lemon, found wedged sadly in the door of the fridge, and half a packet of frozen peas. It's always good.

(Not Quite) Chao Xa Ga

I should make clear at once that this probably has very little to do with authentic chao xa ga, a kind of Vietnamese lemongrass rice porridge (this sounds terrible in English, which is why it isn't the title of this recipe), but it does share most of the same flavours, and some of the same techniques.

Of course, it is really a kind of hearty chicken soup, and an actual doctor once told me that chicken soup has real benefits. That's why I make this: infinitely adaptable and infinitely delicious, it seethes and bubbles and fills the house with soft steam. It's more than the sum of its parts, is absurdly comforting and clean-tasting, and you feel better and more lively for having eaten it.

For 2

1 x 400ml tin of coconut milk

200ml chicken stock (or 1 chicken stock pot/ cube dissolved in 200ml boiling water)

2 tbsp fish sauce

2 tbsp grated ginger (about 6cm)

1 tbsp grated garlic (about 4 cloves)

1 tsp brown sugar

2 tsp white pepper

2 lemongrass stalks (fresh is better, dried is fine)

2 limes

200g kale

Bunch of coriander

Bunch of spring onions

2 red bird's eye chillies

200g jasmine rice

200g cooked and peeled prawns

•• •• • •' • ••• ••• • • •· • ••• • • '•' • •• ••

Combine your coconut milk, chicken stock and fish sauce in a saucepan, and stir to dissolve any lumps. Add the ginger, garlic, sugar and pepper. Stir again. If using fresh lemongrass, chop it into the pan with scissors; if using dried, add the stalks whole. Bring the broth to a gentle simmer over the lowest-possible heat while you zest and juice your limes. Reserve a pinch of lime zest, then add the rest to the broth, along with the juice. Inhale deeply. Feel better.

Tip the kale and coriander into a colander, and rinse them vigorously (both are horribly good at hiding grit). Use scissors to chop them as finely as you can manage, then set to one side.

Rinse and slice the spring onions, then add most to the broth, reserving a few green shreds for garnish. Rinse, slice and de-seed the chillies, and do the same.

This should all take about 10 minutes, and by this time the house will smell beautiful and bright and green. Rinse the rice, then tip it directly into the broth. Cover the pan and cook for 18 minutes, stirring a couple of times to break up any clumps of rice.

Taste: the rice should be soft and sticky, with broth bubbling all around and over it. Stir through the kale and coriander and cook for 2 minutes more. Finally, add the prawns and cook for another 2 minutes.

Decant into bowls: a mound of tender rice, studded with pink prawns and flecks of vivid green, surrounded by a moat of richly scented broth. Scatter with the reserved lime zest, loops of red chilli and hoops of green onion. Serve straight away.

Needs Using Up Minestrone

My fridge is full of good intentions.

I am such an optimist about myself when I shop: I am rich and bounteous and eat acres of vegetables, and I cook something proper from a book every night of the week. I walk through the supermarket convinced that this time will be the time I live up to my trolley, and it never is, and the fridge is where all those good intentions go to die, where they stay until I fish their grim corpses out of the bottom of the vegetable drawer.

This soup is the way to alleviate the guilt. It uses up all that fridge veg, and the Parmesan rind, and the slightly vinegary wine. You could substitute any kind of pasta here – I've made it before with a handful of broken-up tagliatelle ends out of a Quality Street tin – but the little stars and alphabet letters are really lovely. It can take anything you want to throw at it, and it will be good and delicious and hearty. It takes a bit more time, admittedly: you need to peel and chop the veg, and grate some Parmesan, but it's not complicated, and the pasta and beans give it a good whack of energy. Plus, if you're dining alone, it makes enough for lunch tomorrow too.

For 2

1–2 onions

2 carrots

2 celery stalks

150g any other vegetables you want to use up (*I generally seem to have cauliflower, courgette and green beans*)

Oil or butter, for frying

3–4 garlic cloves

1 x 400g tin of tomatoes

1 stock pot/cube (chicken or vegetable)

1 x 400g tin of chickpeas, cannellini beans or butter beans

1 tsp chilli flakes

Pinch of dried thyme

Splash of red wine (optional)

Parmesan, to grate over the top (plus the rind, if you have it)

Handful of tiny pasta shapes: alphabet letters or stars

Handful of frozen peas

Salt and black pepper

Peel and chop your onions. Peel or scrub the carrots and dice them, along with the celery, discarding any grim black bits. Trim or peel the other veg as needed, then cut into florets or pieces about the same size as the carrot and celery. Take a reasonably sized saucepan, add a little oil or butter, and soften the onion, carrot and celery over a low heat, stirring occasionally, for about 5 minutes. Peel and finely chop the garlic, then stir it in too. Cook for 2 minutes.

Put the kettle on. Open the tin of tomatoes, and tip them in. Stir, vigorously. Drop the stock pot or cube into the empty tomato tin, fill it up with boiling water from the kettle and stir to dissolve. Open the tin of beans: if you're using chickpeas, drain and rinse them under the tap; beans can go in with their liquid. Stir in the chickpeas or beans. Swill the stock-tomato water around the tin, and swill it into the empty bean tin too, rinsing both; pour the stock into the saucepan.

Add the chilli flakes, thyme, wine and Parmesan rind (if you have either or both) and a good grind of black pepper. Don't add salt yet. Turn the heat up and bring the soup to a comfortable boil. Turn the heat down a little, add a pinch of salt, and toss in the pasta: it usually takes about 7 minutes to cook, but check the packet just in case. I'd keep testing too, because such tiny pasta shapes can overcook quite fast. When the pasta is almost done, add the frozen peas and cook for 2 minutes, no more.

Ladle the soup into bowls, grate over some Parmesan and grind over some pepper. Pour out the wine. Why not? And light a candle, even if it's just you. You deserve wine and candles, because you made yourself dinner, and it's good, and it's nutritious, and it's hearty, and it will keep you going just as long as you need it to. And you're brilliant. Completely brilliant.

Big Hearty Black Bean Soup

The only effort required here involves grating a couple of garlic cloves and chopping an onion. Everything else is just a chuck-in-the-pan-and-go job. It's got a decent kick to it, is warming like nothing else, and is really rather good for you: plenty of protein and vitamins; lycopene from the tomatoes; vitamin C from the lime, in case you were thinking of getting scurvy; and fibre and iron in the beans, too.

For 4

1 small onion

Oil, for frying (*I use rapeseed*)

1 tsp dried oregano

1 tsp dried thyme

1 tsp ground coriander

1 tsp chilli flakes

1/2 tsp soft brown sugar (*but really, any sugar will do*)

2 garlic cloves

1 x 400g tin of black beans

1 x 400g tin of chopped tomatoes

1 stock pot/cube (*any kind works here: beef, chicken or vegetable*)

1 lime

Salt and black pepper

Greek yoghurt, sour cream or feta (*or Cheddar for a school-dinner chilli vibe*) and fresh coriander, to serve

Take your onion, and chop it as finely as you can be bothered. Put a little oil in a saucepan over a medium-low heat and add your onion. Measure your herbs, spices and sugar straight into the saucepan too. Stir a bit, then grab your garlic cloves. Peel them, then carefully grate into the saucepan and stir again. Cook for 5–10 minutes, stirring occasionally.

Put the kettle on. Open the tin of beans, and tip it in, water and all. And the tomatoes. Save one of the tins, drop in the stock pot or cube and top up with boiling water from the kettle. Stir well, then add the stock to the pan. Turn the heat up a little bit, and grind in a good dose of black pepper.

Cut your lime in half and juice it: squeeze both lime halves over the pan, nice and slowly. Properly thoroughly. But at least you don't have to wash up a juicer.

By now the soup should be coming to the boil. Turn the heat right down again, and let it cook for 15 minutes more. Unearth the hand blender and zizz up the soup in the pan until not-quite smooth (carefully – it's hot). Taste it, tentatively, and add whatever salt it might need. (It's important to wait until now to season, because the beans and stock can both be quite salty.)

Pour into bowls and scatter over whatever yoghurt, sour cream, cheese or coriander you've been able to acquire.

(Ladle any leftover soup into an empty yoghurt tub or other sealable container and stick it in the fridge, then take it with you for lunch the next day, and feel smug and contented.)

Ciao Bella Tomato Sauce
(for Pizza & Pasta)

There's a restaurant I love in Holborn, in central London, called
Ciao Bella, and it feels like it's in Rome. Whenever I go there
with the Tall Man, we sit outside under the heat lamps, growing
like weeds, and they bring us olives, and I can't ever stop myself
quoting that line from Rebecca Lindenberg's poem – 'the round
olives are the green/all green things aspire to be' – and the Tall
Man laughs, because I do it every time.

The waiters are kind, and there is rough red wine, cheaper
than you'd find it anywhere else in central London, and platters
of thinly sliced cured meats with a burrata perched in the centre.
A man in a shabby coat and broad-brimmed hat sits and smokes
a few chairs down, and sketches the people passing by in swift,
deft strokes; a table of women, all blue-rinsed, chain-smoking and
silk-scarved, fall into that raucous, glorious laughter that comes
from loving people for forty years or more. Then they bring out
pasta for me, and pizza for him, and both have this immaculate,
fine tomato sauce. 'Tell me about your tomato sauce,' I say to my
favourite waiter one day, and he pulls up a chair and sits on it
backwards. 'It's so easy, bella,' he says, 'Let me explain.' And it is.

This sauce is not quite that sauce, but the Tall Man's take on
it: he adds wine, swaps the onion for garlic, and (go with me on
this) adds a couple of anchovies. I thought I loathed anchovies,
but, simmered in this sauce, I don't. I don't think you can taste
them, anyway, only a lingering sense of salty depths and darkness.

Fair warning: this recipe makes too much sauce. No matter
how much we get through, there's always a whole bowlful left in
the fridge afterwards, waiting for me to eat it, hungover, with a
spoon. It also freezes well, and this makes enough to freeze for
another, even harder day. With grated Parmesan and black pepper
(and perhaps, if you can make it to the shop, a sprig of basil?),
it's perfect with any pasta, or pizza, or spooned over arancini.
It's perfect, and it tastes like holidays, like weekends, like sitting
people-watching under an orange heat-lamp on a Holborn
pavement and holding hands under the table.

For 4, with leftovers

6 garlic cloves	2 anchovies
100ml extra virgin olive oil	1 tsp chilli flakes
3 x 400g tins of chopped tomatoes	Sprig of fresh basil, plus a few extra leaves
About 250ml red wine	Salt and black pepper

Chop your garlic very finely. In a big frying pan (not a saucepan, unless you only have a shallow frying pan), heat the olive oil. It will seem like a lot, but this seems to be the trick to good tomato sauce – use more oil than you think can possibly be necessary, and keep your nerve. Once your oil is hot, add the garlic. Burnt garlic is nobody's friend, so keep an eye on it and, if you think it's going to catch, quickly dump in your squished tomatoes to bring down the temperature. If you manage to keep the burn at bay, put in the tomatoes once the garlic is starting to go golden. Turn the heat down a bit to avoid spitting, and turn back to your tomato tins.

The aim of the game here is to get all the tomato juice out of the tins with minimal faff and without diluting the sauce. I like doing this with red wine, which would be going in anyway and might as well work for its keep. Slosh about a third of a tin's worth into one of the tomato tins, sluice it around as thoroughly as possible, then pour the tomato-and-wine goop into another tin. Repeat the sloshing and sluicing with the third tin, adding a bit more wine if you fancy, then pour the tomato-y wine into your sauce and you're done. You'll probably end up with about 250ml of wine in the sauce.

Add the anchovies and chilli flakes, along with a good grind of black pepper. The anchovies will break down, so pop them in whole and just have a bit of a stir. Sit a basil sprig on top of the sauce while you get it simmering.

About 20 minutes later, the basil will have sunk and the sauce should be coming together nicely. Give it a stir, taste and add salt (unless the anchovies have made it salty enough for you), then apply to your carbohydrate base of choice. Fish out the wilted basil sprig as you serve and, if you're feeling fancy, replace it with a couple of fresh leaves.

Carbonara, for Caroline

Nigella, in *How to Eat*, says that she makes carbonara for her lovers, like in the movies, and takes it back to bed. I make mine for my best friend, when we're up late, when the men are away; when we're watching bad films at midnight, and the shops are shut, and we need something savoury and salty and good.

Caroline says *men don't eat carbonara*, which is not true, but is true enough that it makes us both laugh, quietly, in the kitchen, with the bright white light of the streetlamp shining down on the Parmesan and the garlic and the linguine on the laminate. I'm beating eggs, and turning the garlic cloves over and over in the pan. Caroline is grating the Parmesan, and I am pretending not to notice that more is going into her mouth than in the bowl.

It is the kind of friendship one doesn't expect to find in the adult world: it's a schooldays, jealous, *'my* best friend' friendship. While I cook, she reads to me from *Flowers in the Attic* and *My Sweet Audrina*. We give each other beloved books for birthdays, and annotate them. *You're going to love this*, or, *NO!*, or, *YOU*, with an arrow, and underlined passages. The books are almost always by women: Laurie Colwin, Judy Blume, the Ephrons. The Mitford sisters. We are always swapping books about sisters: she is a youngest sister, and I am an eldest sister, and we sit sometimes and map that onto our lives. *You want validation because you've always had it; I want attention because I never got it. You assume everyone is looking at you; I am desperate for people to look at me.* We talk about our sisters. We talk, always, about our mothers: we always have. The first evening Caroline came to dinner, the Tall Man (whose friend she was) was late home from work, and Caroline and I sat for two hours, strangers, and ate a piece of Stilton as big as a novel, and laughed a lot, and talked about our bodies, and our mothers. The pattern was set then, I think, for this peculiar, intense friendship that is part motherhood, part wifehood, part sisterhood, and all framed in the shameless joy of eating.

This is not terribly authentic; nothing in this book is (you might have worked this out by now). Real carbonara has no cream, no garlic and no wine; only eggs, pancetta, pasta and Parmesan. That's good too, of course, but it's harder to get right. It took me years before I could make it without scrambling the eggs, and, truly, it's only practice that did it. Not a recipe, not a technique; only practice. I'm sorry... but not that sorry, because, in the ⟶

—→ meantime, there is this: equally delicious, yet far easier. Creamy pancetta-cheese-eggs linguine, rounded off with a hit of white wine and garlic and nutmeg, hitting every single one of the same spots as real carbonara without having to wait to work out how to get it perfect. Because this is always perfect.

For 2

200g diced pancetta
  (or bacon)
A sliver of butter
1 tbsp olive oil
2 garlic cloves
About 80g Parmesan
40ml cream (or full-fat milk,
  at a pinch)

3 large eggs
1 smallish glass of white wine
About 200g linguine
Freshly grated nutmeg, if you
  can be bothered
Salt and black pepper

First take your pancetta: fling it with abandon into a large frying pan with the butter and oil. (If you're using bacon, fry the rashers whole then cut with scissors when cooked.)

Peel the garlic cloves and crush lightly, by pressing down on them with the flat side of a knife. (I learned this trick from the Half-Blood Prince: he was talking about Sopophorous Beans and a Draught of Living Death, but it works exceptionally well for garlic in carbonara.) Put the garlic in the pan with the pancetta and let them cook, stirring often.

While the pig is getting crisp, set a large saucepan of salted water (as salty as the sea) over a high heat to boil and grate vast quantities of Parmesan – you want an extravagant amount of cheese for two people, at least 80g. In a jug, beat together the cream, eggs, most of the Parmesan and a simply astonishing amount of black pepper.

Carefully pour the wine into your pan of pancetta or bacon and garlic – it will sizzle alarmingly. This is what is supposed to happen. What we're aiming for is what Nigella calls a 'salty, winey syrup', and that's exactly what you'll get if you let it reduce.

Your saucepan of water will almost certainly be ready for its close-up by now. Put the pasta in and cook until al dente, stirring your winey-garlicky-piggy syrup occasionally as it thickens. Drain the pasta, reserving a half-mug of its cooking water, and then add the pasta to the frying pan. Stir thoroughly, adding a little bit of the pasta-cooking water to help the sauce cling to the pasta. Take the pan off the heat. Call through that you are *coming back, with food!*

Add a little pasta-cooking water to the cream, egg and cheese mixture – this brings it up to temperature, and stops it from scrambling – then quickly pour it into the pan and toss with the pasta. Divide between two bowls, I suppose, if you're feeling mannered. Eat from the saucepan if not. Grind over more (more) black pepper, scatter with (more) Parmesan and grate over a little nutmeg if you have it.

Pea Parmesan Pasta

This is comfort food at its most simple, so simple it feels almost silly to write a recipe. But perhaps you've had a hard day, and perhaps you need a very simple nursery tea. It couldn't be easier to make. It's also pretty, with a hint of alchemy: together the Parmesan, chicken stock and olive oil make a rich, tender sauce, better than cream – almost like a hassle-less carbonara, studded with little green jewels of peas.

For 2

1 chicken stock pot/cube

Generous glug of your very best olive oil

2 nests of vermicelli pasta

Biggish chunk of Parmesan

Large handful of frozen peas

Flaky sea salt and black pepper

Set a saucepan of water on the stove and bring to the boil, then add the stock pot or cube and a splash of olive oil. Drop your pasta nests into the boiling water – they'll take about 6 minutes to cook.

Meanwhile, grate your Parmesan.

After 5 minutes, add the peas to the pan. I cannot stress enough that you must watch your peas. Frozen peas are horribly easy to overcook: you want to catch them the minute they go that beautiful bright fresh green and float to the surface. (I will not hear a word said against frozen petit pois. I love them. They are not garden peas, but if you haven't got a garden, and it's March, that's irrelevant.)

The instant your peas are the right green, drain your pasta and peas by tilting the pan over the sink, keeping a tablespoon or two of the starchy chicken stock in the pan with them. Quickly stir through the Parmesan. Add a generous glug of olive oil, all melty gold. Stir well. Tip into two bowls, scatter with black pepper and maybe a few flakes of sea salt, then serve.

Marmite Spaghetti

I thought I'd invented this on Study Leave, as a late-night post-revision snack when I was fifteen and doing GCSEs, but I find to my surprise that I'm following in Nigella's footsteps, and she was following in Anna Del Conte's, and I believe that means we all three have exquisite taste.

A handful of long pasta, into salted boiling water.

50g of butter, melted in a saucepan with a teaspoon of Marmite, stirring all the time.

As much Parmesan as you can be bothered to grate.

Drain the pasta, stir through the butter and Marmite, and scatter over the cheese.

Best eaten from the pan, in your dressing gown, after a long evening of some dull but difficult work (like Latin revision).

Uplifting Chilli & Lemon Spaghetti

This is so simple and so beautiful, and is equally viable as a dinner-party dish (with a handful of prawns) or a late-night, low-mood kitchen supper. I make this when I am very sad, and need something to do with my hands: you mince the garlic and shred the chilli – a continuous rocking movement with the knife that is deeply meditative, and thoroughly soothing; then you zest the lemon. At the end of it, you have a little white heap, and a little ruby heap, and a little yellow heap, and you shake them together into sizzling olive oil, and the scent that rises up is about the most uplifting thing I know. It's bright and zingy and vivid, and everything about it is honestly good.

I used to call this recipe Flatly Suicidal Spaghetti, because that was when I most often made it, but the name was too sad: it was me that was flatly suicidal, not the spaghetti. And so I thought again and called it Uplifting Spaghetti, because that was how it made me feel. To make this, and to eat it, is an entirely satisfying, soul-restoring experience.

For 2

4 garlic cloves

1 big fat red chilli
   or 1 tsp chilli flakes

1 lemon

About 2 tbsp olive oil

200g spaghetti

About 50ml white wine
   (a very small glass)

200g cooked and peeled
   prawns (optional)

Thumb-sized nub of
   Parmesan (optional)

Salt and black pepper

. . . .

Take a big, deep pan, fill it with cold water and add a handful of salt. Taste the water: it should be as salty as the ocean. Set the pan over a high heat.

Find a chopping board and a big knife or cleaver, and take your garlic. You want to keep the part of the blade nearest the handle still against the board, and use it as a pivot, rocking the knife through the garlic over and over again, until you have a fine garlicky confetti. (You will need to concentrate on this, which is why it is good.) Take your fresh chilli, if using, and chop that too,

stripping out the seeds and fine white membranes, then dicing the flesh into a pinky heap. Next, your lemon. Take that, and finely grate the zest from about half of it, trying to get as little of the pith as possible.

Pour the olive oil into a frying pan and set it over the lowest-possible heat. Add your garlic, chilli and lemon zest, and stir constantly, watching it like a hawk so it doesn't burn.

Your water should be coming to a good rolling boil now: fat bubbles coming up from the bottom to the top, and bursting, and slinking down again. Add a little splash of olive oil and your spaghetti and cook until al dente.

Meanwhile, keep stirring your garlic just until it's the palest golden colour, then quickly pour in your white wine. Stir it, and keep stirring, letting the wine reduce until it's thicker and a bit syrupy. (Add the chilli flakes here too, if you didn't use fresh chilli.) If using prawns, add these now as well, and gently warm through. Grate the Parmesan, if you're using it.

Using a big slotted spoon or tongs, take your spaghetti from the water, dripping wet, and fling it straight into the frying pan. Stir it through the winey sauce. (If you prefer, you can drain your pasta in the normal way, reserving about 2 tablespoons of the pasta-cooking water, and then add the pasta and water to the frying pan, but I am lazy and recommend the slotted-spoon approach.) Scatter over the Parmesan, if using, and a good grind of black pepper, and stir well.

Decant into bowls, pour the wine, sit at a table and eat with a fork and a spoon, because you deserve to sit at a table, and you deserve to have a nice supper and be looked after.

Blackened Broccoli & Bittersweet Almonds (on Toast)

Please: bear with me here. I know. You hear 'broccoli on toast', and despair. But this is so much better than that. I can eat it by the fistful, dredging the toast through the roasting tin.

For my twenty-second birthday, the Tall Man took me to a pub on the edge of Hampstead Heath. It had been a long, strange year: I had spent the year slowly, infinitesimally pulling myself out of the depths. I had learned in that year to love food, and to love eating – which is at heart, for everything else it is too, just the simple mechanics of living – and so we went to a pub that's famous for its food, and ate piles of charcuterie and cheese, and a dish a little bit like this.

That broccoli was not blackened, but I like to think it's an improvement. There's a cauliflower cheese over the page where the florets are seared before being baked, and a beetroot soup on page 85 that involves burning things too, so this is the third in that trilogy: blackened broccoli, with bittersweet almonds. It's grown-up and subtle, and it tastes, bizarrely, more like broccoli itself than it would if it hadn't ever been burned. There's a metaphor there, but I think it might be clumsy to make it. So I won't: I'll make broccoli instead, and heap it on toast.

For 1 greedy person, or 2 as a double-duty carb-and-green side dish

220g broccoli (either Tenderstem or chopped)

50g flaked almonds

2 tbsp extra virgin olive oil

2 garlic cloves

$^1/_2$ lemon (or 1 tbsp lemon juice)

2–4 thick slices of good bread

About 1 tsp chilli flakes

Flaky sea salt and black pepper

· · ·· · · · · · · ·· · · · · ·· · · ·· · · · · · ··

Pre-heat your oven to 180°C, and rinse your broccoli. Leave it to dry in the colander, while you toast your almonds over a high heat in a dry frying pan. Give the pan a shake every so often, leaving the almonds alone to get toasted on the hot pan in between shakes, until they're a nice golden colour; try not to let them burn much, but don't worry if they do.

Tip out the almonds (you needn't be too fussy) into a dish and set aside. Add the olive oil to the pan, along with the whole peeled garlic cloves. Turn the heat down to low and cook for 2 minutes to infuse the oil with just a hint of garlic.

Tip the broccoli into a roasting tin, and pour over the garlic-infused oil, shaking to coat the broccoli in the oil. Scatter over 1 teaspoon of salt and a good grind of black pepper. Squeeze over the lemon and shake again. Roast for about 15 minutes: the broccoli should be tender, but not soft; firm, but toothsome; and the fronds at the ends should be blackened and crispy.

Take two slices (per person) of the best bread you can find, and toast them a little bit less than you'd ordinarily like. Slip the toast into the roasting tin among the broccoli, and return to the oven for 5 minutes more, so the toast absorbs all the salty, green-tasting olive-oil juices.

Put the toast onto plates and pile the broccoli on top, pouring over the garlicky oil from the roasting tin. Scatter with the golden-brown almonds and the chilli flakes.

Slightly Charred Cauliflower Cheese

This is a sort of amalgamation of the regular Sunday-lunch cauliflower cheese that I have always loved, a mad fontina and cauliflower dish they serve at this restaurant called Polpo, and an absolutely amazing cauliflower cheese I once ate in a pub as a starter and enjoyed so much I ordered it again as my main course.

I make this recipe in two ways: either I cook it in a medium-sized skillet, which saves on washing up, and do everything except the cheese sauce in it, and then serve it as a good show-off side-dish; or I make four little dishes for nights in the future when I really can't be bothered to cook. I freeze it in those same little dishes (blue and white enamel) at the point they're ready to go in the oven, then cook it from frozen – just for ten minutes longer, keeping a north eye on it.

The secret to really good cauliflower cheese, I believe, lies in understanding that cheese (and cauliflower) is always better a bit burnt: those blackening bubbles of burnt cheese that one has to peel off the grill pan after making a toastie; the gorgeous dark completeness of cheese cooked to a crisp; the golden-brown on the top of a really good lasagne. In this recipe, I like to use a cast-iron skillet, to get as much browning as possible – maximum char.

What you end up with is tender, fluffy cauliflower and nutty browned butter, with a salty, savoury, umami cheese sauce poured over, then topped with crispy, chilli-blitzed breadcrumbs and extra cheese, all blistered and burnt in the most delightful way. Bring it to the table with one big spoon for serving – or smaller spoons for eating straight out of the pan, with the heat from the skillet radiating along your forearms as you dip and dive for a second mouthful. You'll likely want nothing more for supper, perhaps just a hunk of bread to wipe around the pan afterwards, and who could blame you? ⟶

For 4

1 medium cauliflower
(or about 250g ready-
prepared florets)

3–4 tbsp salted butter

About 250g cheese – I like
about 150g Gruyère, 50g
Parmesan and 50g good
strong Cheddar

4 tbsp plain flour

200ml full-fat milk

3 tbsp panko (or any other
dried breadcrumbs)

1 tsp olive oil

Pinch of chilli flakes

Salt and black pepper

•• •• • • • ' • • •• ••• • • • •• • • •• ••• • • '• • • ' •• • ••

Pre-heat the oven to 180°C and stick the kettle on.

Break the cauliflower down into small florets, the better for
getting cheese on every conceivable surface, then put into a
saucepan with a bit of salt. Cover with boiling water from the
kettle and cook over a medium heat for 4 minutes exactly.

Tip into a colander, and leave to drain while you make the cheese
sauce: it helps the cauliflower to char if it's really dry, so it doesn't
matter if it sits for a little while.

Wipe the saucepan dry, and put it back over the lowest-possible
heat. Add 2 tablespoons of the butter and let it melt slowly, while
you grate all the cheeses into a bowl – keep a bit of the Parmesan
separate, ready for sprinkling over the top later. Whisk the flour
into the melted butter, and keep whisking for a few minutes to
cook the flour.

When you have a thick roux, slowly add the milk, whisking all the
time, to make a smooth sauce. Bring to a simmer over a medium
heat and cook, stirring constantly, for about 2 minutes or until the
sauce thickens. Add the cheese and stir until melted.

Put a cast-iron skillet or ovenproof frying pan over a low heat.
Throw in your breadcrumbs, a pinch of salt and a good grind of
black pepper, then drizzle lightly with olive oil and stir. Add a
pinch of chilli flakes – but go easy, and remember to open the
window and turn the extractor fan on, if you have one. Frying
chilli can be suffocating if you're not careful.

Cook for about 4 minutes, shaking the pan from time to time, until the breadcrumbs are golden and lovely. Tip them out into the bowl that once held the cheese.

Put the skillet back on the heat and add a tablespoon or two of butter – it will foam and brown almost immediately. Quickly add your cauliflower and cook for 4 minutes, stirring once or twice so that all sides of the florets get exposed to the hot pan: you want the cauliflower to get just a touch of lovely, glossy brown.

Pour the cheese sauce over the cauliflower in the pan (or transfer to small ovenproof dishes); scatter over your breadcrumbs; sprinkle over the reserved Parmesan and bake in the oven for 20 minutes until bubbling and well browned.

Bread; wine; somebody lovely; cheese. What could be nicer?

(Nothing, probably.)

Fridge Drawer Salad with Decent Dressing

You can make a pretty good salad out of pretty much any vegetables you have, provided you dice them as finely as you can be bothered, and then you dress them with a good sharp dressing. I also recommend a handful of nuts scattered over the top, to provide the crunch that some fridge veg can be missing.

The basis for most salad dressings worth eating is oil, salt and acid. There's a kale salad on page 201 that thrives on just a spritz of lime and a pinch of salt (the margarita approach) – and if you've got very fresh vegetables, all they really need is some good olive oil, a little balsamic vinegar and a bit of salt: this is great. But it won't work for older vegetables, for cheaper vegetables, or for any that have been lingering just a little too long; for those, you need a decent dressing to gussy things up.

When I was a nanny in Paris, the father of the family called his version 'De La Sauce', and he made a vat of it every weekend: the children and I would then have it with our salad starters every single night, dipping raw carrots straight into the tub. (It was Paris: of course the children were expected to eat starters every night.) It is delicious, versatile and a bit like magic the way the oil and vinegar come together. The thing about vinaigrette is that you're always trying to get water (in the vinegar) and oil (in the, er, oil), two things which hate each other, to become one unified whole, and that's why it splits – but mustard and salt stop it from splitting and make it into an emulsion. Then you can add whatever you like for extra flavour – such as garlic, or Parmesan or anchovy – but you don't need to. I have before now swapped the vinegar for red wine, which is brilliant. And a finely chopped shallot is really good here too.

The basic De La Sauce goes like this: one part vinegar, in a jar; one part mustard; a pinch of salt; and two parts olive oil, whisked in slowly, slowly, to form an emulsion. Once you've got the hang of making an emulsion like this, you can pretty much do what you like. Me, personally, I like the one on the page opposite.

Makes enough to dress a salad for 4

1 garlic clove

20g Parmesan

¹/₂ lemon

1 tsp Dijon mustard

1 tsp red wine vinegar

About 4 tbsp extra virgin
   olive oil

Salt and black pepper

· · · · · · · · · ·· · ·· · · · · · · · · · ·· ·· · · ·· ·· ·

Finely grate the garlic, Parmesan and the zest of the lemon half
into a jar with a lid. Add the mustard and vinegar, and squeeze in
the juice from the zested lemon half. Add salt and pepper to taste,
then immediately follow with the olive oil. Screw the lid on the
jar and shake until the dressing is thick and emulsified. If you're
making this in a bowl, slowly drizzle in the olive oil, whisking
constantly, until the dressing is thick and emulsified. It will keep
in the fridge for a few days.

Imaginary Granny's Latkes

When I was a little girl I used to pretend to have a grandmother. Really, I already had two grandmothers, and three great-grandmothers, all of whom were beloved, but still: I conjured an imaginary one, and her name was Yvette.

Yvette was small, precise, bird-like, and Jewish. I did not know anybody Jewish when I was little – I lived in a very rural, very small, very un-diverse Midlands village – but nonetheless, Yvette was. I suspect, now, that she grew out of a couple of books: *100 Assemblies for Primary Schools*, in which the story of Passover was easily the most compelling; and *Children of Britain Just Like Me*, in which the observant Jewish girl child-of-Britain-just-like-me had her name written into her carpet in bold pink letters, and was preparing for her bat mitzvah, and I thought both of these things were wonderful.

Yvette wore berets, and smoked thin, lilac cigarettes; she had small hands. She cooked (in my head) with a kind of tense, contained, distracted fury, like an elastic band pulled taut, and she made food I had never eaten, but read about in the books. Schmaltz. Bagels. Latkes. I could picture her quite clearly. She didn't take any nonsense, and she had a very straight back.

In Yvette's honour I bought big books on Jewish cooking, and read them all. This recipe does not come from those books, however, but by way of my wonderful friend Fiona, whose very real, unimaginary Jewish grandmother taught her to make these, and she has very generously allowed me to include the recipe for them here.

These are Fiona's grandmother's latkes, but they have quite a lot in common with the late, great Laurie Colwin's rösti, and that is why they are in this chapter: in her brilliant book *Home Cooking*, she recommends rösti as the thing you most want to eat when you get home from a disappointing dinner party that has 'dragged on way past the closing time of most pizzerias'. I love this, and I love that her recipe starts with 'take off your coat', as all good late-home recipes should.

I like to imagine Fiona's grandmother cooking these latkes in her kitchen, and Fiona cooking them in Paris where she lives, and Laurie Colwin cooking potato pancakes to her mother's recipe. Cooking these myself makes me feel part of a chain of women, mostly real (but one imaginary), and I hope you'll think of us all when you make them: Fiona, her grandmother, me – and my imaginary, fragile, tough-as-nails Jewish grandmother, with her small hands, shredding potatoes to make latkes.

For 2

1 big russet potato	1 tsp paprika
1 fairly small onion	1 tbsp oil (or, if you're very
1 egg	lucky, chicken fat)
20g plain flour	Salt and black pepper

. . . .

Using a coarse grater, grate the potato and onion into a heap. Scoop them into a sieve set over the sink and press as much water as possible out of them. Do this at least twice: squeeze, let sit; squeeze, let sit. ('No water in the latkes!' Fiona says, sternly.)

Crack the egg into a large bowl, and add the flour, along with the paprika, a big pinch of salt and a good grind of black pepper. Tip the potato mixture from the sieve into the bowl and stir until well combined.

Put your oil into a skillet over medium heat – or an ordinary frying pan. ('If you can't find schmaltz,' Fiona says, 'any oil will do.') Take small handfuls of the potato mixture and drop into the pan. Give them some room to spread and don't over-crowd the pan. Flatten them slightly with a spatula as they cook. Once they're golden and crisp on the bottom, carefully flip them with a spatula and cook until they're golden and crisp all the way around.

Lift the cooked latkes out onto kitchen paper to drain, and let them cool for a minute or two before eating. ('Some people prefer sour cream, some people like caviar,' Fiona says, 'But I can't account for the taste of fools. I'm an apple sauce girl all the way.') I like mine just as they are: crisp and delightful and home-late perfection.

Goat's Cheese Puff with Salsa

This is not a storecupboard supper in the strictest sense, but it is so quick and easy and delicious that I couldn't leave it out – and if you happen to live somewhere where you can grab some puff pastry, goat's cheese and prosciutto on the way home, so much the better.

As kids we mostly ate this after swimming lessons. It was, and is, my mum's staple: made with thyme and fancy olive oil for dinner parties, or Heinz ketchup for post-swimming suppers. This is a meal for the damp-haired and pink-cheeked, and for the chloriney, grey June days counting down to the holidays. Which is almost certainly why, cycling home from the pool today, I thought about this meal; that, and the sort of days (damp and chlorinated) when only soft melted cheese in crisp pastry will possibly do.

I am an enormous fan of hot cheese. Hot cheese is one of life's better small pleasures. Cold cheese is marvellous, but bubbling soft, salty cheese is a different joy entirely: Lebanese cheesebreads, on which I mainly lived for the two years I was at school in the Middle East; whole baked camembert studded all over with chilli and slivers of garlic; these puff-pastry parcels of cheese and ham and whatever else you feel like putting in there.

I've taken to serving this with a very simple salsa. I call it a salsa, but I'm not sure it is: it's incredibly good, and incredibly spicy, and by dint of being the exact opposite of hot cheese makes the hot cheese somehow hotter and cheesier, while the hot cheese makes the salsa taste even brighter and spicier. I have yet to find anyone who doesn't like this supper, and it is what my heart sings for every time I come home after a swim, and it is a small and gorgeous pleasure – and the very best thing is that you can have dinner ready in about half an hour from the moment you get in. ⟶▷

For 2

1 x 320g packet of pre-rolled
   puff pastry

4 slices of prosciutto

1 small round soft goat's
   cheese

Good splash of olive oil

Decent pinch of thyme leaves

2 tsp pesto (optional)

1 egg, beaten

Salad leaves, such as rocket
   and watercress

For the salsa

4 tomatoes

3 big red chillies

1 large red onion

5 spring onions

A few basil leaves

1 generous tsp chilli sauce
   (or chilli pesto, or hot sauce)

Splash of extra virgin olive oil

$\frac{1}{2}$ lemon

Flaky sea salt and black pepper

· · · · · · · · · · · · · · · ·· · · · · · · · · ·· · · · · · · · · · · ··

The thing about dinners in half an hour is that they require you to be a little bit organised. In this case, that organisation means this: wash up your chopping board, your sharpest knife and your scissors, and pre-heat your oven to 180°C.

Unroll your pastry neatly and speedily onto a clean chopping board; you want to cut it into two squares, each large enough to accommodate two slices of prosciutto. Lay two strips of ham across each pastry square, like this, like that, a delicate hammy kiss. Slice the goat's cheese around its middle into two discs, then sit one, cut side up, on each square where there is 'double ham'. A splash of olive oil. A scattering of thyme leaves across the whole fiasco. A dollop of pesto, if you like.

Fold the corners of each pastry square into the centre, like you're making a paper fortune-teller, only all the fortunes are cheese. My mother sort of scrinkles the pastry up in the centre; I like to pleat mine where the pastry edges meet, because it is remarkably satisfying to both make and eat symmetrical things. Pinch closed the pleats, or the scrinkle, and brush with beaten egg. Lift onto a baking sheet and bake for 15 minutes, or until crisp and golden.

Meanwhile, make your salsa. Cut the tomatoes into quarters. De-seed the chillies. Into a bowl with them. Finely dice the red onion. Bowl. Slice your spring onions. Bowl. Rinse the basil. Bowl. Now take your kitchen scissors, and snip and chop everything in the bowl. Chopping with scissors is the best kitchen trick I know, and I don't know why it isn't more widely accepted – you can, with things like this, get them much finer and neater. When everything is nicely chopped, give your salsa a little stir with the blades of your scissors; add the chilli sauce and stir again. A little olive oil; the juice of your lemon half; a solid pinch of flaky sea salt. Stir. Stir. Cover. (This will keep very well in the fridge for about 12 hours, improving all the time – the flavours sort of meld into each other in a very pleasing way.)

When your pastries are ready, deposit a heap of salad leaves onto each plate, a heap of salsa on top of that, a goat's cheese puff on top of that, and a sufficient quantity of wine into each glass. Lo, be comforted. Flaky pastry, bright salsa, hot cheese. A small and perfect supper. A small and perfect pleasure.

Nice Little Nibbly Things

This is good for impromptu parties, but also good for the evenings when you just want to graze gently as you potter. The inspiration for this came from a 1970s 'Food of the Middle East'-type cookbook I rescued from a box of free books: it was battered, had both covers and half the pages missing, and really I picked it up just so I could be mean about what passed for Middle Eastern British cuisine in those days. Happily, I was being a millennial idiot: the book was delightful. And, more to the point, accurate. I have mislaid this book somewhere along the way, but it was written, I think, by an ex-serviceman who had spent time in the Middle East during the war. And there he had grown to love za'atar, aubergines – 'which aren't just for decoration,' he noted, cheerfully – lemons, and above all, chickpeas.

Roasted chickpeas, he asserted, would soon be the 'entertaining housewife's best friend'. And I can confirm that they do indeed make a better hors d'oeuvre than peanuts in every conceivable way: crisp and crunchy chickpeas, puffed up so they're fudgy-textured inside, sharp with lemon and warm with toasted spices, and with a punchy hit of chilli; all spiked with dense, salty, bitter olives and speckled with vivid-green parsley and coriander. Incidentally, this is also the recipe that converted me to liking parsley, which I hated for years, so do try it if you have always felt the same. $\longrightarrow$

For 2, over the course of an evening's grazing,
with a good bottle of wine

Big handful of olives, any kind
(*I like a mixture, starring
Kalamata*)

2 lemons (unwaxed, if you can
get them)

1 x 400g tin of chickpeas

2 tsp cumin seeds

2 tsp coriander seeds

2 tsp fennel seeds

1–2 tsp chilli flakes, to taste

1 tsp black pepper

2 tsp extra virgin olive oil

2 tsp smoked flaky sea salt

Handful each of flat-leaf
parsley and coriander leaves

•• •• • •• • • • •• •• • • • •••• •• • • ••• • • ••• • •• ••

Pre-heat the oven to 210°C, and put your biggest baking tray into
the oven to heat up with it. Ideally you want a tray big enough to
hold the chickpeas in a single layer, or they will steam rather than
roast, and end up soft, not crisp: this isn't a disaster, but I think
they're nicer crunchy.

Briefly rinse your olives, and set aside in a bowl that's much too
big for them, as you're going to add everything else to keep them
company in a minute. Rinse your lemons too. (If you've only
been able to get waxed lemons, you can get rid of the wax by
scrubbing them with a scourer and washing-up liquid in the
hottest water you can stand; just make sure you rinse them
thoroughly afterwards.)

Drain your chickpeas in a colander and rinse them well. Shake
the colander vigorously, then pat the chickpeas dry with kitchen
paper. (If you have no kitchen paper – something we seem to
get through at an alarming rate – just leave the chickpeas in the
colander over the sink while you do the next bit, popping up every
so often to give them another shake.)

Take a dry non-stick frying pan and set it over a medium heat.
When the pan is hot, add the cumin, coriander and fennel seeds,
and toast them for 2–3 minutes, watching them closely and
stirring every so often so they don't burn. You'll be able to tell
when they're done, partly because of the glorious smell coming
from the pan, and partly because of the rich tobacco-red colour
of the cumin seeds.

Tip the warm seeds into the bowl with the olives, and turn to your lemons: slice them into quarters, and then into the thinnest slices you can possibly manage. (You could use a mandoline here, if you have one. Personally, I don't trust myself with anything that sharp.) Add the lemon slices to the bowl, along with any juice that has collected on the cutting board, the chilli flakes and the black pepper. Stir thoroughly, then add the chickpeas and drizzle over the olive oil, stirring as you go.

Working quickly now, take the hot baking sheet out of the oven, and shake the chickpea mixture onto it, spreading it out evenly. Sprinkle with the smoked salt, then roast for 35–40 minutes, until the chickpeas are puffed up, and the lemon slices are blackened and twisting.

Meanwhile, finely shred your parsley and coriander. When the chickpeas are ready, stir in the herbs and decant into little nibbly-sized bowls. Serve anywhere between piping-hot and room temperature.

Parmesan Popcorn

This is not really a recipe, but I wanted to put the idea into your head. For each person, you'll need 20g popcorn kernels, 20g really good Parmesan and 1 tsp extra virgin olive oil. Pop the popcorn as per the packet instructions: I just do mine in a saucepan with a tiny bit of oil. It will take about 5 minutes to pop most of it, which is just enough time to grate the Parmesan and find the extra virgin olive oil. Toss everything together, and eat in front of the telly.

Three Ideas & an Egg: Quick Ways to Make Dull Meals More Interesting

You cannot make interesting meals all of the time, no matter how well stocked your fridge or your cookbook shelves. This is a fact. Sometimes you are just hungry and out of inspiration, and you throw something together without a recipe that kind of works, but could be – you know this – so much more. (I am thinking particularly of the kind of meal that relies heavily on lentils, pasta, tinned tomatoes and fridge-drawer vegetables.)

There are four things you can do, immediately, to make this better – to make a meal that feels a bit special, a meal worth taking a picture of, a meal worth savouring.

Saffron Yoghurt

The first is saffron yoghurt: golden, subtle and smooth, and sounds much fancier than it is. This is especially good with lentil dishes, such as dals and soups, but can be pressed into service with almost any rich, deeply flavoured stew or casserole. This, plus a little chopped parsley, is beautiful against a dark background.

Pinch of saffron threads

1 tsp boiling water

1 tsp flaky sea salt

2 tbsp full-fat plain thick yoghurt

Finely grated zest of 1/2 lemon

1 tsp extra virgin olive oil

• • • • • • • ••• • • • • • • • •• • • •• •• •• • ••• • •• ••

In a little bowl, mix the saffron with the boiling water and salt. When the salt has dissolved, stir in the yoghurt and lemon zest. Cover with cling film and leave for at least 45 minutes – the longer you leave it, the richer the egg-yolk-yellow colour it will become.

Salsa Verde

The second is salsa verde: vividly green, punchily bright and endlessly delicious. It's wonderful as a dressing, to drizzle over cooked meat (lamb chops love it) or fish, or to use as a marinade. It also works as a dip, or spread thinly on toast. Wildly, wildly good with new potatoes. I usually use the herbs in a ratio of 2:1:1 parsley to coriander to basil, but feel free to tinker according to your taste.

This lasts a few days in the fridge, and freezes really well in an ice-cube tray, to be used as needed.

Large bunch of flat-leaf parsley	A few capers, if you like
Small bunch of coriander	1 tbsp mustard
Small bunch of basil	Juice of 1 lemon
1 garlic clove	1 tsp vinegar
2 large anchovies	4 tbsp extra virgin olive oil

Rinse the herbs and tip into a food processor or blender, stalks included, then add everything else. (Don't, for God's sake, add any salt, especially if you're using capers.) Blitz until smooth.

Pangrattato

The third is pangrattato, which means 'breadcrumbs' in Italian, but is so much more than that. Essentially it's crispy, chilli-y, zesty breadcrumbs: dash it over a risotto, scatter over linguine with olive oil and a fried egg, chuck into salads for a bit of added pizzazz.

2 thick slices of the nicest, stalest (or toasted) bread you have	2 tsp chilli flakes
	2 tsp olive oil
1 lemon	Flaky sea salt and black pepper

Tear the bread into chunks and zest the lemon, then chuck into a food processor or blender. Add the chilli flakes, a teaspoon of salt and a few big grinds of black pepper, then blitz to fine crumbs. Set a big, non-stick frying pan over a low heat, add the breadcrumbs and drizzle over the oil. Stir. Cook, stirring every now and then, until just the charred side of golden.

Put an egg on it...

And the fourth thing you can do is put an egg on it. Just put an egg on it. Fried or soft-boiled (see pages 59 and 62–3 if unsure how), either/or. An egg is protein, and an egg – especially one fried in fat so the edges are lacy – is beautiful.

Weekend Cooking

Someone I knew once told me that you always cook for the number of people in the family you grew up in: I cook for six, at least. Always. There were six people in the family I grew up in – me and my three sisters, and my mum and dad – and I don't seem to be able to stop myself. It never matters, because there's always someone to eat it: someone dropping by to pick up a book, or borrow a book; someone coming with a guitar to sing; someone who just had a rough day and wanted to come and be comforted. 'Come and be loved,' I find myself saying, to my friends, when they are sad, and what I mean is, 'Come and be fed.'

There is a kind of magic to these evenings in the Tiny Flat: a golden, shining, infinite kind of magic that keeps me sane in the cooking and (I think) everyone else sane in the eating. We are all there together, all safe, all beloved, a disorganised playlist of everybody's favourite songs on Spotify; me stirring at the stove, them peeling or chopping on the kitchen sofa, all companionably bickering about Disney's *Hercules*, the relative merits of musicals, and whether 'really big jumps' could ever be as good a superpower as flying. (Obviously not, Tall Man, you idiot.)

I love these evenings: I have never felt safer or happier or more loved than knowing I'm only ever five days away from a night like this. And this is what I wish for you too: weeks with endings as beautiful and infinite as these. For this is *weekend* cooking.

You can't do this every night, of course; life gets in the way. But that's what weekends are for, and what this chapter is about: weekend cooking. The kind of cooking that needs maybe a bit of time, in the shopping or the chopping or the proving.

Things that might be quick in the cooking, but with what the Tall Man calls a 'hero' ingredient: a beautiful piece of meat; a pair of neat little poussins; a pile of perfectly fresh, bright-eyed, salty sardines, or a heavy net of clams. Things you need to shop for specially, in maybe a fish shop, or a butcher's, or just a big supermarket.

Or things that are fun, but fiddly, like making your own pasta, and kneading the egg-yolk yellow dough and rolling it fine, and spreading it out to dry; or things that need a whole day of keeping half an eye on, like a slowly simmering ox-cheek ragù.

Or things that just don't make sense Monday to Friday, like making your own pizza dough, and letting it rise and prove slowly for the best-possible flavour.

Nothing is difficult here, but all of it is best tackled on those weekend days when you feel like getting stuck in, and making enough for everyone: for a dinner party, or a date night, or an impromptu 'why not tonight?' gathering.

When I was a little girl, and we lived in the countryside, I would sometimes be allowed to stay up when my parents had dinner parties. My parents entertained a lot, but never in a very formal way: mostly, my dad would cook a vat of curry on a Friday night, and everyone would pile into our kitchen after the pub. It can only have been six or eight people – three or four couples – but it always seemed to me as if the whole village was there. In my heart, I think it's those Curry Nights that I have always wanted cooking to feel like: someone standing by the stove, spoon in hand; someone else perched on the benchtop, chatting. Music, plenty of booze and plenty of laughter. Someone eating the ingredients before they make it into the pan, and enough food that it doesn't matter. Enough food that it doesn't matter who drops by, or comes back, because there's always enough.

This is a chapter about enough: about having enough time to do it really properly, and to enjoy every second of it, in the cooking and the eating, while the house fills up with good smells and warm air.

Happy cooking. Happy weekend.

Rare Roast Beef for Two

A secret: I am terrible (really terrible) at cooking full roast dinners by myself. It's the pressure, I think. The last time we had people for Sunday lunch, I spent the afternoon weeping in my bedroom, and one of the guests, in helpful mode, put my best non-stick muffin tin on the hob and scorched the bottoms out of it. I have never quite forgiven him – although, to give him his due, the resulting Yorkshires were superb. The time before, nothing was ready until eleven at night. I can never remember when things have got to go in, or come out; the oven is never the right temperature for anything; the goose fat gets everywhere. I am always thrown by the meat needing to 'rest' (so do I, usually, by that bit); the leeks always seem to catch just as I need to be shaking the potatoes; and my Yorkshires always go too tall while I'm thinking about other things, and puff up, and catch.

Which is a shame, because I love all the bits of roast dinners individually: I love the Yorkshires, I love the little chippy roast potatoes, I love carrots and parsnips and creamed leeks. I love rare roast beef; above all, I love the leftovers from Sunday dinners. I think, maybe, I am just a leftovers person. I like nothing better than to pick gleefully through a happy pile of burnt crunchy bits, and the bloody end of the joint, and pack it all into a hot little roll with butter and mustard and horseradish. I would go to the ends of the earth for a really good rare roast beef sandwich.

And then I had an extraordinary revelation, and it was this: a person could decide to cook a joint of beef just for sandwiches. A person could even – given enough good butter, those little part-baked rolls (for which I am a total sucker), mustard (only Colman's will do) and horseradish, and some rocket or sorrel or other sharp little leaves – serve this for dinner, without any of the hassle of potatoes, or fretting about puddings, or any of the pressure that often seems to go with roast dinners. You just rub the beef with salt and pepper, maybe some finely chopped rosemary (the Tall Man calls this 'rosemary lichen', and it's his recipe really), and roast it in one of those disposable foil tins, then stick the bread rolls in to finish baking while the meat rests, and that's it. Generous glasses of red wine, light some candles, and it will be the best romantic dinner you've ever had. ⟶

$\longrightarrow$ We tend to have this just for the two of us, and I love that: a full roast dinner for two always seems like too high a faff quotient, and this is the perfect compromise. We have quite a chaotic life, when I stop to think about it. And it's nice, sometimes, to bar the door, and roast this beef, and put some music on, gently squabbling over whether we use his playlist or mine, and sit together in the candlelight, making hot little sandwiches with our bare hands, and getting a little bit tipsy, and being totally content. The Tall Man wrote this recipe, because he is much better than me at roasting big bits of meat.

For a sandwich roast, I like beef topside: it's uncomplicated, it carves evenly and you don't end up with gaping holes where the fat has melted away or chunks of suet-y horror where it hasn't. Try to get a piece that's nicely barded with fat on the top, because it'll save you having to baste.

If you only remember one thing about roasting beef, let it be this: you can always put it back in for a bit. This is especially true when you're roasting for sandwiches – no carefully coordinated side dishes means there's no need to put the meat in the oven three years ahead 'to make sure it'll be done'.

All that said, of course, sometimes there's enough of you that a Sunday roast seems like the right thing to do; some autumn Sunday with leaves falling and rain starting to drizzle against the window, and a piece of meat that seems to merit the full hoorah. Plus there's a huge sense of accomplishment in pulling off a Sunday roast, no matter how many people you grab to help. And do grab people to help: rope in everybody and anybody to peel things and chop things and keep an eye on things. Also, if you never cook the whole lot, you'll never have leftovers – and these make particularly good leftovers for late-night fridge raids and next-day sandwiches: creamed leeks; roasted carrots with honey, cumin and orange; and little chippy roast potatoes.

For 2

1kg piece of topside

1 tbsp black peppercorns

1 tbsp flaky sea salt

2 tsp mustard powder

A little mild-flavoured oil

Part-baked bread rolls and
horseradish sauce, to serve

•• •• •• • •• ••

First, pre-heat your oven to 200°C. Before things get too hot, make sure you've got a rack in the middle of the oven so you can put your joint in without it catching on the top of the oven.

Pop your peppercorns into a mortar and grind with the pestle. I like doing this in two stages, so you get some finely ground pepper and some coarser pieces. Add the salt and mustard powder, and stir until you have a sort of murky gravel.

Lightly oil the beef and treat it to a good coating of the mustard rub; for ease, you can tip the rub out onto a chopping board and roll the joint through it. Make sure you don't neglect the fat on top, because that's going to melt and carry your flavours all through the meat.

Get your beef into a disposable roasting tin – honestly, use them once and you'll never go back – and give it 25 minutes in the oven (or about 10 minutes per 450g if you're cooking a bigger piece of beef), reducing the heat to 180°C after the first 5 minutes. *Do not forget this bit*; otherwise, you might end up with well-done beef.

When the time's up, remove your beef from the oven and let it rest under some foil and a tea towel for 10 minutes – this is the time to put your part-baked rolls in the oven – and then carve, being aware that butcher's twine loves to ping hot fat into your face when you cut it. If, by any chance, you find the meat isn't done enough for you when you cut into it, remember you can always put it back in the oven for a little longer.

Pile the rare roast beef into your warm bread rolls. Eat with horseradish sauce and feel immensely smug.

...*with* Marky Market's Creamed Leeks

I arrived in London in a yellow dress, nineteen and newly in love, and the Tall Man met me at the gate of the Eurostar, and we walked out into the filthy air around King's Cross. I thought it was the most beautiful place in the world (probably because I was nineteen, and newly in love). And then we went home. Home, then, was one room with a single bed in Wood Green: it was dirty, cramped and beloved, and had the inestimable advantage of belonging to a person who would become (I didn't know it then) one of our London touchstones.

His name was (and is) Mark, a former ad-man who had, in the recession, become instead a sort of sausage salesman. All meat, really, and fish if you wanted: he bought for supper-clubs and restaurants and for anyone who wanted it. Cheaper than a high-street butcher, better quality than the supermarkets. He liked food, he told me, that first night, and he liked going to the markets while everyone was sleeping, and it paid the bills, with enough over for a pint and a packet of fags. Mark smoked all the time, and Mark cooked all the time, and his food was extraordinary. Mark cooked the way I love best to cook: glass of wine in one hand, spoon in the other, and with leftovers to glory in. He would leave notes on the side, which we would find when we woke up, hours after he had left: 'Half a side of home-cured Gloucester Old Spot in the fridge. Needs eating.' 'Feel free to eat all cold roast beef.' 'Sausages in Tupperware: please cook and take with you.'

We were horribly poor: I'd left my job in Paris to come to London, and London is not a good city to be poor in. Unless you have a Mark. He let us the one room, at the kind of rent that doesn't exist in London any more. Looking doubtfully from the Tall Man's six-foot-six heft to the single bed and back, we told him, quite confidently, that we would be fine (and we were). And he gave us good food, and he taught us things.

The Tall Man was already a good cook, but I wasn't. I stood with the Tall Man behind me, and we learned to make Mark's creamed leeks, and now I am teaching them to you: they are ambrosial, and I have never known a person not want a second helping. (Thanks, Mark. I owe you.)

For 4

3 big leeks	250g Parmesan
Knob of butter (if unsalted, a pinch of salt too)	2 tbsp double cream
	Black pepper

• • • • • • ••• • •• • ••• •• • •• • •• • •• •• •• • •••• ••• ••

Take your leeks. Run a sharp knife down their long sides to make one straight slit, so they open out, and run the cold tap vigorously through them: leeks hold onto grit and mud like nothing else, and this is the best way I know of cleaning them properly.

Slice them into fine almost-rings (the slit stops them being proper rings), and set them over the lowest-possible heat with a knob of butter in a wide pan. You must stir them and watch them for about 20 minutes: burnt leeks can go horribly bitter, which doesn't work here at all. Glass of wine in one hand, spoon in the other. Cooking à la Mark.

Tell someone else to grate all that Parmesan for you. Don't skimp.

After 20 minutes of stirring and watching, taste the leeks: they should have a modicum of bite to them, but mostly just be tender and lovely. At this stage you can take them off the heat if you have other things to bring to fruition, because creamed leeks hate sitting.

When you're about 5 minutes away from serving, return the leeks to the heat, and add your cream and your Parmesan. Stir properly, then grind plenty of black pepper over the top once the cheese has melted.

These are so simple, and so absurdly delicious, and you can eat them the next day in a leek sandwich with a lot of horseradish and extra pepper.

...*with* Sticky Cumin & Orange Carrots

I have been known to eat these on toast, with a quick pesto made in the blender from the carrot tops. They are utterly more-ish, and the best way I know to eat carrots.

For 4

2 blood oranges	1 tbsp olive oil
400g carrots	1 tbsp cumin seeds
4 garlic cloves	1 tsp cracked black pepper
1 tbsp honey	1 tsp smoked flaky sea salt

Pre-heat your oven to 180°C.

Scrub the blood oranges with a scrubby thing, hot water and washing-up liquid to get rid of any wax coating, then cut them into quarters.

Peel, top and quarter the carrots lengthwise. You want them thin, so if your carrots are on the thick side, you might need to cut the quarters into thinner slices too.

Put the carrots and six of the orange quarters into your most useful roasting dish. Push the unpeeled garlic cloves into any spaces.

Squeeze the juice of the two remaining orange quarters into a glass or small bowl; whisk in the honey and the oil, then drizzle liberally over the carrots. Scatter over the cumin seeds, pepper and smoked salt.

Roast for 25–35 minutes, keeping an eye on them in case they need a shake; you want them to be tender and a little caramelised on top.

...*with* Goose Grease Roast Potatoes

These are the best roast potatoes. They are almost chips, and make bloody good chips if you slice the potatoes up that way. It's very easy, safer than frying and extremely delicious.

For 4

8–12 potatoes, depending on size

2 tsp salt

1–2 tbsp goose fat

· · · · · · · · · · · · · ·· ··

Take your potatoes, and set people to peeling. If you've got people coming for Sunday lunch, they ought to be given jobs, so enlist several friends to peel potatoes for you, and turn the oven to 200°C.

Cut the peeled potatoes into halves or quarters, depending on their size: probably quarters for most potatoes, because more edges means more crispy bits.

Put the potatoes into your biggest pan with a lid, and cover with cold water. Add the salt, put over a decently high heat and bring to the boil. (The salt will be absorbed by the potatoes, a bit like that osmosis experiment everybody does in GCSE Biology – this is perhaps the only useful thing I have retained from GCSE Biology.)

Your oven should have come to temperature by now: take a big roasting tin, and put in it a big dollop of goose fat. Stick it in the oven, so the goose fat melts.

Boil the potatoes vigorously for about 5 minutes, until they are soft enough to stick a fork in, but not soft enough that you could serve them as is, and drain, returning them to the pan. Put the lid back on, then lift the pan, and shake, shake, shake for a minute or two, bashing the newly softened potatoes against each other and the sides of the pan. We're after roughened edges, because that also means more crispy bits.

Quickly but carefully, take the roasting tin out of the oven, tip the potatoes in and shake again, covering them with the hot goose fat. Return to the oven to roast: about 40 minutes should see you right, and the potatoes crisp, crunchy and golden.

Fat Little Harissa Poussins

These are not difficult at all, but finding poussins is rather a faff for a weeknight, and you're unlikely to have them in on a whim, which is why they are here. A poussin is really only a young chicken, but it sounds fancy, and that's half the battle. The other half of the battle, I think, is to douse them relentlessly in harissa and olive oil and sesame seeds and sea salt, and roast them until the skin is crisp and brittle, and the meat tender and flaking away from the little bones. Fancy as you like, and really very little effort.

I like to roast these on top of sweet potato hash – which is so good that I've given it as a separate recipe, for days when you don't have poussins.

For 4

2 tbsp harissa paste	1 tsp white pepper
1 tbsp olive oil	2 x 450g poussins
1 tsp grated ginger	1 tbsp sesame seeds
2 garlic cloves, grated	1 tbsp fennel seeds
Finely grated zest and juice of 1 lemon	Flaky sea salt
1 tsp sumac	Sweet potato hash (see page 192) or salad, to serve

•• •• • • •• • • •• • • •• • • •• •• • • •• • •• • •• ••

Combine the harissa, olive oil, ginger, garlic, lemon, sumac and white pepper in a lidded jam jar. Shake vigorously (or stir hard with a fork). Pop your poussins in a big bowl, and pour over the contents of the jar: rub the dressing into every crevice, working it in well. Cover loosely with cling film, then set aside to marinate for about 1 hour (this step can be skipped if you're in a hurry).

Pre-heat your oven to 200°C. If you're making the hash, which I highly recommend, set the poussins on top of the pressed-down hash; if not, just sit the birds in a roasting tin. Either way, scatter the poussins with the sesame and fennel seeds and salt, then roast for about 40 minutes, or until the juices run clear when you stick the point of a knife into the thickest part of the leg.

Serve immediately – either with the hash, or a nice, bright salad: rocket and basil with slivers of bitter chicory or wedges of fennel.

...*with* Five a Day Sweet Potato Hash

I conceived this hash as a backing band for Fat Little Harissa Poussins (see page 190) – but then I thought it deserved some space to itself. This is because it is the kind of delicious thing that you find yourself eating with a spoon while you're trying to serve it. I have written this recipe with the vegetables I most often use, but there's wriggle room: it's a flexible kind of dish, as hashes always are. Try to stick with the thyme-coriander combination, if you can, though: it might sound uncomfortably 'fusion', especially with the Parmesan, but the two herbs work together beautifully and addictively against the sweet-bitter tangle of leeks, the liquorice kick of roasted fennel, the fudgy close-textured bite of sweet potato, and the meaty heft of paprika-scented chorizo.

Chorizo lends the salty, savoury umami tang of cured meat to the whole, mostly vegetable hash. It's wonderful. But please don't let this stop you making the hash if you're vegetarian: just leave out the chorizo, and add a hefty shake of smoked paprika instead – and maybe a pinch of porcini dust from the end of a packet of dried mushrooms, for extra oomph.

If your frying pan has an ovenproof handle (or you don't mind transferring it to a roasting tin), you can put the hash under the grill for a few minutes at the end to melt the cheese, but it's not essential.

For 4

1 tbsp extra virgin olive oil

75g chorizo, diced

2–3 sweet potatoes (or a 270g pre-prepared bag of mixed sweet potato and squash)

3 leeks

2 fennel bulbs

2 red chillies

1 head of broccoli

1 lime

1 tsp black pepper

1 tsp white pepper

250g kale

Handful of coriander

4–6 stalks of thyme

25g Parmesan

You'll need a big, heavy-bottomed frying pan that you can cover (if you don't have a lid, you can improvise with an enamel plate or foil). Put your pan over a low heat and add the olive oil. When it's hot, shake in the chorizo, and let it start to cook while you get on with chopping. (What you're aiming to do here is render out the lovely, scented, scarlet chorizo fat, so that you can cook everything else in it, and it's easiest to do that slowly.)

Peel and dice your sweet potatoes, if you're not using ready-chopped. Cut your leeks into quarters lengthways, then cut crossways into shorter lengths: you should end up with leeks that will tangle in the pan, but not be a complete pain to eat. Rinse them thoroughly and set to one side while you dice and rinse the fennel. Chop the chillies (de-seeding them if you want). Add the fennel and chillies to the pan with the chorizo. Stir in, then add the leeks. Turn the heat up slightly and leave to cook: you want the leeks to catch on the bottom of the pan a little bit, for that lovely, slightly bitter char.

Meanwhile, rinse the broccoli and then chop very finely – I use a cleaver to essentially turn it into broccoli dust. Cut the lime in half and squeeze the juice.

Check on the leeks: when they're soft and slightly charred, add the black and white pepper, the broccoli (stir) and sweet potato (stir again). Pour over the lime juice, then cover reasonably tightly – you're essentially steaming the sweet potato – and cook for about 25 minutes or until just about soft.

Rinse and finely shred the kale and the coriander, and strip the leaves from the thyme. Grate the Parmesan.

When the sweet potato is ready, stir through the kale and herbs, then cover and cook for 5 minutes. Scatter the hash with the Parmesan – and put under a hot grill for 5 minutes to melt the cheese, if you like. Dish up, or, if you happen to be by yourself, eat straight from the pan, with a spoon.

(If you're making the harissa poussins too, skip the grilling and – unless your frying pan is ovenproof – transfer the hash to a roasting tin, pressing it down. Scatter with the Parmesan, sit the poussins on top, and follow the roasting instructions on page 190.)

Stuck in a Bookshop
Salmon & Sticky Rice

I was hungry, and it was raining, and I was stuck in a bookshop.

I don't mean stuck there in the normal way of bookshops – the too many books, too little money, too little time way – or even locked in. I mean stuck there because I was scared and I couldn't work out how to overcome it. I was scared of the dark outside. I stood in the corner of the bookshop in a full body stutter: one step forward, two steps back, trying to will myself home. Come on, I thought, come on, come on. And I didn't.

It's like a temporary paralysis. The best way I can think of to explain it is this: could you step off a cliff? Of course you could, but you wouldn't. That's what it feels like. What kind of idiot would step off a cliff? What kind of idiot would step out into the dark street? The flesh is willing; the spirit is weak.

And I was scared, and I was stuck. It was ridiculous, laughable: sometimes anxiety is. Often it is. It doesn't make it any less real, or any less difficult to manage. I have walked that street a hundred times; this time, I just couldn't.

And then I could. Forty minutes of pacing the bookshop, looking at the sky outside, and then I did it: opened the door, and went out into the street, counting the steps to distract myself from the gathering sky. And on the way home, I thought of this: something as far from November evenings and rush-hour Tubes and panic as could be. Bright. Clear. Uncomplicated. Warm and spicy and sweet. Pink salmon, barely seared. Red chorizo. Black rice, white coconut. Ginger, chilli, pepper, honey. Soy. And when I got home I made it, and it was good.

I don't have any explanations for why I sometimes get stuck, or why, if this happens to you, you get stuck. I don't have a way to fix it, either, except to cook through it, to press through it, to trust that I will, somehow, get through it, and it will, somehow, be over. And you will, too. This will not last forever for you, either. And the supper was wonderful: a small victory. And we should celebrate small victories, I think.

This supper is complete on its own, but what makes it so wonderful for weekend cooking is the variety of extras you can make to go with it: hearty butternut squash mash (see page 198); tender aubergines cooked in gingery miso broth (see page 200); and a very good, light kale and coriander salad (see page 201) that I could happily eat by the fistful. ⟶

For 4

4 salmon fillets

2 tbsp soy sauce

2 tbsp shaoxing rice wine
  (or dry sherry)

2 tsp honey

1 lime

For the sticky rice

50g chorizo

4 garlic cloves

Splash of mild-flavoured oil,
  such as groundnut

1 x 400ml tin of light
  coconut milk

200ml stock, from a cube or
  stock pot is fine (*I usually
  use chicken because it tends
  to be what I have*)

5cm knob of ginger

2 tsp chilli flakes

1 tbsp Thai fish sauce

200g Thai black rice

· ·

The first thing to do is marinate the salmon. Measure the ingredients into your bowl like an alchemist: 2 tablespoons each of soy and shaoxing, 2 teaspoons of honey and the juice of a whole lime. Stir well, then plunk in your salmon fillets and spoon over the marinade. Cover the bowl and leave your salmon to marinate for at least 20 minutes; you can leave it for longer than this if you have time, but you'll need to stick it in the fridge.

For the sticky rice, finely dice your chorizo and grate your garlic. Take a large-ish heavy-bottomed frying pan, set it over a medium heat and add a splash of oil. Add the chorizo and garlic and fry them off, letting the garlic turn golden as the chorizo releases its paprika-scented fat. (There's something absolutely Spanish about the smell of frying chorizo – it always makes me feel holiday-ish.)

Take your tin of coconut milk, tip it into a heatproof jug and add your stock: I do this by tipping 200ml boiling water into the jug with the coconut milk, and whisking in a stock pot. Trust me, it works. Peel and grate the ginger, straight in, and shake in the chilli flakes. Stir them in, along with the fish sauce. Inhale the steam. Feel the chilli in it catch at the back of your throat, and the ginger warming you all the way down.

Go back to your frying pan, give the chorizo and garlic a stir, then tip in your rice and stir well. That dark, nutty smell of black rice toasting is something rather special. Stir the rice for a moment or two to coat each grain in the chorizo-garlic oil. Turn the heat down as low as it will go, tip in half of your coconut-milk stock, then cover with a lid or foil and leave to cook for 15 minutes.

When the time is up, take a look at the rice: if it has absorbed all or most of the liquid, add a little more stock; if not, don't. Stir well, cover again and let it cook for another 10 minutes.

Test the rice: it should stick briefly in your mouth and taste nutty-sweet, a little sharp, a little sour; dense and dark, yet strangely wholesome – like a risotto in a black hole. When you're happy with your rice, spoon it out into a heavy serving bowl and then cover with foil to keep it warm.

Give your frying pan a quick scrub to get the last grains of rice out, then set it over a medium-high heat. If your frying pan isn't non-stick, add a very small splash of oil. Lift your salmon fillets out of the marinade, and fry them, skin side down, for 4 minutes. Turn them, and fry for 2 minutes on the other side. You want the salmon to be just barely seared, so that the fat pinkish flakes of flesh fall apart when you stick a fork in: crisp on the outside, soft and yielding inside.

Spoon the rice onto four plates, then very carefully lay the salmon fillets onto the rice, with their silvery skin facing up. This is an incredibly beautiful supper: minimalist, muted and clean. Nothing complicated or difficult. A tiny triumph. Look at those whorls, though. Aren't they gorgeous?

...*with* Baked Butternut Squash Mash

I stopped dieting when I went mad. I had been on a diet for all my life, on and off, until then; and then I stopped, cold turkey. I needed to enjoy the things I could enjoy about being alive, like cooking and eating, and writing about both. And once I'd twigged to that, it was hard to mind being a bit plump.

I had never achieved much by being on a diet, anyway: I have been on various diets in my life – for most of my life – and not much good came of them. Happily, however, this recipe did. If my brief flirtation with following the precepts of a popular slimming club left me nothing else (I remain exactly the same roundish shape I've been all my life), it left me this: butternut squash mash has more flavour than potato mash, and is better for you. Although I am not sure this recipe really counts as 'slimming' (what a horrible word), because of the coconut milk. Ah, well.

For 4, as a side

1 butternut squash
  (or 400g pre-chopped)
1 tsp cumin seeds
1 tsp coriander seeds

1 x 400ml tin of coconut milk
$^{1}/_{2}$ lime
Handful of coriander

· · ·· · · · · · · ·· · · · · · ·· · ·· · · · · · ·

Pre-heat your oven to 180°C.

Take your butternut squash, and peel it (a standard peeler won't work nearly so well as a big knife for this). Use a spoon to scrape out the seeds, then chop into medium-sized chunks.

Take a flameproof casserole or ovenproof pan with a lid and set it over a medium heat. Add the cumin and coriander seeds and dry-fry for a minute or two until fragrant, keeping them moving so they don't burn. Add the butternut squash and a tablespoon of water, then put the lid on, pop in the oven and cook for 20 minutes.

Take the lid off and let the steam evaporate for a few moments, then return to the oven, uncovered, for another 20 minutes, so the squash caramelises a little.

Remove the pan from the oven and set it over a low heat: the squash should be soft enough to break up with a fork – but don't just yet. Slowly add your coconut milk and mash gently with a potato masher. When the mash is smooth and heated through, stir in the juice of your lime half and a handful of freshly chopped coriander.

Serve in great big dollops with the salmon and sticky rice on page 195; it's also very, very good with pork belly.

...*with* Miso Ginger Aubergine

There is a wonderful book called *The Flavour Thesaurus*, by Niki Segnit, which I urge you to acquire swiftly – and I vaguely remembered, while on holiday and unable to check, a couple of lines about aubergine going well with ginger. This is what I made then, based on that vague recollection, and what I always make now, because I love it. We call it 'sog', and I wish we didn't: nonetheless, there it is. Tender aubergine sog, with ginger and soy.

For 4, as a side

2 medium aubergines

Thumb-sized knob of ginger

Small splash of mild-
  flavoured oil, such
  as groundnut

2 tbsp shaoxing rice wine
  (or dry sherry)

1 tbsp light soy sauce

1 tsp dark soy sauce

Brown rice, to serve

•• •• • • • • •   • • •   • • • • • •• • • •• • •• ••

Dice your aubergines, leaving the skin on, as small as you like. Peel the ginger with the back of a teaspoon (just rub it with the wrong end, the skin will come right off).

Pour a little bit of oil into your wok (or a large frying pan) and shove it on a medium-high heat. Add the aubergine and stir-fry briefly. Take your peeled ginger, and grate it right into the wok. Stir that too, and keep stir-frying until all is golden. You might need a tiny bit more oil, but probably not: go easy, because aubergine *absorbs*.

Add your shaoxing wine and soy sauces, and loosely cover the wok with foil, like a little hat. This lets it steam and keep all the flavours in, and I kind of love it as a cooking technique, because it always looks a bit inept. Lid on too, if you have one.

After 15 minutes, taste it: if the aubergine is tender, and all the liquid has been absorbed, you're good to go.

A dollop of rice on each plate, then a dollop of aubergine – and perhaps the salmon on page 195, or some crispy pork belly. Bingo.

...*with* Bright & Brilliant Kale Salad

I hope, by now, that I have established my credentials as a lover of fat and butter enough that you'll trust me when I tell you this is the best salad I know: that raw kale, done like this, is not only very, very good for you, but the kind of salad you want to eat by the spoonful, the kind you can't stop eating. The kind of salad where, without noticing, you've eaten almost a whole bag of kale before supper is even served. It's good, because kale grows year round: this is a salad to brighten up the glummest of winter days. It's fresh and zingy, and I love it. It's also absurdly simple, as some things should be. It has a ratio of about 2:1 kale to coriander, plus deep-pink pomegranate seeds, sticky sweet-sour pomegranate molasses, sharp lime and flaky salt. It isn't complicated, but it does take a while to shred a bag of kale and a bunch of coriander, which is why it's in the weekend chapter. Utterly addictive, it's worth every second of the chopping.

For 4, as a side

200g kale

100g coriander

1 lime

Big pinch of flaky sea salt

2 tsp pomegranate molasses

Handful of pomegranate seeds (about $^1/_2$ pomegranate)

• • • • • • • • •• • •• • • •• •• • • •• •• •• • •••• ••• • ••

With the biggest cleaver or knife you've got, shred your kale finer than you think it could possibly be shredded. It's a sort of chunky kale dust you're after, and the same with the coriander. Tip the lot into a big bowl.

Cut the lime in half, squeeze the juice into the bowl and stir with your hands (always stir salad with your hands). Sprinkle over the salt and the pomegranate molasses. Scatter with the pomegranate seeds just before serving.

That's it. That's the whole thing. It's so much more than the sum of its parts, and it's clean and bright and brilliant.

First Night Fish Finger Sandwiches

We moved into the house I grew up in – the house that I mean when I say 'my childhood home' – on a chill November evening, almost twenty years ago.

The front-door key was big and old (like the key that opened the door to *The Secret Garden*, I thought), and there were four little stained-glass panels set into the door (like the greenhouse in *Tom's Midnight Garden*, I thought), and in my room there was a wardrobe of old wood that was too heavy to be moved, and a hidden door that let to a little secret room under the rafters.

Outside my window was a streetlight, and across the street stood a tall stone cross and a church with a tower. No cars came by, except our own, ferrying the last bits and pieces to our new home. We did not unpack.

The house was very cold, and the Rayburn would not light. Eventually we got it lit, and although it struggled to heat the house, it got hot enough to cook fish fingers on, and we sat on the packing cases, my sisters, our friends, my parents and I, and ate them in white bread rolls with tomato ketchup. We all wore fleeces over fleeces to keep warm. The fish fingers, salty and crisp, steamed in the cold air, and they were perfect. Perhaps it was because we were all hungry, or because we were all cold, but I have rarely eaten anything so delicious: I never really liked fish fingers much before then.

I still remember them vividly, and I have never eaten fish fingers since without thinking of that evening, when I was six years old. And then we slept, of course. More fleeces, and a little oil-fired radiator in my room. Hot water bottles.

You could, of course, make these fish finger sandwiches as we did, by the simple expedient of pushing fish fingers into bread rolls and lathering them with ketchup, but you know how to do those, anyway. These are a bit more grown-up, a bit more sophisticated: gently spiced and golden, and sort of exciting, thrust into a baguette spread with green harissa. ⟶

For 2 (makes about 8 fish fingers)

250g white fish fillets, such as pollock or cod

1 egg

30g shelled unsalted peanuts

1 tbsp fennel seeds

Salt and black pepper

30g Japanese panko or any other breadcrumbs

Green harissa (see opposite) and baguette, to serve

. . . .

Set yourself up with a production line: first, lay the fish fillets out on a plate. Beat the egg in a wide shallow bowl, and set that next to the fish.

Take the peanuts and blitz them in a spice grinder, if you have one, or a coffee grinder (blitz a piece of bread in there first, to take away the coffee taste). You could also crush them by hand with the end of a rolling pin, but a grinder will get them finer: you're aiming for a fine peanutty dust, with the occasional crunchy bit. Tip this onto a plate and mix in the fennel seeds, a pinch of salt and a grind of pepper; this is your second plate; line it up by the egg.

Spread out your breadcrumbs on the third plate.

Finally, put a large baking sheet, lined with baking paper, at the end of the line.

Pre-heat your oven to 180°C.

Cut your fish fillets into eight fish-finger-like strips. Taking one at a time, dip each strip of fish into the beaten egg, roll it in the peanut-fennel dust, then coat it in breadcrumbs, pressing them in with your fingers. Lay the eggy-peanut-fennel-breadcrumbed fish finger on the baking sheet, and repeat with the rest.

When all your fish fingers are lying neatly in a row on the baking sheet, bake them for 20 minutes or until crisp and golden.

While they are cooking, make the harissa, then cut your baguette in half – or hollow it out – and slather with harissa.

Pack the hot fish fingers into the harissa-ed baguette and eat with your hands, perhaps sitting on packing cases.

...*with* Exceptionally Easy, Fast Green Harissa

I thought for a long time about what to call this recipe. I solicited suggestions from anyone who would listen. 'Hope Springs Harissa' I quite liked. Ditto 'Harissa Explains It All'. But in the end, someone suggested I call it exactly as I'd described it to her: exceptionally easy, fast green harissa. Because it is all those things. So I did.

Makes a 200g jar (in my case, one of those empty Nutella glasses)

60g bunch of coriander	1 tsp chilli flakes
20g bunch of curly parsley	Finely grated zest of 1 lemon
Pinch of salt	2 garlic cloves
1 tsp ground cumin	$1^1/_2$ tsp olive oil
1 tsp ground coriander	

· ′ ·· · · · · · · ·· · · · · · · ·· · · ·· · · · · · ··

Rinse the coriander and parsley, then chuck them straight into the blender, stalks and all. Add the salt, cumin, coriander, chilli flakes, lemon zest and the whole peeled garlic cloves. Lid on the blender. Blitz until everything is finely chopped, then drizzle in the olive oil through the hole in the lid, with the blender still running.

That's it. Exceptionally easy. Fast as you like. (Also, there is very little washing up involved, because there is no chopping – just the blender.)

Eat this with whatever you'd normally eat harissa with. The fish finger sandwiches opposite, or the sweet potato hash on page 192. Or stir into cooked basmati rice for a slightly punchier accompaniment to things. Whisk with a little oil to make a salad dressing. It's a condiment. Go wild.

Crispy Lemon Sardines

Please immediately put all thought of tins out of your mind. Thank you. These sardines are not those sardines. These sardines are seaside sardines: little, fresh slippery morsels, scattered with breadcrumbs, rosemary and lemon zest, and grilled until crisp and golden.

I always think of this as a holiday recipe: I tend to make it at my mother-in-law's house by the sea, because the sardines there are so wonderful, and also her grill works. Mine smokes relentlessly, like an old-school journalist, and so grilling things is a rare and delightful treat.

These are pretty quick and easy, but because of the faff involved in getting sardines, and asking the fishmonger to butterfly them for you, I've put them in the weekend chapter.

For 4

2 tbsp black peppercorns

2 tbsp white peppercorns

2 lemons

2 tsp flaky sea salt

4 big sprigs of rosemary

4 tbsp breadcrumbs

16 sardines, butterflied (ask the fishmonger to do this)

2 tbsp extra virgin olive oil

Samphire (see page 208) and green beans (see page 209) or salad, plus crusty bread rolls and butter, to serve

Turn on the grill to high (if possible; mine only has 'on' or 'off'). Line a big baking sheet, or the grill pan, with baking paper.

Roughly grind the peppercorns in a pestle and mortar – not too fine, you want to get some real crunch and flavour coming through. Scrub and zest the lemons, and mix into the pepper, along with the salt. Strip the leaves from the rosemary and chop them very, very finely, then add to the mortar. Stir through the breadcrumbs.

Lay the butterflied sardines, skin side down, on the lined baking sheet or grill pan. Drizzle with olive oil. Allocate each sardine a scant teaspoonful of the pepper, crumb, lemon and rosemary mixture, lightly pressing it in to form a crust.

Grill for about 7–8 minutes, or until the crusts are golden and the sardines are cooked all the way through.

Serve with the samphire or a green salad (dressed with lemon juice, a splash of oil and a bit of Dijon mustard), some crusty white rolls and plenty of butter.

...*with* Chilli, Garlic & Brown Butter Samphire

If you can get hold of samphire, it's very much worth it. I get mine from the fishmonger, but it's also starting to turn up in supermarkets. I'm not exactly sure what it is: it's sometimes called a 'sea vegetable', but the dictionary says it's a 'succulent halophyte', and it's been compared to asparagus, a thick grass, or even a tiny spineless cactus. These are all fair descriptions, but the most important thing to know is that it's delicious: enormously salty, crisp and tender, like eating the sea itself.

I like to eat it raw, but I like it best just warmed through and then tossed with brown butter, garlic and little specks of chilli. Absolutely do not be tempted to add salt. Don't do it. Don't even think about it.

For 4, as a side

25g butter

3 garlic cloves

250g marsh samphire

2 tsp chilli flakes, or to taste (*I usually use more, but then I like a real kick*)

• • • • • • • • • •• • • • • • • •• • • •• • ••• • • •• •• •• • ••• • •• •• ••

Put the kettle on and set a frying pan over a low heat. Add the butter and let it melt and foam until it turns brown: gorgeous and nutty and dark gold. Add the whole peeled garlic cloves (you're looking to infuse the butter with the garlic flavour without interrupting the texture of the samphire) and turn the heat down to the lowest possible.

Thoroughly rinse the samphire under running water, picking out any stubbornly grubby or gnarly looking bits. (There will be quite a few; that's just how samphire is.) Pinch any longer stems in half, then rinse again.

Sit your samphire in a large heatproof bowl and pour over freshly boiled water from the kettle to cover. When the water is cool enough to touch, the samphire will be warmed through. Drain and tip out onto a serving plate, then drizzle over the brown butter (leaving the garlic cloves behind in the pan) and scatter with the chilli flakes.

...*with* Parmesan Green Beans

When I was a little girl, I went to visit my father and my stepmother in their house outside Warsaw. I was ten, I think. Maybe a little older, but not much. It was a big white house, with a black-and-white-tiled veranda that stretched along the front, and steps up to the front door, and four floors. It seemed excessive for the two of them and their son (my half-brother); there were a lot of empty rooms. I thought a lot of my own home in the little village where I spent most of my childhood, where there was rarely a room that wasn't occupied by a sister, a parent or a solitary cat in a sunbeam – and I tried to pretend I didn't mind. And I didn't, much: it was an adventure.

And my stepmother made these beans, and I have kept making them ever since. They're very simple, and all the lovelier for it: the chlorophyll-y greenness of the beans gets to be the star, supported by the quieter greenness of good olive oil and the subtle, low note of Parmesan.

For 4, as a side

250g green beans

1 tbsp really good extra virgin
  olive oil

25g finely grated Parmesan

Big pinch of flaky sea salt

· · · · · · · · ·· · · · · · · · · · · · · ·· · ·· · · · · ·.

Bring a saucepan of water to the boil and add the beans. Cook for 2 minutes or thereabouts, so the beans still have a decent bite.

Drain, then toss in the hot pan with the oil, Parmesan and salt. Serve immediately, straight from the pan.

Saturday Afternoon Charred
Leek Lasagne

Lasagne, I think, is the truest weekend food: the Saturday dinner, the Sunday lunch. You can make it in a rush on a weeknight, but it won't be nearly as good, and scrambling to get it ready takes all the fun out of it.

You want half a day to devote to it really. Say Saturday afternoon some time in autumn, or maybe spring, and the kitchen to yourself, with some music on, and a glass of wine in your hand all the time you're cooking – a leisurely half-day of stirring and grating, assembling and baking, and dipping a lazy forefinger into the sauce.

Lasagne can be party food, picnic food or leftovers, but most of all it is proper comfort food. Done well, it's both a joy to eat and a joy to cook. It's not like a Sunday roast, to which stress can attach itself like a remora; endlessly flexible, this is lazy, lovely weekend cooking.

This version is vegetarian, which I prefer. Both lighter and more grown-up than its meaty counterpart, it's also beautiful: the deep umber of sweet squash, green-and-gold slivers of charred leek to temper the sweet with the bitter, punchy green kale for vitamins and to cut the fat a little, all layered with rich, melty, nutmeg-y béchamel (or something like it, anyway) infused with Parmesan rind, peppercorns and a bay leaf.

I make this in my trusty old tin with the measurements written on it: 12 inches long, 8 inches wide and 2 inches deep – that's about 30cm x 20cm x 5cm. Once it's assembled, the lasagne can be kept in the fridge, covered, until you're ready to cook it. With a sharp side salad (think chicory, rocket, fennel, lemon) and a little glass of white wine, this is a perfect meal.

For 6

About 300g no-cook lasagne
  sheets, depending on the
  dimensions of your dish
1 x 125g ball of mozzarella
25g Parmesan
Freshly grated nutmeg
Black pepper
Salad or garlic bread, to serve

For the vegetable filling
800g squash, such as
  butternut (but any is fine)
1 garlic bulb
Olive oil, for drizzling
50g butter
Small handful of thyme

2 tbsp white wine
3 large leeks
400g kale

For the cheese sauce
60g Parmesan
60g strong Cheddar
40g butter
40g plain flour
600ml milk
200ml double cream
6 black peppercorns
1 bay leaf
1 Parmesan rind
Salt

. ′ . . . .

Pre-heat your oven to 180°C.

First, make the filling. Peel your butternut squash – a big knife
works much better than a standard peeler for this. Use a spoon to
scrape out the seeds, then chop into dice. Tip the dice into a large
roasting tin. Take your garlic bulb, and slice the top off to expose
just the very tips of the cloves. Wrap in foil, like a parcel, leaving
it slightly open at the top. Drizzle the tops of the garlic cloves with
olive oil, then seal the parcel and tuck in the tin with the squash.
(I sometimes do a second bulb of garlic in this way too, because
roasted garlic is so useful to have in the fridge during the week.)

Cut half of the butter into tiny cubes and dot among the squash.
Grind over some pepper, then strip the thyme leaves from their
stalks and scatter them in. Pour over the white wine, then put in
the oven to roast for 40 minutes or until the squash is good and
caramel-y. $\longrightarrow$

$\longrightarrow$ Meanwhile, turn your attention to the leeks. Split them lengthways and rinse thoroughly under the tap (leeks are great at hiding grit and mud). Chop roughly, then muddle with your hands to separate the leeks into their constituent layers. In a large frying pan over a medium-low heat, melt the remaining 25g butter and allow it to brown slightly. Give the leeks a last shake dry, and tip them in. Stir to coat in the brown butter, then leave them to lightly char (maybe 20 minutes), giving them a stir every so often – this adds a lovely rich bitterness to balance the sweetness of the squash.

Rinse the kale, and chop roughly with scissors. That's all you're going to do to the kale. Leave it be.

When your squash has been in the oven for about 20 minutes, check on it: it should be happily doing its thing: if it looks like it's burning, spoon over some of the juices from the bottom of the tin and loosely cover with foil, before returning it to the oven for the remaining 20 minutes.

Next up, the cheese sauce. Grate both the cheeses – you can mix them together; it's fine.

(Give your leeks a stir.)

Melt the butter in a saucepan over a medium-low heat, and when it's foaming, add the flour, stirring to form a golden-coloured paste (breathe in – it smells amazing). Cook your roux for a couple of minutes, stirring constantly, then remove from the heat.

(Stir your leeks again – they should be softened and starting to catch by now.)

Gently and slowly introduce the milk to your roux, stirring the whole time. You want to pour with one hand, and stir with the other, to avoid lumps. Keep pouring. Keep stirring – you can get any lumps out by stirring. When your sauce is smooth, stir in the cream. Add the peppercorns, bay leaf, Parmesan rind and a good grating of nutmeg. Bring up to a simmer, stirring constantly, then cook for about 10 minutes. Turn off the heat, and fish out the peppercorns, bay leaf and Parmesan rind. Add the grated cheese, stirring until the cheese has melted and the sauce is smooth. Taste – you might want salt.

Check your squash, which should be very soft with caramelised edges by now; your garlic too should be soft, like butter left out on a warm day. Remove, but leave the oven on.

Squeeze the soft garlic into your cheese sauce and stir well to fully incorporate. Decant the squash into a bowl and take the leeks off the heat.

Dig out a tin or baking dish about 30cm x 20cm, and 5cm deep: it's time to assemble your lasagne. Squash in first, a thin layer; next, a handful of kale, then lasagne sheets in a single layer, followed by cheese sauce, then leeks and more kale. Another layer of squash, lasagne sheets, cheese sauce, leeks and kale; then a final layer each of squash and lasagne sheets, followed by the end of the cheese sauce, spreading it right to the corners of the tin.

Tear the mozzarella and scatter over the top, then grate over the last 25g of Parmesan, some nutmeg and a twist of black pepper.

Bake for 45 minutes or until the pasta is soft and the cheese is golden-brown and bubbling.

Serve with a sharp side salad (or garlic bread) and cold white wine.

Life Affirming Mussels

There is something special about mussels. They are surprisingly cheap for something that feels so utterly decadent, and they taste very much and very simply of the sea, no matter how you cook them.

They require a level of commitment that is the hallmark of all the best dinners: hands-on murder, hands-in devouring, and plenty of wine. You can't eat mussels half-heartedly. With mussels, you need to make your peace with eating things that were once alive, and that are now dead, and that you killed to eat; it's a circle. I like this peace-making – it seems fairer, somehow, than buying lumps of supermarket meat.

I cooked these mussels for the first time just before my first big breakdown, and strangely enough I have always loved them for it: they were a little glimpse of what my life ought to be like, and something to hold on to as I came back. The weekend before my big breakdown – which happened on a Monday – my parents came to dinner, for my twenty-first birthday, and this is what we made.

'Can you do this?' said the Tall Man to me, and I didn't know. But they had come a long way, and we had promised, and I loved them.

We cleaned the mussels, me holding the colander, the Tall Man pouring out the gritty water. 'Are you all right?' said the Tall Man to me, and I didn't know, and we sat together on the sofa looking at the maps on the opposite wall. I thought that one day I'd like to write about those maps. I thought that one day I'd like to write about my parents, and I thought that one day I'd like to write about these mussels: how they simmer and seethe in white wine and chorizo and sautéed onion, and how you can't eat them without getting stuck in.

I was pleased my parents were coming. I so wanted to be well. I so wanted them to see I was well. 'Let's do it together,' said the Tall Man to me, and I nodded my head: *yes, let's do it together*.

So we did, and we fed my parents and my grandparents with mussels and French bread, and it was a perfect evening. It was in many ways the calm before the storm, and the mussels were salty, hot and boozy. I hung onto these mussels, and that evening, for a long time – and I try, now, to fill my life with the kind of evenings I could hang on to if things went south again: the kind of evenings full of laughter and wine, and the salty kick of the sea, the sweetness of onion and the meaty bite of a really good mussel. $\longrightarrow$

For 4

1.5kg mussels	1 tbsp butter
1 red onion	125ml dry white wine
6 garlic cloves	2 baguettes, to serve
200g chorizo	

Take a bowl big enough to hold your mussels; fill it with the mussels and cover with cold water. Look blankly down at the bowl. Wonder what you're supposed to be doing next. Ask the Tall Man. He says:

'How long you need to purge your mussels depends on how they grew and how confident you are in their freshness – rope-grown mussels need less cleaning, and potentially dodgy ones need as long as possible to disgorge their muck and, ideally, expose themselves as dead and horrible before you accidentally eat them.

Because I've had mussel poisoning and I never want it again, I prefer to soak them in maybe five changes of water, leaving them for 20–30 minutes each time (although longer is fine if you're busy). After the fifth bowl of water – slightly gritty and smelling like a beach just after the tide's gone out – has been poured away, find yourself a drink of something and start debearding. This will require an extra bowl, and a bin, close at hand.

Each mussel needs to have its beard (if present) yanked off with your fingers; the beards are made of a strong, fine filament that the mussel uses to anchor itself to its rock/rope, and legend says that if you weave it into cloth you can make a pair of ladies' gloves that will fit inside half a walnut shell. If there's no beard, don't worry about it – but if the mussel is open, even a little bit, throw it away. Well-bred mussels stay shut in strange environments, and a gaping shell is a sure sign of a mussel that has died. Conversely, when you serve them, make sure you throw away any that haven't opened.

When you have a bowl of closed, beardless mussels, you can start worrying about cooking them.'

While the mussels are in their last change of water, you can start preparing everything else. Take the onion, and dice it finely; the same with the garlic. Take the chorizo, and if not pre-diced, dice it.

Then you can go back, and follow the Tall Man's instructions for debearding the mussels. When they are debearded, they can sit for a minute in their colander, while you take a big heavy pot with a close-fitting lid, and fry the onion, garlic and chorizo in the butter until golden.

Ramp the heat up to medium-high, chuck the mussels in the pot and pour over the wine. Cover quickly, shout '*Three minutes to dinner!*', and get everyone else to fetch the bread and the bowls, and another big bowl for empties. You need no cutlery – this is an 'eating with your fingers' spectacular, is what I'm saying.

If your pan has a glass lid, you can watch the mussels opening; otherwise, lift the lid and take a peek after 2 minutes. As soon as they are all open, which is usually about 3 minutes – you'll see them winking orange or white at you, depending on their provenance – whisk off the lid and decant into bowls. Make people come to you, holding out their bowls like little Mark Lester (*Oliver, Oliver, never before has a boy asked for more!*). Big heap of mussels, big ladleful of the sauce, rich with chorizo and onion; half a baguette each.

DIY Linguine alle Vongole

I have never lived alone, and never really been alone. In some
ways, I wish I had. I think I'd be rather good at it. I am the eldest
of four sisters, and grew up in a loud, chaotic farmhouse in the
countryside. When I was seventeen, I fell in love with the
Tall Man, and when I was nineteen, I moved in with him, in
a new country (I lived in a tool shed with my friend for the
time in between).

Sometimes when the Tall Man is out, I imagine what it
might be like to live here by myself, the only mess my own, the
only clothes on the airer or in the laundry my own, and I like it;
although when he is not here, I miss him dreadfully. It is a fantasy:
the same kind of fantasy that leads me to wonder about booking
weeks away in tumbledown shrines, or running off to live alone
in a little house on a deserted pebble beach.

I am, in fact, a terribly solitary person, the introvert to end
all introversion: the nights the Tall Man goes out are some of my
favourites. A kind of full-body sigh of finally, finally being alone –
of being able to sprawl across the sofa, and turn the telly on to the
kind of cooking documentaries the Tall Man hates, and spread my
papers across the floor, and scribble down notes, and read five or
six books at once, and eat the kind of dinners the Tall Man hates.
The Tall Man is not much of a one for pasta, nor is he much of
a one for the kind of meal 'where you have to use a *fork* and your
hands', nor for creamy sauces. I love all three of those things.

This is that dinner: a romantic dinner for one, and I want
you to read that in the least salacious way possible, although I
understand it is difficult when reading about solo adventures with
seafood. Somehow seafood and sex are always tied up together –
there's no getting away from it – but the bubbling, delicious,
decadent pleasure of buying a bundle of clams just to eat alone
is too gorgeous not to write about. I will draw a careful veil over
the actual eating of this dish: it's a fingers-and-fork, sticky-and-
salty, clam-juice-dripping-down-your-chin sort of eating. The
sort where you open a dozen clams at once, and pin them with
your fork in a coil of fat linguine; the kind where you dredge bread
through the sauce and sup on it like a Tudor. It's the sort of eating
best done alone, or with someone who loves you just as you are.
It's glorious, and it's messy, and I won't apologise for either of
those things. Devour it properly, and enjoy every single second.

Because I mostly cook for other people, this feels like a kind of rebellion: a chance to shout, loudly and expensively, 'I deserve this, too!' The greatest things I learned in therapy are that having compassion for other people is no good unless it is accompanied by compassion for yourself, and you cannot give all of yourself over to another person. Otherwise you become useless and empty, exhausted, broken and brittle. As my mother says, 'Fasten your own oxygen mask before attending to those of others.' And this is how I do it.

And when the Tall Man comes home, I will greet him with open arms and real joy, as he deserves. I will have missed him, and I will be better, and I will be happier. I love it when the Tall Man is gone, but I love it most when he comes back. Not least because it's the Tall Man who does all the washing up.

For 1, of course

500g clams

6 fat garlic cloves

1 large onion

1 celery stalk, with any stringy bits pulled off

Knob of butter

Absolutely tons of black pepper

100g linguine (*or see page 232 if you want to try making your own pasta*)

1 tbsp crème fraîche or cream

1 large glass of white wine

• • • • • • • •• • • •• • • •• • •• • • •• • •' • • •• •• •• ••••• ••• •

First soak the clams. Put the clams in a colander that will fit inside a large bowl, then fill the bowl with cold water: this makes it very easy to change the water, which you have to do four or five times, about 25 minutes apart each time. Discard any clams that won't close when lightly tapped.

When the clams are in their last change of water, chop the garlic (a frankly prodigious amount of garlic), onion and celery. Do it fine, because it's satisfying like that – and it keeps your hands busy. Put a large pan of salted water on to boil.

Set a flameproof casserole with a close-fitting lid over the lowest-possible heat, then add the butter and garlic. You really don't want the garlic to catch: watch it like a hawk and never let it alone. ⟶

$\longrightarrow$ The minute it looks as if it might catch, throw in the onion and celery. Stir, then grind in lots of black pepper (but no salt, as the clams will release their salty juices as they cook).

Put the linguine into the pan of boiling water and leave to cook until al dente, about 9 minutes. Deep breath – you now have about 90 seconds to prepare yourself for the hectic few minutes coming up. Lay the table and get the crème fraîche out of the fridge. Ready?

Drain the clams and tip into the casserole with the garlic, onion and celery, then pour over the wine. Clamp on the lid and leave to cook for 3 minutes.

Lift the lid. Are the clams open? Let's go: with a slotted spoon, transfer all the open clams into a bowl (and throw away any that stubbornly refuse to open). Dollop the crème fraîche into the casserole and whisk vigorously until you have a creamy sauce.

Scoop the linguine out of the pan, using a spaghetti spoon or tongs, so it drips that lovely thickish salt water, and throw into the casserole. Quickly toss the pasta through the clam-garlic-cream sauce, then transfer to a warm plate and take to the table, along with your bowl of clams.

Eat alone, cheerfully, not minding your manners much at all.

And for Sharing...

This recipe makes an extraordinary, decadent, greedy meal for one – but the quantities here can easily be doubled or quadrupled, and when I do that I usually serve it with the kale salad on page 201, so you could do that too, if you wanted. When serving time comes, I put a reasonable dollop of the linguine onto each warm plate in the kitchen, and then I just take the bowl of clams to the table and let people help themselves; plenty of bread and napkins for everyone.

Marital Harmony Sausage Pasta

The first Christmas after I left home, my family gave me a cookbook. They had written it. My sisters, my parents, my grandparents: there were pictures and diagrams, and my mother had copied out notes she had written to herself in the margin of her own cookbooks. Some about the food; some about the days she had cooked it. 'Girls revising – stressy day! Pie for tea.' Or: 'DGR in kitchen all day. Worth it!!'

DGR is my dad, and this is the way he cooks: alone in the kitchen. Most Sundays, a little before lunch, my dad would pour himself a glass of wine, take down a heavy cookbook from the shelf above the sink, turn to a pre-chosen page (the groceries having already been bought, in readiness) and shut the kitchen door. We were absolutely not allowed in. When we were thirsty, there was the garden tap. When we were hungry, there were apples on the trees, if it was autumn; honey in the nettle flowers, if spring; fennel fronds in the earth, if summer. If winter, tough. The kitchen was off-limits. The sound of the radio, and the low roar of an AGA at full tilt, would burble through the door, and in time, smells too: sometimes good, occasionally unsettling, because my father cooked (like the dad in Neil Gaiman's *Coraline*) to a recipe.

Many recipes, in fact. My dad, like me, owns too many cookbooks – but, unlike me, my dad tries them all. I am terrible at following orders, but my dad is precise and demanding and ambitious. He will try any recipe once, and he is an exemplar for following the recipe exactly. His chocolate mousse cake (Nigella) won the office bake-off, and his curries (each spice measured precisely by the teaspoon) are things of beauty.

This is not how my mother cooks. My mother cooks, I think, because she has a family to feed. Left to her own devices, my mother might live on tiny exquisite dishes, a sliver of this, a perfect pipette-drop of that.

And so, in the cookbook that my family made me, there were two recipes for this pasta dish. Two recipes that come to much the same thing: sausages simmered with tangly sweet onions, tomatoes, rosemary and red wine. Then cream and Parmesan. And big fat penne-ish pasta. (I often use this lovely kind called lumaconi, or 'snail shells', as they make perfect little pockets for the sausage-bits. However, I have recently learned that lumaconi are not meant for this sort of thing at all, but rather you are

supposed to stuff and then bake them. Hang it. They work well like this, even if an Italian would have me hanged.)

One recipe is my mother's: it is fourteen lines long (like a sonnet) and takes twenty minutes. She drains off the fat from the sausages and halves the cream. (In the margin, in little cramped handwriting: '22/4/07– Forgot cream – DGR gutted.')

The other is my dad's: it is three pages long and takes two and a half hours. It has all the fat and all the cream. It wants nutmeg and demands sea salt. It even specifies Chianti. (His marginal note: 'Great Sunday dish. Only one pan to wash up. Happy sausages, happy Sunday, early to bed. 19/2/06.')

This is my compromise. It takes about an hour, from start to finish, and I will see how quickly I can write it. (Unlike both my parents, I have never had a knack for brevity.) It's called Marital Harmony Sausage Pasta partly because of this, and partly because it is the quickest recipe for marital harmony I know.

I should tell you now that although my parents both called this 'sausage pasta', I believe it is really onion pasta. You could omit the sausages and still make something marvellous: it's the alchemy of the onions that really makes it. I put in lots more onions than my parents, perhaps because I'm not feeding four fussy children, and it's absolutely magic.

It is very, very easy, and it tastes delicious, and best of all it will make the house smell wonderful: I am not sure if there is any scent better than an intemperate quantity of onions cooking *very* slowly in butter and oil. Onions, like heartbreak or fine wines, only get better with time. ⟶

Feeds 4, generously

3 biggish red onions	1 big sprig of rosemary
1 tsp butter	1 generous tsp chilli flakes
1 tsp olive oil	100g Parmesan (with the rind, if possible)
4–6 sausages	
2 x 400g tins of chopped tomatoes	300g fat penne-ish pasta
	2 tbsp double cream
300ml red wine	Salt and black pepper

Take a large knife and a chopping board, and your onions. Cut the onions in half, and then into half-moons: press with your finger so each half-moon separates out into little arcs. You will have a lot of these. This is good.

In your largest frying pan, melt your butter on the lowest-possible heat and add the olive oil (this stops the butter scorching). Stir, then dump in all your onions, and leave to cook slowly, giving them a stir when you think they need it, but don't worry too much. The worst thing that can happen to a slowly frying onion is that it turns to caramel, and that is delicious.

While the onions are cooking – and, really, they must cook for at least 15 minutes (although longer is always better) – at some point, take your sausages, and cut each one into about six little bits. 'The recipe calls for skinning them,' my mother writes, 'but I'm sure I never do.' I never do, either: I am my mother's daughter. You can, if you like.

When the onions are soft and caramelised, throw in your bits of sausage. Let them brown for about 10 minutes, turning them every so often. When they're nicely brown all over, open your tins of tomatoes and empty them into the pan. Rinse the tomato tins out with the red wine, by the simple expedient of half-filling each tin with half of the wine, sloshing it about a bit until the wine has picked up all the scraps of tomato that cling to the inside of the tin, and then sloshing it into the frying pan. Chuck in the rosemary and chilli flakes – and the Parmesan rind, if you have it.

Give everything a good stir, then leave to simmer gently for 20–35 minutes at a bare minimum. I cannot imagine any possible harm would come to this if you let it simmer for an hour, or even two, except that the sausages might disintegrate and merge into the sauce: I think this would be very delicious too.

In any case, the only thing you *must* do in this time is grate the Parmesan; and when you think you're about 20 minutes from serving, put a big pan of salted water on to boil; and when you think you're 10 minutes away, put the fat penne-type pasta into the salted water to cook.

While the pasta is cooking, stir the sauce again, taste it, add a big pinch of salt if it needs it, and an absolutely enormous grind of black pepper. Sloop in the cream – using a little less (like my mother) or more (like my dad), depending on how much you have. Chuck in two-thirds of the grated Parmesan, and stir like billy-o until it's all incorporated: it will be a marvellous soft orange colour, like a violent sunset.

Check the pasta: when it's al dente (and for this it really must be al dente), drain it, and toss it into the sauce in the frying pan. Again, stir like billy-o. You want, ideally, all the little hollows and whorls of the pasta to be full of sauce. Stir, stir, and summon everyone to the table.

Demand someone refresh the wine glasses (that's what the rest of the bottle is for) and tell someone else to get the cutlery. You will want napkins. Dollop into four large bowls (trying not to give anyone the cheese rind or the rosemary stalk), grind over a bit more pepper, and pass around the rest of the grated Parmesan, so people can help themselves. Receive, after a gratifying and satisfied silence, boundless praise.

Proper Ragù

What follows is three recipes in one: a basic ragù, an ox-cheek ragù, and fresh pasta. One story; three parts.

If you really, really pushed me, I would tell you that my favourite thing to cook is ragù.

Ragù, what we mostly call in England 'bolognese' (and has nothing to do, really, with what the Italians call bolognese, which is full of milk and white wine), is my best comfort food. The ritual of it all: the chopping of onion, carrot and celery into fine confetti; the way the wine and tomatoes come together to make something greater than the sum of their parts; the beef, either simmered until falling apart or browned and savoury; just the beef, beef and pancetta, or beef and pancetta and chicken livers. The way it can have four ingredients, or a dozen, and both will be good; the way it simmers and bubbles and changes through a thousand shades of red and sharpness, mellowing down into something rich and soothing. This is what makes ragù such good weekend cooking, even at its simplest: it takes time, and it takes thought, and it's sort of alchemical.

It is, I think, the easiest thing to cook, and it's a really good place to start cooking proper meals, because you can taste it all the way through: you can dig a spoon in whenever you like, once the meat has browned. You get to learn how to cook properly, not just follow instructions: you discover how food goes from being raw ingredients to a real dinner, and how each of those shades of red the ragù turns corresponds to a shade of taste.

Bolognese: The Shortcut

Ragù can be as complicated or as simple as you like. At its
simplest, it goes like this: you know it must be extremely
simple, because the recipe is literally four tweets long. Tweets!
I know. I think they might be my best four tweets ever. I sent
them to a friend looking for a beginner's proper dinner, and an
unlikely number of people saved those tweets, and they send me
(gloriously, and gloriously often) pictures of the ragù they make
following them. This is it. It is so simple, and I include it here
to prove to you that anyone can make a good ragù:

1. Sauté: 2 chopped onions + 4 garlic cloves (chopped fine) +
   packet pancetta + olive oil.

2. Don't burn it.

3. Add 750g beef mince until it's brown, 2 glasses of red wine,
   2 tins of tomatoes, a shake of balsamic vinegar, black pepper
   and salt, lid on, simmer for an hour.

4. Taste it. Lid off. Thirty mins to reduce. Basil, Parmesan,
   fancy dinner.

A fifth tweet urged my friend to put in a Parmesan rind (my love,
my saviour: I try never to buy Parmesan pre-grated, because the
rind is so useful in every kind of savoury dish) just before the lid
goes on.

And that is it. If you are new to cooking proper dinners, start
with this one: it is very easy, and it's fairly foolproof, and although
it's simple it holds its own against anything, and nobody will ever
think it's a shortcut.

Serve it with linguine (miles better than spaghetti, if you ask
me) and garlic bread, and everyone around you will praise you yea
unto the skies, and they will never believe that bolognese could
get better than this.

But it can. It absolutely can. That's the shortcut: let's call this
next version the scenic route. It is, perhaps, the best ragù I have
ever eaten, in or out of Italy. It is the purest expression of umami
I know. It's also fun to make, and everyone is very impressed by it.

Bolognese: The Scenic Route

You need about six hours, and a good butcher, and you need to be ready to get a little bit comfortable with – deep breath – offal. I know. I know. Would it help if I told you that I have been squeamish about offal my whole life, and it's only because this ragù is so good that I can even bear to look it in the face? The face, coincidentally, is exactly what you want here: an ox cheek. A big, fat, cheap ox cheek, prepared by your friendly butcher. You're going to want livers too. Chicken livers. I know. I hate liver, and I hate offal. But I promise you, this won't make your ragù taste offally; the livers are only really there for texture – they add a sort of melting, buttery softness.

I usually do the pepper for this in a pestle and mortar, because I think it tastes better, and also because I use such a lot of it: maybe *twelve* peppercorns. If you aren't sure how many you'd like to use, put in six peppercorns, crush them to hell in the mortar, and you can always add more later.

You can serve your ragù with shop-bought pasta, or make your own (surprisingly easy) for extra smug points – and extra taste points, because home-made pasta is a completely different beast. You don't salt the dough, but you cook it in water as salty as the sea and it becomes sleek and flavourful, and absorbs sauce like nothing else.

That's why this is in the weekend cooking chapter: because a slow-cooked ox-cheek ragù, with pasta you made yourself, is worth a Saturday spent in pursuit of it. I hope by now you trust me enough to know that I'd never, ever tell you to faff about for something that wasn't worth it. This is worth it. This is a pull-out-all-the-stops, look-at-me-go, fancy, *fancy* dinner – and the recipe is dedicated, with love, to my friend Duncan Vicat-Brown, who ate it first. $\longrightarrow$

Makes loads – easily enough for 6, with fabulous leftovers if you're lucky

3 red onions

2 carrots

2 celery stalks

Splash of good olive oil

1 whole garlic bulb

150g diced pancetta (or lardons)

200g chicken livers

Flour and mustard powder, for sprinkling

1 ox cheek, prepared (ask the butcher to trim off the sinew and skin)

3 x 400g tins of chopped tomatoes

250ml red wine

Handful of dried porcini mushrooms

Handful each of rosemary and thyme

1 tsp balsamic vinegar

4 squares (maybe 15g) dark chocolate

Salt and black pepper

400g pappardelle (or see page 232 if you want to make your own) and grated Parmesan, to serve

. . . .

Some 6 hours before you are thinking of eating – or longer, if you're an organised soul – take a sharp knife and a chopping board, and dice your onions, carrots and celery as finely as you possibly can, to make a kind of glorious confetti. (You may want to de-string the celery first; the Tall Man always does, I don't.) Known as 'soffritto' once it has been slow-cooked until meltingly soft, this confetti always reminds me of those pictures of sand, close up: a thousand tiny crystals.

Set the biggest flameproof casserole with a lid that you have (a cast-iron one is ideal) over a medium heat and add a decent splash of olive oil. When the oil is hot, turn the heat down right low and add the onion, carrot and celery. Leave your soffritto to cook for about 10 minutes until soft, giving it a stir every now and then.

Finely chop your garlic, then add it to your soffritto, maybe with a splash more oil. Stir well, then go and find your meats.

The pancetta can go straight in. Stir it around, so it comes into contact with the hot casserole and starts cooking. The livers

I prepare like this: I rinse them under the tap, then snip off any bits that look manky with the kitchen scissors. Any white fatty bits go, and any stringy bits too. And then I chop them to a size I like, again with the scissors, dropping them straight into the casserole. Add a big, big grind of pepper. Stir, stir, stir, then leave to cook for about 15 minutes, stirring occasionally, until the livers go from being purplishly livery to looking like cooked meat.

Mix together a little flour and mustard powder in a shallow bowl and season with salt and pepper. Drop the ox cheek in it, turning it to coat nicely. Clear an ox-cheek-sized space in the middle of your soffritto, and pop the ox cheek straight in. When the underside is nicely browned, flip it over. Press it idly against the hot casserole and hear it sizzle. This is almost the hard bit over with, now. Thank you for going along with this mad idea.

When the ox cheek is sufficiently browned – or you have watched it for long enough – add the tinned tomatoes, red wine (swilling it around the tomato tins first to rinse them out), porcini mushrooms, herbs, balsamic vinegar and chocolate. Put the lid on, make sure the heat is as low as it will go, and walk away. Give it $4^1/_2$–5 hours, and the windows will steam up with promise. Stir it occasionally, and dip in a spoon for a taste: add salt if it needs it, and more pepper if you like it. The only thing to watch out for is the ox cheek sticking – if it does, add a splash more oil, and flip it over. You will only be able to flip it during the first 3 hours; after that it will start to disintegrate. (This is exactly what you want it to do, and a sign that everything is going well – you can even help things along by poking the ox cheek with a spoon.) If it sticks later on, a vigorous stir should sort it right out.

This is the hard part completely over with: congratulations!

From here, it's pretty much plain sailing, even if you're planning to make the pasta yourself. If you are, you'll want to make a start an hour or so before you think you're going to eat: I usually do it at the point the ox cheek starts to fall apart, after about $4^1/2$ hours. Either way, when you're ready, cook the pasta.

Dish up: a spaghetti spoon of pappardelle, two enormous ladles of ragù, a good grating of Parmesan. A bit more black pepper, maybe.

This ragù really is worth it, and I hope you'll love it as much as I do.

How to Make Pasta

I learned from the great Marcella Hazan that pasta should be, basically, flavourless: it is a vehicle that makes sauce taste better. Pasta is simply eggs and flour; no salt, only eggs and flour. Taste it on its own, and it will be strange and bland, quite unlike shop-bought pasta. But with sauce? It is the absolute best thing ever. Making your own pasta is not hard, and you can completely do it, without anything but a rolling pin (or a clean wine bottle) and a bit of nerve.

For 4

240g 00 flour, at least
(keep the bag to hand)

4 large eggs

• •• • • ' • • •• • •• • • •- • •• • ' '• ' •• •• •

Wash your hands thoroughly. Put the flour onto a clean bench or table, piling it into a mound. Make a hollow in the middle and crack in the eggs. Using a fork, gradually draw the flour into the eggs, blending in as little or as much flour as you need to make a firm dough. Perhaps a shake more flour? More flour. More flour. It is astonishing how much flour four eggs can drink up. When there's no visible egg left on show, get your hands involved, kneading and mixing. It will come together, slowly, into a tough, flexible dough. Knead the dough for at least 15 minutes. Pull it, push it, work your fingers through the tug and warp of it, crimping and pleating, the heel of one hand to the palm of the other. Feed it with the stress and tension in the back of your neck, sending it down your arms and into your fingers: stretching, pulling, turning. Feel it stretch; hold it by one edge and let it swing, hanging. Flip it and turn it. Isn't this remarkably pleasing? When you have a smooth, elastic dough, divide it into eight pieces.

Roll out the first piece of dough on the largest clean surface you have – I use the kitchen table, well scrubbed. Give it a turn (in other words, move the dough, so it doesn't stick) and then roll it out again; keep rolling until it's as thin as you can make it, and as long as you can make it. (I don't have a pasta machine, but this would be a brilliant place to use one, if you do.)

Slice your sheet of pasta into pappardelle-ish strips (think fat and long), laying them out on tea towels to dry. (Ideally you will have enough space to dry all your pasta on tea towels: practically speaking, you're probably going to have to resort to coat hangers, clothes horses and chair backs. Don't worry about it.) Repeat. Repeat. Repeat. Repeat. Repeat. Repeat. Repeat.

Leave your pasta strands to dry for about an hour, and then set a great pan of heavily salted water on to boil. When the water is boiling, gently slide the pasta into the water and cook for approximately 3 minutes, until just cooked through. Drain and serve immediately.

Blackberry Pizza

There are weeks that are made for steamed vegetables, and weeks that are made for nuts and grains, and then there are weeks that are made for absolutely nothing but pizza.

'I think,' the Tall Man said, sort of thoughtfully, one Friday afternoon, 'I think the thing I like best in the whole world (excluding you) is pizza.' It had been the kind of week where it had rained every time on my walk home. That's a pizza week if ever I saw one.

So we dedicated Saturday to pizza making, and this was the pizza we made, and it is the pizza I have been making ever since. The dough (rye) needs a while to rise, and the oven needs time to get as hot as it can go, and it's entirely worth it.

It is a little bit thinner and cracklier than a lot of pizza, and a little bit spicier and deeper than a lot of pizza, and a little bit sexier than nearly every pizza in the world.

This is pizza for grown-ups. And the blackberries: well, they are simply the best topping I know to put on pizza. They have the same sweet-sharpness you get from the very best tomatoes, but with a richness and depth all their own. Teamed with soft goat's cheese, maybe a little butternut squash sautéed with caraway seeds or a handful of oyster mushrooms, you have perhaps the greatest pizza ever made.

This recipe makes a dozen small pizzas (like, paperback-book-sized – I never worry too much about making them round), which will probably be more than you need. However, I've given these quantities for two reasons: first, because it's hard to halve a sachet of instant yeast; second, because if you freeze half of the dough (in six small balls), then you can have home-made pizza on a weeknight, and that feels like a miracle in every sense of the word. ⟶

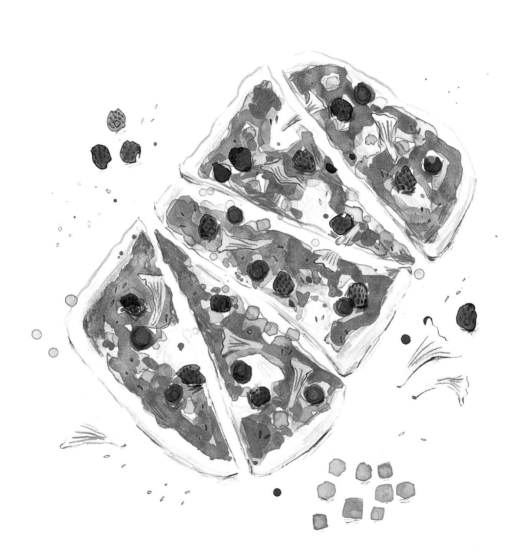

Makes about 12 smallish pizzas

For the dough	For the toppings
200g rye flour	1 quantity tomato sauce (see page 148) or a jar of pesto
300g 00 flour, plus extra for dusting	25g caraway seeds
1x 7g sachet of instant yeast	250g diced butternut squash
300ml warm water	Splash of olive oil
2 tbsp olive oil, plus extra for oiling	Oyster mushrooms
Good pinch of fine salt	Saucisson sec
	Soft goat's cheese and/or mozzarella
	Blackberries

• • • • • • ••• • •• • ••• •• • •• ••' • •• •• •• •••• ••• ••

You can make the dough by hand, or by stand-mixer-with-dough-hook. Sift your flours into a biggish bowl – or the bowl of your mixer. Stir in your yeast, then make a well in the centre and pour in the warm water and the 2 tablespoons of olive oil. Stir briefly, then let it sit for a few moments. Sprinkle in the salt, and then either get your hands in there (you know how to knead – fold the dough over and under itself until the gluten stretches and a dough forms), or flip the mixer-with-dough-hook switch to the lowest-possible setting. About 10 minutes of hand-kneading, or 8 minutes of machine-kneading. And then... that's it. Take your dough, and pop it into an oiled bowl (I just oil the mixer bowl, post-facto), cover with a clean tea towel and leave to prove in a warm place. In my case, this is under the table, with the space heater on. Which, coincidentally, is my favourite place in the whole flat, but I don't mind sharing it with pizza dough.

Wait for 4 hours, possibly a little longer, until the dough has doubled in size. Resist the urge to peek too often because lifting up the tea towel lets the warmth out of the bowl.

Meanwhile, make the sauce, if you're doing your own, and prepare the other toppings.

For the toppings, you can, obviously, use whatever you like. It's your pizza. But those listed here work well, arranged so that everyone can add their own. The butternut squash is absolutely gorgeous: toast the caraway seeds in a dry frying pan until fragrant, then add the squash and a generous splash of olive oil. Cover with a lid or foil and cook, stirring occasionally, for about 10 minutes. Finely slice the mushrooms and saucisson; slice or tear up the cheese.

If you want your pizza Roman-pizza-cart crispy, about an hour before the dough will be ready, turn your oven on as high as it will go, as Felicity Cloake recommends. (This works beautifully, but it is a bit wasteful of electricity, and it won't be the end of the world if you don't do this and just pre-heat your oven the usual 15–20 minutes beforehand.) Put a baking sheet or pizza stone (fancy) in the oven to heat too.

Take the tea towel off your dough and prepare yourself a work space: a clean surface big enough to wield a rolling pin in, dusted lavishly with flour, and a rolling pin. Divide the dough into twelve roughly equal-sized pieces. Roll each one into a ball, and – unless you're feeding a crowd – put six of them into a freezer bag and freeze immediately.

Take one ball of dough, and by some unholy combination of tugging and pulling and rolling with a pin, form your pizza base. As thin as you like. Go on, a bit thinner. Don't worry about the shape, so long as it fits on your baking sheet. Mine are almost aways rectangular.

Using oven gloves, take the hot baking sheet or pizza stone out of the blisteringly hot oven. Rest it on the unlit hob, a trivet or other heatproof surface – be careful, it will be *seriously* hot. With some combination of luck and unexpected dexterity, flip your pizza base onto the hot baking sheet or pizza stone, then spread with sauce or pesto and add your choice of toppings.

Carefully slide into the oven for 6 minutes if very hot, 12 if not. Have plates or wooden boards at the ready. Oven gloves on: one pizza out, another one in.

Eat and repeat. Have a glass of wine, and another slice of pizza. That's how you turn a week around; that's why some weeks are pizza weeks.

Beginner's Chicken Curry, for Harry

Harry Harris arrived at my house unexpectedly one afternoon, when the Tall Man was still at work. 'He invited me to dinner,' Harry Harris said, through the crackly intercom, standing on my doorstep. 'He and I used to work together?'

The Tall Man and I had not been together very long, and I did not know anybody he knew. 'I've got my guitar,' said Harry Harris.

Now I came to think of it, the Tall Man had said something about a dinner party. Something... something... I had not been paying attention. And now I was in my pyjamas, and there was a man on my doorstep. 'Should I... should I go away?' said Harry Harris.

I was quite shy then, and I have never been good with strangers. But something about Harry Harris made it easy, and so I held my breath and jumped in. 'Come up,' I told Harry Harris, and he did, and I liked him on sight. We sat and listened to the radio, and we talked, and he helped with the curry, which was the first one I had ever made, and was the first thing in the cookbook I had all the ingredients for. Ish. I improvised: this is not an authentic curry. It's not authentic in any way. But it is simple and very delicious, and it eases you into the whole business of curry making. It's also fabulous for parties, and you can have a nice time while it's doing its thing. This fogs up your windows and cooks all by itself while you sit and sing with a glass of wine in hand. And afterwards, you can feed the five thousand, as it scales up beautifully – I once made this for twenty people at a party in our Tiny Flat.

I don't have a lot of recipes for curry, not least because there are so many people who do it better. Meera Sodha. Madhur Jaffrey. Anjum Anand. But this one is mine, and I love it. This recipe is for Harry, with whom I have been friends ever since, with infinite affection and gratitude.

For 4

1kg chicken thighs and
  drumsticks

2 tsp chilli powder

1 tsp paprika

2 tsp salt

2 tsp black pepper

2 onions

4 garlic cloves

Thumb-sized knob of ginger

1 tbsp mild-flavoured oil,
  such as groundnut

2 tsp garam masala

6 cloves

6 cardamom pods

2 x 400g tins of chopped
  tomatoes

500ml chicken stock

Rice and/or naan, to serve

· ·

Take the skin off the chicken and trim away any fatty bits, then rub it with some of the chilli powder, paprika, salt and pepper, and leave it to marinate while you get chopping.

Assemble your onions, garlic and ginger. Dice the onions, finely chop the garlic, and peel and grate the ginger. Put the oil into a wok or large frying pan over a low heat and add your onions. Fry them, stirring every so often, until they are starting to soften, then add the ginger and garlic and fry for a few moments. Add the rest of the chilli powder and paprika, the salt, pepper, garam masala and cloves. Bash the cardamom pods with a pestle and mortar or the end of a rolling pin and add those too.

Now add the chicken and let it get brown on all sides – the browner, the better. This will take about 15 minutes, giving you time to breathe, and sit down.

Add the tomatoes and the stock. Bring to a simmer, then turn the heat down low and clamp on the lid (or cover with foil). Done.

Open the wine; gather friends. Sit on the sofa, getting progressively happier, and warmer, and drunker. Sing.

At some point, about an hour later, when the chicken is falling off the bone, take the lid off and let the curry reduce until it is thick and saucy.

Serve with rice, and naan, if you like. Give everyone a bowl of chicken curry. Give everyone a spoon. Sit down. Eat. Eat. Eat.

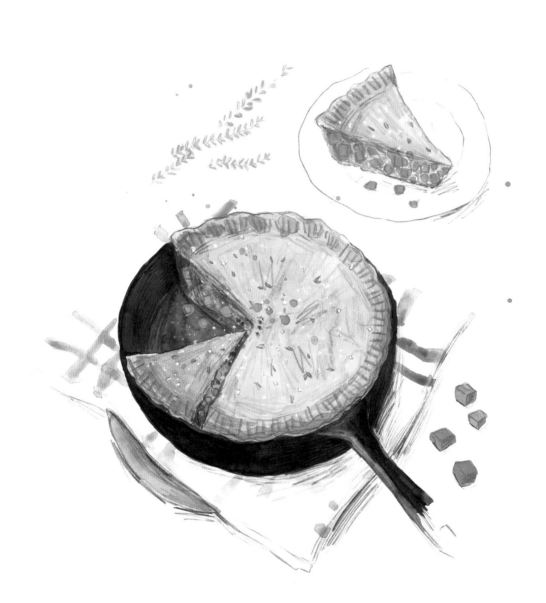

Squash Skillet Pie

I do not have many principles, as a cook, but chief among those I do have is this: I will go to the wall for pre-prepared ingredients. Cooking is not a contest or a virtue test, and it is not only for those with plenty of time. Cooking is for everyone, or it should be. And anything – anything – that makes that more likely (pre-chopped vegetables, ready-rolled pastry, a stock cube or pot) is to be applauded, wholeheartedly.

You can't always do everything, and you should know that even people who make a living from cooking do not always start from scratch. Prepping is work, and it takes physical strength sometimes, and mental strength sometimes, and energy always, and if it's easier on you to buy pre-prepared ingredients, do it. Consider this permission, if you need it. You do whatever you need to look after yourself. This does not make you any less of a cook. This does not make the success of your meal any less your success.

Carl Sagan once said that you couldn't make an apple pie from scratch unless you first invented the universe: all you're doing is starting a little further down the road than most. There is no shame *at all* in buying pre-rolled puff pastry. I have never met anyone who made their own puff pastry, and if I did I'd wonder (with more than a touch of envy, obviously) if they didn't have anything better to do. There is no shame in buying cooked chickpeas: you can't always know exactly what you're going to eat twenty-four hours in advance. And there is no shame in buying pre-diced squash: chopping squash is hard, especially if you have shaky hands.

This pie is made with ready-rolled pastry, pre-chopped squash and tinned chickpeas, and it's brilliant. Really. It's one of my favourite meals in the world – and with a glass of cold white wine and a crisp salad (or some petit pois), it's even better. ⟶

For 4

2 red onions

4 garlic cloves

1 tsp butter

1 tsp olive oil

540g pre-chopped squash
  (*that's 2 bags of the stuff from
  the supermarket – sometimes
  it has sweet potato in it too,
  and that's fine*)

1 tsp black pepper

2 good gratings of nutmeg
  (or 1 tsp ground)

3 stalks of fresh thyme
  (or 1 tsp dried)

Little glass of dry white wine

1 x 400g tin of chickpeas

50g Parmesan

1 egg

100ml double cream

1 x 320g packet of pre-rolled
  chilled puff pastry

Flaky sea salt

Salad, to serve

· · · · · · · · · · · · ·· · · · · · · · · · · ·· · · · · · · ··

Slice your onions and chop your garlic. Grab a cast-iron skillet
or ovenproof frying pan (mine is 26cm across), and set it over a
medium-low heat. Add the butter and oil, and your onions and
garlic. Cook for 15 minutes, stirring every so often until the onions
are all beautiful and tangly, then chuck in your squash.

Let the squash sear against the hot skillet for a minute or two, and
then, working fast, add the pepper, nutmeg, the leaves from two
of the thyme stalks (if you're using dried thyme, add it all now)
and the white wine. Cover immediately with a lid or foil, then turn
the heat down to low and leave the squash to cook for 20 minutes.

Meanwhile, open the tin of chickpeas, rinse in a colander and
leave them to drain in the sink. Grate your Parmesan (unless
you've bought pre-grated, which is – say it with me – also fine)
and beat your egg.

Take the lid or foil off your squash, and taste: it should be tender
and lovely. Add the chickpeas, Parmesan and cream. Give it a good
stir, and taste again: add salt if it needs it, and maybe more pepper.
Remove from the heat and let it cool for 10 minutes.

Pre-heat your oven to 180°C.

Unroll your pastry on a sheet of baking paper, and cut out a circle slightly bigger than your skillet – I use a dinner plate for this, as a template. Using the baking paper to help you lift it, slide the pastry lid over the top of the squash, then carefully use a fork to seal the edges of the pastry against the sides of the skillet. Prick a hole with the fork in the centre of the pastry lid, then brush with beaten egg and scatter with sea salt and the leaves from the remaining thyme stalk. Transfer the skillet to the oven and bake for 15 minutes, or until the pastry is golden and glossy.

A trivet on the table. Get someone else to pour the wine, put out knives and forks, and maybe make a salad. (I mean, empty a bag of leaves into a bowl, maybe whisk up a little olive oil with lemon juice and balsamic vinegar: this is a lazy meal, remember.) Maybe light a candle. Take the skillet to the table – be very careful around the skillet, as it will be hot – and let people serve themselves, chinking glasses in the candlelight.

Sweet Things

L et me start this chapter with a confession: I don't really make a lot of sweet stuff. Please don't get me wrong – this isn't a moral position, or a health position. It is a position born entirely out of not wanting to be stuck in the kitchen making pudding when everyone else is deep into bottle four. It's also a position based on not having much of a sweet tooth myself (unless I'm feeling really sad), and on not being a very confident baker. Somehow it always seems very complicated, understanding 'crumb' and 'humidity' and measuring everything, and I'm never quite sure it's worth the faff.

However, the sweet things here are, I swear, worth the effort – of which there isn't much at all. These are the only puddings I make, and most of them are humiliatingly easy, with an effort-to-reward ratio carefully calibrated for maximum enjoyment and minimum bother. Every pudding in this chapter can be made in advance and then put in the oven to warm, or left in the fridge or freezer until serving time.

There's a lot of spice and a bit of salt, plenty of sharp notes and caramelised edges, or a hit of dark smoky caramel itself – and I'll admit to being partial to a booze-spiked sauce. There's one grandmother's recipe for apple pie (the same apple pie I have for my birthday every year), and the other grandmother's recipe for a proper, richly spiced gingery parkin: sturdy enough to hold in one hand with a book held open in the other. There are little baked goods that you can stick a candle in for an easy birthday 'cake' or pack in a picnic: American-style crisp and chewy choc-chip cookies; whiskey-spiked and star-studded rye blondies; and luscious brownies with a molten heart of chocolate buttons and salted caramel shards. And a deep, dense Christmassy walnut and cardamom cake, heavy with syrup and glossy with roasted clementines.

There is the easiest and best three-ingredient lemon posset, which can become a cheesecake with the swift bashing of a bag of shop-bought ginger nuts. Those same ginger nuts are transformed into elegant, grown-up petits-fours by the addition of some whipped and peppery goat's cheese swirled with golden olive oil, before being dusted with icing sugar and served with a glass of port.

And two ice creams: the first Crunchie-flavoured, briskly trashy, super-sweet (yet utterly moreish) and unbelievably simple. The second, and the only remotely faffy recipe in this chapter, is a patient, meditative meander: gin and tonic in one hand, standing gazing out over the garden, while deftly folding a sour-sharp rhubarb and ginger ripple through freshly made custard.

There is, I think, something for every season and mood; nothing to make your heart sink with the effort of it all (or with the amount of washing up), and everything to gladden it. So, here we are: recipes for the sweet things that genuinely bring me joy – to cook and to eat and to serve.

Et Cetera Apple Pie

This is the best apple pie in the world. I mean that. My grandmother on my father's side taught me how to make it, and she learned it from her grandmother, and perhaps she learned it from hers. The pastry would always be crisp and flaky, even on the bottom, and the apple was green-skinned and never too sweet. On the top, little sugar crystals glistened like stray jewels and the initial letters of our names were cut out of the leftover pastry: E T C, for me, my sister and our half-brother.

I have never had a birthday without an apple pie like this. My grandmother doesn't make it for me any more; I do. When I was eighteen, I ran away from that side of my family, and in my haste, much got left behind: my Doc Martens, my plum-coloured hat with the veil, my stepmother – and my grandmother.

But people – unlike Doc Martens – don't just disappear; everyone leaves a trace. My grandmother used to say that the ghosts of Aunt Soggy and Aunt Stone, two long-gone spinster ancestresses, were always in the kitchen with us when we made this pie together; and now, as I make my own, I can almost believe that my grandmother, in some ghostly form, guides my hands. That is what I love most about cooking: in the kitchen I can resurrect that which was lost: the warmth of the oven, my grandmother's cool hands over mine, and the smell of good sharp apples, plainly cooked and encased in homemade pastry. It is not a sweet apple pie – there's no sugar, except a scattering on top.

It's especially lovely for me, because my great-grandmothers, grandmothers and mother all made good pastry, and so I can be with all of them at once. My mother is not an especially enthusiastic cook, but she knows her pastry. She had a cookery teacher at school in the 1970s, and the cookery teacher was ghastly, but she knew pastry too, and she taught my mother. I don't remember a time when I didn't know 'half fat to flour, more white fat than yellow, a teaspoon of iced water for each ounce of flour; mix and chill, and roll with short sharp strokes running forward.' 'I hope she's dead now,' my mother said, thoughtfully, 'but her pastry was very, very good.' $\longrightarrow$

Makes 1 large pie

450g plain flour, plus extra
  for dusting

125g lard

100g unsalted butter

Mug of iced (or very cold)
  water, with 1 tsp lemon
  juice added

6 Bramley or 8 Granny Smith
  apples (Bramleys are better,
  but you can't always get
  hold of them)

1 egg, lightly beaten

1 tsp granulated sugar

Thick cream, to serve

•• •• • •• • •• • •• • •• •• • •• • •• •• • •• • •

Start by making the pastry. Put your flour into a large bowl and chop your lard and butter into little dice – the slight unevenness of their measurements, with more lard than butter, is called 'the wrinkle'; my grandmother taught me that.

Run your hands under very cold water (the cold tap, run until it's icy-cold), then dry them. Use your fingertips to rub the fat into the flour, letting it sift and fall between your fingers, until it resembles breadcrumbs. Pastry cannot be fudged or hurried. Bind the pastry together with a splash of iced water, gathering it into a fist-sized lump. Add some more iced water if it won't come together, but only a little bit. Handle it lightly. Wrap in cling film, then put into the fridge to chill for half an hour.

Meanwhile, pre-heat your oven to 180°C and lightly grease an enamel pie plate or tart tin. Peel your apples and chop them into pieces about the size of your thumbnail. (If you can get the peel off in one long spiral, you are supposed to throw it over your shoulder, so it will reveal your true love's name. I have never been able to do this, but fortunately I am pretty sure I know the name of my true love, and I think it is beyond the capabilities of apple peel to spell – rather a lot of spiky letters in 'T-A-L-L M-A-N'.)

Put the apples into a stainless-steel saucepan with absolutely nothing else. You may, at a pinch, add a splash of water to stop them from sticking. Let the apples simmer for 10–15 minutes, giving them a stir now and again. When about half of the apples have broken down into apple sauce and are coating some still-pretty-solid pieces of apple, spoon the lot onto a plate, spreading it out evenly, and leave to cool completely.

Lay a sheet of baking paper on a clean table or work surface and dust with flour. Tear off a second sheet of about the same size and set it to one side.

Run your hands under the cold tap again. Dry them, and with your newly cold, ice-queen fingers, set half of your pastry onto the flour-dusted baking paper. Put the other sheet of baking paper over the top, and roll it out, with those short, sharp strokes running forward, into a rough circle about the diameter of your pie plate (I usually set the plate on the rolled-out pastry, to check) and the thickness of a ten-pence piece. Peel away the top sheet of baking paper, then carefully flip the pastry onto your pie plate and peel off the baking paper.

Roll out the other half of the pastry in the same way – this will be the lid of your pie.

Spoon in the apple mixture, and place the lid on top. Trim all the way round with a sharp knife, then use your thumb and fingers to crimp the edges together, making a seal. Prick the centre with a fork and – if you like – fashion your initials out of the pastry off-cuts and press them on top; or you can cut out leaf shapes for decoration instead.

Brush your pie with beaten egg, sprinkle with sugar and bake for 35 minutes, until crisp and golden on top. Serve with good thick cream, the kind that's so good and dense as to be almost yellow.

Reading in the Rafters Parkin

Here's a cake for the runaway in you; a cake for the oyster-solitary, scrambling-through-the-rafters child in your heart, or your past (which might be the same thing). It's a dense, dark cake – not heavy, somehow, but solid and satisfying – for a grey low day when the clouds bash the chimney pots. It's dark and treacly, a little bit toffee-burnt at the edges, sweet and sticky at the centre. You could take a hunk of this cake and shimmy up into the rafters, paperback book between your teeth like a pirate in a story, and you could stay there all day with this and that and a bag of apples, and nobody would know you were there.

Which is exactly what I did when I was growing up. I had a lot of sisters, and we had a lot of friends, and it was the sort of childhood where people were always in and out. All my life I have been torn between liking to be part of a pack, and desperately wanting to be left alone. My favourite place was up in the rafters of the barn, which I reached by stacking up old chairs and bits of lumber to make a ladder. I knew we weren't allowed up there because it was dangerous, and that is perhaps why I loved it so much.

I still go there, in my head, sometimes, trying to recapture that feeling of being of, but not in, the world. As a child, I read and re-read stories about children who see without being seen, children who find things and fix things and love things: *Harriet the Spy, Tom's Midnight Garden, The Secret Garden, Swallows and Amazons, The Children of Green Knowe* and *Alice in Wonderland*; Sara Crewe, Arabel and Matilda. All of which left me with a deep and pervasive sense that the world is vaster and more intricate than we know, and that it might not take much for your ordinary life to tumble and fall, whirling, down the rabbit hole.

This is what you learn to see, when you sit alone in a forbidden place, reading faster than you can turn the pages. You learn how very strange and lovely the world is and can be. How there is always more to find out, how there is nothing new under the sun – and that you are not alone, not really, not ever, with a book. That you can scramble as high and as far as you like, but if you've got a book it's impossible to believe that your own sadness or rage or fury is anything new, or anything special; rather, you are part of a long line of people, and all of those people are unlikely and complicated in ways that you both can and cannot imagine.

And this is the perfect cake to take with you on such adventures: it doesn't crumble when you clutch it tight in one hand, and it's delicious and sturdy and life-affirming.

Makes 1 large loaf

100g salted butter, plus extra
   for greasing

100g light muscovado sugar

100g treacle

100g golden syrup

150ml semi-skimmed milk

2 eggs

125g self-raising flour

100g rolled oats

4 tsp ground ginger

2 tsp ground cinnamon

1 tsp ground mixed spice

• • • • • • • •• •   • • •   • • • •   •• •   • •• •• • • • •• •• •• • ••• • • •• •• •

Pre-heat the oven to 180°C and find yourself a 900g (2lb) loaf tin. Lightly grease the tin with butter, then tear off a sheet of baking paper and press it into the tin, using the butter to stick it all the way up the sides – this makes it easier to get the parkin out later. I usually hold the paper in place with an elastic band around the outside of the tin until I have poured in the batter.

Take a saucepan and weigh in your butter, sugar, treacle and golden syrup (digital scales are very useful here). Set it over a low heat and stir gently until everything has melted into a smooth, dark, sweet syrup. Remove from the heat and leave to cool slightly.

Measure the milk into a jug and crack in the eggs; beat lightly until smooth. Weigh out the flour, oats and spices into a big bowl.

When the treacle mixture is barely warm, pour it into the flour mixture, and stir to make a stiff dough. Slowly add the egg and milk mixture, stirring with your other hand: yes, it's supposed to be that thin. Pour the batter into the lined loaf tin and ease off the elastic band. Slide into the oven and bake for 40–50 minutes, or until a skewer comes out almost clean – parkin should be a bit sticky in the middle. The top should be a deep reddish-brown, cracked across and risen high; it will feel solid, and should come away easily from the tin. Sit it in its baking paper on a wire rack to cool.

Let it cool before you cut a slice, or it will crumble – perhaps 20 minutes. A mug of tea, a good book, a plan for an adventure, and a big, damp, dark slice of treacle cake.

Whiskey & Rye Blondies

We climbed the hill together: the Tall Man and me, Harry Harris and his girlfriend, and Fiona, our token American, in pristine wellies. It was dark. It was Bonfire Night, and we were going to watch London burn.

We had a picnic: a midnight picnic, for eating in the cold and the dark, our mittens tinged with smoke. We had acquired some mulled wine from a pub on the way up and decanted it. We had samosas, ineptly folded, but spicy and strong. Tiny hand pies. Blondies, studded with sea salt and crisp, half-melted sugar, still warm. We had sparklers, matches and good boots. Scarves and gloves. The Tall Man had a bottle of ginger wine in his pocket. I think it was Fiona's first Bonfire Night, although I am not sure. People were singing 'American Pie' as we climbed the hill, and I had been thinking of the same song earlier when I was baking these blondies: dense rye crust, and the sharp-sour tang of whiskey in among the sweet white chocolate.

'So… it's to burn the Catholics?' Fiona asked, and we sort of shrugged, silhouetted against the city lights. Kind of? Maybe? Not at all, once you get right down to it: it's about fire, really, like every other festival that comes to hold back the dark.

We lit our sparklers and wrote our names in fire, as we always have, and always will. I wrote our initials entwined in a heart. The afterimage stayed on my retinas for a long time, and I felt like a teenager. Flippant, silly, dangerous, with everything mine for the taking: the whole world bright at my feet, bright with fire.

Then there was an enormous bang, close by: the real teenagers had sent an illegal roman candle into the hedgerow. The police came swiftly, and in the shadows cast by their blue lights, so clean and so ordinary, we slinked away, down the hill, through the long grass, and surreptitiously ate our blondies in the pub. They were (and are) so good: toffee-ish, a little blackened at the edges, dense and fudgy inside, with a crackled sugary crust. Sea salt. Whiskey and rye. The gold sugar stars caught on my teeth. I leaned against the Tall Man, breathed in the smoke from his coat, closed my eyes and wished it would last forever.

Makes 24 blondies

200g unsalted butter, plus
    extra for greasing

200g golden caster sugar

200g molasses sugar

2 tbsp whiskey (if you don't
    like whiskey, just leave
    it out and add an extra
    teaspoon of vanilla extract)

1 tsp vanilla extract

2 large eggs

250g rye flour

150g white chocolate

2 tsp flaky sea salt

2 tsp 'golden stars' sugar
    decorations (optional, but
    you can get them from most
    major supermarkets, in the
    baking aisle)

· · · · · ·   · · · · · ·   · · ·   · ·   · · · · · · · · · ·   · · ·   · · · ·

Pre-heat your oven to 180°C and butter a brownie tin (about
30cm x 20cm) or other similar-sized tin.

Weigh the butter into a large saucepan and set it over the lowest-
possible heat. You're going to melt it, then brown it, and this will
take about 7 minutes: keep an eye on it. It will go through solid to
liquid, to foaming, to rising, to sinking back on itself, and you will
be able to see the colour change.

Meanwhile, weigh out your sugars separately. (You can tinker
with these a bit, as long as you keep some dark sugar in there.
Molasses sugar is splendid, but can be hard to find; using
demerara instead will give you a lovely, paler blondie, while
substituting the golden caster sugar with granulated can make the
crust even crunchier, with that classic crackled finish.)

When the butter is a nut-brown colour, add your sugars to the
pan: golden caster first, and then molasses. Whisk with all your
strength to dissolve the sugar, and simmer over a low heat for
about a minute. Add the whiskey and/or vanilla, and whisk until
you have a smooth, glossy, dark mixture. Remove from the heat
and leave to cool for 5 minutes.

Crack both eggs into the cooled butter and sugar mixture, and take
up your whisk again. Whisk, whisk, whisk. Keep whisking until
the eggs are thoroughly incorporated, then gently fold in the rye
flour; you can do this with the whisk too, just go gently. $\longrightarrow$

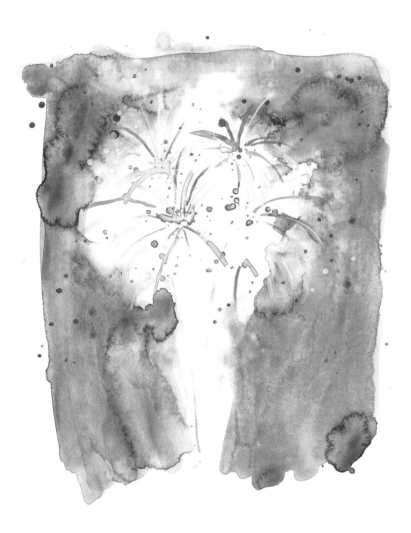

⟶▷ Break up your white chocolate into little pieces or shred it with a big knife or cleaver. Quickly stir the chocolate through the blondie batter, not minding too much if it melts, then decant into your buttered tin, squidging it down into the corners. Scatter with the sea salt – and the gold sugar stars, if using.

Bake for 25 minutes, then leave to cool completely in the tin. Score into 24 small squares: these are very sweet and very rich, which is why they are so good on a cold night. If you can, store in their tin, as they stay fudgier that way – just cover with foil, and lever out as needed. Or lever out half a dozen and wrap in foil, then take them up the hill to see the fireworks and the stars.

Walnut, Clementine & Cardamom Cake for Christmas

This is not a Christmas-cake Christmas cake, but it is a cake for Christmas.

A Christmas cake is a big, elaborate fruitcake that needs three months to mature, and nobody eats that much of it (except me), and it's all steeped in tradition, and you never quite know when to cut it (Christmas Day? Before?), and you need dried fruit and brandy and time, and then you're still eating it in March.

This cake is not like that. This is a cake for Christmas-time, for people popping round to drop off a card or stick a present under the tree, for taking with you to dinner parties at the wrong end of the year, and for emergency 'you *really* shouldn't have got me anything' gifts. It's got walnuts and clementines, like the toe of a stocking, and the deep green scent of cardamom running through it. Dense and chewy on the outside, the cake is tender, yielding and syrupy, and is decorated with walnut halves and jewel-like roasted clementine slices.

It's quite quick to make – you don't even need to pre-heat the oven. The finished cake fits beautifully into an oblong one-litre Tupperware container, and if you leave it in the baking paper it looks authentically and charmingly artisanal to present as a gift. It also makes your house smell beautiful, just like Christmas: oranges, spices, roasted nuts and molten sugar.

Makes 1 cake, in a 450g (1lb) loaf tin

150g walnuts, plus 3 extra halves for decorating	2 clementines
14 cardamom pods	1 lemon
50g stale sourdough bread	4 eggs
200g brown sugar	175ml olive oil, plus extra for oiling the tin
2¹/₂ tsp baking powder	60g granulated sugar

· ′ · →

⟶ First, briefly blitz your walnuts and the seeds from six of the cardamom pods in a spice grinder or food processor – you want some of the nuts to remain a bit chunky, to give the cake texture. You might need to stop the machine and give the nuts a stir, as they have a tendency to clump. Tip the walnuts and cardamom into a large bowl. Blitz the stale bread to fine crumbs and add to the bowl, along with the brown sugar and baking powder.

Scrub your clementines. Set one aside and finely grate the zest of the other one into the bowl. Juice the zested clementine and set the juice aside for the glaze later. Scrub your lemon and finely grate the zest of half of it into the bowl. Juice the zested half of the lemon and set this aside with the clementine juice.

Lightly beat your eggs and combine with the oil, then add to the bowl and stir to combine everything.

Oil and generously line your loaf tin with baking paper. You want plenty of overhang so you can wrap the finished cake in it, and to help with removing the cake from the tin.

With a very sharp knife, carefully cut your second clementine into thin slices. Pour the cake batter into the prepared tin and lay the best, most round clementine slices on top (you can eat the rest, if you like). Put into a cold oven, turn it to 180°C, and bake for 1 hour or until a skewer inserted in the centre comes out clean and the clementine slices are starting to blacken a little.

About 15 minutes before the cake is due to come out of the oven, put the granulated sugar, reserved clementine and lemon juices and 100ml water into a stainless-steel saucepan. Split the remaining eight cardamom pods, and shake the seeds into the pan. Set over a medium heat, and bring to the boil, then turn the heat to low and simmer for about 10 minutes until thick and syrupy. (You could strain the syrup here to remove the cardamom seeds; I'm very sorry, but I just never do.)

Take the cake out of the oven and carefully lift it out of the tin by firmly taking hold of the baking paper at either end. Set it on a plate, then break the three extra walnut halves into pieces, and scatter over the top of the cake.

Using a skewer, puncture the cake all over with little holes. Slowly pour over the warm syrup, and let the cake absorb it; you really will want all the syrup, even though it seems too much. If it pools on the surface of the cake, simply make more holes beneath the puddles, and let it drain into the cake.

This cake is very good served warm from the oven, with a dollop of good yellow cream, but it's even better the next day, when the syrup has set to a deep, glossy, chewy coat, and the flavours have had a chance to develop. Stored in an airtight container, it will keep well for several days, if you can resist it for that long.

'Three Lemons for the Healing' Lemon Possets

I got the idea for this recipe off the back of a condensed milk tin. Bear with me here. I had had the sort of culinary injury cooks are prone to (finger; blender). The doctor who fixed it was a tiny Italian lady who looked like a mouse pretending to be a person. She kept up a steady, soothing chatter, mostly under her breath, but occasionally, as she lunged for a steri-strip or a bit of gauze, I'd catch what she was saying, and what she was saying, very seriously, was this: 'I cannot prescribe, they will not let me prescribe on NHS, but you must take... three lemons – for the healing, to heal. Three lemons you must eat. Every day you take three lemons. Very good for healing, very good for nutrition also. For the healing.'

As it happens, I eat a lot of lemons, especially in winter when everything seems grey and dull and doom-y, and they do seem sort of healing. This is the most lemony thing I know, and is absurdly easy to make: three ingredients, four if you grate a bit of nutmeg over the top. One bowl. A sharp, delicious mouthful, it is simple and elegant and tastes like it ought to have taken you hours in the kitchen with egg whites and whisks and goodness knows what else – and, yes, it does feel kind of healing, and comforting, and bright. There are four lemons in this recipe, not three, which I think probably makes it even more magical.

For 6

250ml double cream	4 lemons
1 x 397g tin of condensed milk (the shorter tin, not the taller one)	Freshly grated nutmeg, if you like

Pour your cream into a big bowl, tip in the condensed milk and whisk them together.

Scrub your lemons in hot water, with a scourer and washing-up liquid, then rinse well (this removes any wax coating, which is not something you want in a posset); or you could splash out on unwaxed lemons and skip this step.

Finely grate the zest of the lemons, then cut them in half and juice them. Reserving a teaspoon of the zest for later, add the rest of the zest and all the juice to the bowl of cream. Whisk until everything is combined – the posset will literally thicken before your eyes. It's magic, actually, this bit. Don't worry if it still looks a bit thin when you've finished whisking, though: it will thicken up properly in the fridge.

Spoon into six ramekins and scatter with the reserved lemon zest and (if liked) a grating of nutmeg. Cover tightly with cling film and put in the fridge to set for 1 hour. Serve just as they are, a ramekin per person.

Quick Lemon Cheesecakes

Make a quick cheesecake base with equal parts crushed ginger nuts and melted butter, and press into the base of each ramekin before spooning in the posset. When my grandmother makes these (it turns out she's been making them for years and I never knew), she also puts crushed ginger nuts and a mint leaf on top, but I eat them just as is: a three-spoonful, glorious, perfect thing.

Paris Cookies

Before I came to London, I lived in Paris. I was eighteen, and I lived in a tool shed there, with my best friend in all the world. Her name was Cornelia, and she had better clothes than I did, and more nerve. By day we looked after three boys: L, who was seven, E, who was five, and little P, who was three. And by night Cornelia and I would go out to the kind of parties I had always dreamed of going to, in apartments high above the Seine, in bookshops and old music halls, or alongside the Canal Saint-Martin, where the cool kids hung out, and pretend to be older and wiser than we were. We would come back on the night bus, horrified at our own daring; tiptoeing through the door, we'd tumble into the kitchen for *tisane* and a handful of cookies, and so to bed.

There were always cookies, because we made them. We were not great cooks, either of us, but we suddenly had possession of a kitchen, a great deal of free time in the middle of the day (once we had done the school run and tidied up), and three boys to entertain and feed. That lovely yellow kitchen was where I started to want to cook, I think. Partly, at least, because cooking there seemed different: contrary to everything I had ever thought about French cooking, it turned out to be, in that household at least, something you did because you enjoyed it, and if it all went wrong, well, *bof!* There was always the butcher's shop, with trays of ready-made suppers; the greengrocer, with crisp little lettuces and sharp leaves of chicory; and the baker, with excellent, still-warm baguettes.

Our Parisian family was so kind to us. They took us to a cheese shop that sold the most delicious raw milk, straight from the farm, and were astonishingly tolerant when we drank it all. They let us feed their children the most extraordinary diet, part frozen Tater Tots, part vegetable experiment. We liked going to the market, and we'd come home with vegetables no French person would ever eat, like parsnips. But they ate everything we made. For the father's birthday, we baked a Victoria sponge without a single raising agent, and they couldn't have been more charming. They just pretended we'd meant to do it that way, and fed it to their guests as *le petit déjeuner anglais*, toasted, with jam. I am still not sure if they actually enjoyed it: either way, it all went. $\longrightarrow$

$\longrightarrow$ What they did enjoy, however, and I know this because they ate them in prodigious quantities, were these cookies. We made them every day. They are very easy, easy enough for the children to make with us on rainy afternoons; and fast, fast enough to make between picking one child up from nursery school and collecting the others from the big school. We would have them warm for *goûter*, the fourth French meal that children have after school, with chocolate milk in bowls; and cold, when we stumbled in at weekends a little tipsy; and frozen, as cookie dough, on the long, lazy afternoons when the children were all at school, our own work was done, and we had nothing better to do than be eighteen and eat cookie dough.

These are American-style cookies, and they are the best I have ever tasted: chewy, crisp and amenable to all manner of adaptations and tweaks. I have given two ideas for variations at the end, just to get you started, but this recipe will stand up to a fair bit of tinkering, so please feel free to play with it.

I recommend them to you heartily, and I would like to dedicate this recipe to that family, who took me in as a waif and stray, and loved me when I most needed it.

Makes about 24 cookies

170g salted butter	250g plain flour
300g sugar (*I like demerara*)	1/2 tsp bicarbonate of soda
1 egg, plus 1 extra yolk	150g chocolate chips
1 tsp vanilla extract	Flaky sea salt

• • • • • ••• • •• • ••• •• • •• •• •• • •• •• •• •••••• ••• • ••

Pre-heat the oven to 180°C and line a large baking sheet with baking paper. Melt the butter in the microwave, or in a small saucepan over a low heat.

Put the sugar into a big heatproof bowl, add the melted butter and beat until the sugar has dissolved – a stand mixer makes light work of this. Add the egg, the extra yolk and the vanilla, and keep beating until smooth. (If you use very coarse sugar – some of the rougher brown sugars are like little granules – it won't get smooth, and your finished cookies will have a crunchy, sugary texture: this is not bad, per se; in fact, I prefer it, but I tell you to warn you.)

Tip in the flour and bicarbonate of soda and keep beating until you have a smooth dough, then gently fold in the chocolate chips.

Place dollops of the cookie dough on the prepared baking sheet, about a dessertspoon per cookie, spacing them out so they have room to spread as they bake – I usually get about eight on a baking sheet. (Don't worry too much: even if they do merge together in the oven, they always break apart beautifully. I used to let the three-year-old do this, which tells you how unfussy you can be here.)

Scatter with sea salt, then bake for 10 minutes. They will have puffed up and may look underdone, but as they cool – which they *must* do on a wire rack (you can slide them, baking paper and all, straight onto the rack) – they will become firmer and will crack across the top, like a proper cookie. (Remember, you can always return them to the oven for a little longer if they are under-baked for your taste, but an overdone cookie is a heartbreaking thing.)

Repeat with the rest of the dough. Try to resist eating the cookies as they come out of the oven – they are best after about 10 minutes of cooling and hardening time. I know this, yet still I tend to eat them so hot that the chocolate burns my lips, gulping them down with cold milk, just like any American movie kid.

Oatmeal, Molasses & Banana Cookies

Substitute the egg yolk with 2 tablespoons of mashed banana, use molasses sugar, and use 200g rolled oats and 50g flour in place of the 250g flour. Melt the sugar in the microwave or pan with the butter, beat in the banana, and then continue as per the recipe.

Double Chocolate Cookies

Replace 70g of the butter with 70g chocolate: put both in a heatproof bowl set over a saucepan with a little water in the bottom – make sure the base of the bowl isn't touching the water. Set the saucepan over a very low heat, and stir the butter and chocolate until melted and combined, then proceed with the recipe.

Whipped Goat's Cheese & Ginger Nut Creams

These are a slightly more subtle and grown-up version of something the Tall Man and I ate on our first date: ginger nuts sandwiched with chunks of goat's cheese and dipped in port.

It was the kind of serendipitous thing you can only invent out of necessity. We were very young and very poor, and we somehow had to make a date-worthy meal out of the items on the 'reduced' shelf at the supermarket. We were lucky (then, as in so many things), and the supermarket had drastically cut the price of a bottle of post-Christmas port, a bashed-up packet of ginger nuts, and some cheese that was almost past its sell-by date. That, plus a packet of sausages and a loaf of sliced bread, cleared out both our bank accounts. And so we went back to the little room we were renting in Wood Green, and made these, and they were – like the date – unexpectedly, wholly brilliant. The sweetness of the biscuits and a dusting of icing sugar brought out the sweetness inherent in the goat's cheese and black pepper, while the vivid olive oil – green and warm and clean – sang to the ginger.

We moved into our own flat a few weeks later, and the recipe for these little petits-fours came with us too: they have evolved, and changed, just as we have. I have made my own ginger nuts (and include the recipe here, in case you want to do the same), tried different cheeses to sandwich them together, even incorporated them into a trifle. But these are genuinely best, I think, as a last-minute dessert, with ordinary, shop-bought ginger nuts. They look lovely on a plate too, perhaps on a doily, in the ruby light reflected through a glass of port; I haven't put the port in the recipe, but I do recommend it – that, or a black coffee, to end a dinner party. ⟶

Makes 12 ginger nut creams

1 tbsp black peppercorns
250g soft goat's cheese
1 tsp flaky sea salt
1¹/₂ tbsp olive oil
24 ginger nuts (bought
  or home-made)
Icing sugar, for dusting

For the ginger nuts
  (makes about 24)
100g salted butter
1 tbsp (about 30g) golden
  syrup
350g plain flour
100g demerara sugar
100g light muscovado sugar
1 tsp bicarbonate of soda
1 tbsp ground ginger
1 egg

. . . .

If you're making the ginger nuts yourself, start by pre-heating the oven to 180°C.

Weigh the butter and golden syrup into a saucepan and set over a low heat to melt, stirring occasionally. Remove from the heat and leave to cool for 5 minutes.

Put your flour and both kinds of sugar into a large bowl, then stir through the bicarbonate of soda and the ground ginger. Crack the egg into a glass or small bowl and beat lightly. Add it to the bowl, along with the cooled butter and syrup mixture, then mix to a stiff-ish dough – you might need to get your hands involved and give it a decent knead, just to bring it together.

Wrap the dough in cling film, stick it in the fridge to chill for 10 minutes, and dig out a baking sheet.

Divide the dough into quarters. Take one of the quarters and roll it out between two sheets of baking paper until it's the thickness of a ten-pence piece. Peel off the top sheet of paper and stamp out circles with your smallest cutter (mine is about 4cm across). Cut the biscuits out with a bit of space between them, so that if they spread a little as they bake you'll still be safe.

Lift away the excess dough, leaving behind the cut-out circles (just like peeling the white parts off a sheet of stickers). Carefully lift the bottom sheet of paper, laden with stamped-out biscuits, straight onto the baking sheet. Re-roll and repeat with the excess dough.

Bake your ginger nuts for 12 minutes: they should be golden, and still tender to the touch, but they will harden up as they cool. Slide the finished biscuits onto a wire rack to cool.

While your first batch is in the oven, take a third sheet of baking paper and repeat the whole process: roll out, stamp out and then slide onto the baking sheet when the first batch come out. Do the same with the other two quarters of dough.

When you're ready to make your goat's cheese and ginger nut creams, crush the peppercorns pretty roughly – using either a pestle and mortar or the end of a rolling pin.

Trim any rind from your goat's cheese, then put it into a large bowl and add the pepper, salt and olive oil. With electric beaters, whip the cheese for 2 minutes until it's light and fluffy.

Sandwich together pairs of ginger nuts with a teaspoonful of whipped cheese.

Arrange the ginger nut creams on a plate and cover loosely with cling film until you're ready to serve. Dust lightly with icing sugar just before serving.

Salted Caramel Brown Butter Brownies

In my head, I call these 'It Gets Better Brown Butter Brownies', and every time I make them I am reminded that things do, indeed, get better: not all the time, but enough of the time that it's worth going on. These brownies are worth going on for, I think. They are everything a brownie should be: dense and fudgy on the inside, chewy and caramelised on the outside, and studded with walnuts, chocolate buttons and shards of salted caramel – frozen first, so that little pockets of molten toffee form as they bake. This is the most wildly extravagant recipe in the whole book.

Makes 12 brownies

400g brown sugar

150g cocoa powder

80g plain flour

250g unsalted butter, plus extra for greasing

2 tsp vanilla extract

125g walnuts

4 fridge-cold eggs

1 x 30g packet of chocolate buttons

For the salted caramel

100g demerara sugar

4 tbsp salted butter

3 tbsp double cream

Good pinch of flaky sea salt

. . . .

For the salted caramel, put the sugar in a large saucepan and set over a medium-high heat. Melting sugar to make caramel is a lovely thing: the granular turning, pleasingly, into liquid. Stir it, if you need to. Keep cooking the caramel until it's a coppery-brown colour, then stir in the butter, mixing it in thoroughly. Take it off the heat and let it cool for a minute. Then spoon in the cream and sea salt and mix again. Return it to the heat, stirring while it spits and bubbles and foams astonishingly. You're looking for it all to incorporate into a rich, smooth sauce. This is far easier than you think and you are not going to ruin it. Be careful – it's very hot and will cling to everything it touches.

Line a large plate with baking paper, then lightly grease the baking paper. Pour the caramel onto the greased paper and scatter over some more sea salt before it cools. Transfer to the freezer and leave for 40 minutes.

Meanwhile, pre-heat the oven to 180°C and grease a twelve-hole muffin tin. (If your tin is not non-stick, you might also want to use paper muffin cases to make your life easier.)

Lift the frozen caramel, baking paper and all, onto a chopping board and cut it into smallish shards.

For the brownie batter, put the sugar and cocoa into one bowl, and the flour into another.

Take the pan you made the caramel in and put in the butter. Set it over a medium heat to melt, letting it turn golden and darken until it's a nut-brown colour and gives off a wonderful, warm nutty scent. Swiftly remove it from the heat, then stir in the sugar, cocoa and vanilla and a tablespoon of cold water. Whisk briskly until you have a beautiful, glossy ganache-type thing, then leave to cool for 5 minutes (to stop the eggs scrambling when you add them). Use this time to coarsely crush the walnuts.

If possible, grab a friend and hand them the egg-box. Ask them to pass you the cold eggs, one at a time, as you crack and whisk them into the shiny mixture. Tip in the flour, and whisk and whisk until your arm falls off – and you have a smooth brownie batter. Stir in the walnuts and the chocolate buttons.

Working quickly, so nothing melts, spoon about two-thirds of the batter into the muffin tray, dividing it as evenly as you can between the holes. Press a shard of salted caramel into each one, then cover with the rest of the batter and press a second shard of salted caramel on top.

Bake for 12 minutes, then leave them to cool in the tin for *at least* 10 minutes. I am not joking, nor am I usually one to wait for things to cool. If you don't let these cool, they'll collapse and it will be a disaster. After that, however, perfect – and even better the next day.

Crunchie Ice Cream

My mother used to make this for dinner parties, and I have stolen it. She in turn stole it from Ali James. The Jameses were friends of my parents from the village one over, and they used to come for dinner often; they'd come round on Saturday nights, and the house would be full of noise and laughter and beer. I loved those nights: I have modelled my life after my parents' Saturday nights.

I used to tiptoe downstairs the morning after and scrape out the bowls, because I loved it so much. I am not sure, now, I could eat much of it as it's quite sweet, but a little portion is exactly right – incredibly moreish, incredibly bad for you and incredibly glorious.

It requires nothing from you but a little rage: enough rage to reduce a stack of Crunchies to rubble. The ice cream will only take about ten minutes to make, but you'll need to allow about eight hours for it to freeze. Remember to take it out of the freezer and leave on the counter about half an hour before you want to eat it, to give it time to soften slightly.

For 6

6 x 40g Crunchie bars
1 x 397g tin of condensed milk
 (the shorter tin, not the
 taller one)

240ml double cream

Start by smashing up your Crunchies (this is a deeply satisfying task, especially for the furious; I am always a little furious).

Deconstruct them into a pleasing combination of golden powder and little splinters of chocolate.

Whip together your condensed milk and cream to soft peaks. Resist eating it all.

Stir in your Crunchie shards. Spoon into a Tupperware container and freeze for about 8 hours, or until firm.

That's it. I told you. The laziest, most glorious thing.

Rhubarb & Ginger Ripple Ice Cream

This ice cream came from a glut of rhubarb one summer, and to me it tastes not only of rhubarb and ginger, but also of freedom. It had been a tough few months, and we were staying by the sea until we felt better. The kitchen had an ice-cream maker, and so it seemed necessary to make this, and I did, and it was a step towards better-ness. For the first time in a long time, I felt that happiness was truly possible for me. It's not technically a ripple – leave that to proper ice-cream people – but you know what I mean. It's also utterly delicious.

This is a frozen-custard kind of ice cream, but don't let that frighten you: custard is not complicated, it just needs an eye keeping on it in case it curdles; and if you're worried about it, you can add a little cornflour, which stabilises it further. It's a bit of a faff to make this without an ice-cream machine, but it can be done.

The finished ice cream goes beautifully with meringues, which you can make from the leftover egg whites, or is gorgeous just scooped into cones or small dishes and eaten with the wind in your hair and salt-spray in your eyes. It's a holiday ice cream, and it's a recipe that makes me happy every time.

Makes about 500ml (the same amount as a standard tub)

6 rhubarb stalks

6 balls of stem ginger, plus
    2 tbsp syrup from the jar

1 tbsp soft brown sugar

250ml double cream

250ml full-fat milk

2 vanilla pods

5 egg yolks

75g caster sugar

2 level tsp cornflour
    (optional)

• • • • • ••• • • • • • • • •• • • •• •• • •• •• •• ••••• •• • ••

Rinse the rhubarb and pull off any tough stringy bits, then chop quite finely. Put the rhubarb into a stainless-steel saucepan and add the ginger with its syrup, the sugar and a tablespoon of water. Set over a low heat to simmer and soften for about 12 minutes. Give the rhubarb a stir every so often, and add a tiny bit of water if it seems to be sticking. When it's just tender, remove from the heat and leave to cool. ⟶

$\longrightarrow$ In a second saucepan, combine the cream and milk. With your thumbnail, split the vanilla pods and scrape the black seeds into the white cream mixture. Set the saucepan over a low heat. Heat until it's just simmering (don't let it boil); keep stirring the whole time and inhaling the beautiful, buttery, almost boozy scent of real vanilla. Let it cool for a few moments until it's lukewarm.

In a large heatproof bowl, beat your egg yolks together with the sugar (and the cornflour, if using). Now for the tricky bit: stirring constantly, slowly pour in the warm cream. Keep stirring, or it will curdle – don't take your eye off it for a second. When all the cream has been incorporated, pour the custard back into the saucepan and return it to a medium-low heat. Stir constantly while you bring it up to the boil. Keep stirring, but you've almost done it! Let the custard simmer until it thickens: when it's ready, it should coat the spoon, and cling there when you twist the spoon in your hand – about 4–5 minutes of stirring. Remove from the heat.

Quickly wash and dry the bowl you used for the egg yolks and sugar, then pour the custard back into it.

Blitz the rhubarb and ginger in a food processor or blender to make a thick, sharp sauce. Taste it: depending on your rhubarb, you might want to add a touch more sugar.

Lightly fold the rhubarb through the custard, then pour into an ice-cream machine and follow the manufacturer's directions.

If you don't have an ice-cream machine, pour the mixture into a large Tupperware container and freeze for 6–8 hours, removing it every hour and beating until smooth. This might sound like a pain, and it is – but I do think the ice cream is worth it. I think it's worth most things, to be honest.

Three Last Things

1. Wash up as you go along.

2. If it smells fine, it's probably fine.

3. It's probably *all* going to be fine
(in the end).

This may have looked like a cookbook, but what it really is is an annotated list of things worth living for: a manifesto of *moments* worth living for. Dinner parties, and Saturday afternoons in the kitchen, and lazy breakfasts, and picnics on the heath; evenings alone with a bowl of soup, or a heavy pot of clams for one. The bright clean song of lime and salt, and the smoky hum of caramel-edged onions. Soft goat's cheese and crisp pastry. A six-hour ragù simmering on the stove, a glass of wine in your hand. Moments, hours, mornings, afternoons, days. And days worth living for add up to weeks, and weeks worth living for add up to months, and so on and so on, until you've unexpectedly built yourself a life worth having: a life worth living.

Your life is like a stockpot, simmering with all these minutes: everything you've ever learned and everything you've ever loved. Every time you're in the kitchen you're alive with all the people whose books you've read, and the people who taught you, and the people who loved you. Nobody is born knowing how to cook. It all comes from people, breaking bread together, and talking, and loving, and sharing, and it is probably terribly trite, but I can't think of anything more important than this.

Taking Stock

This is the last recipe in the book, and you can make it with the leftovers from the very first. Only a chicken carcass and a handful of whatever vegetables you have in the fridge drawer, plus salt, pepper and a few herbs, but it becomes something beautiful. A golden thing. Alive and shimmering, and the most nourishing, life-affirming thing I know. Something to build on, but enough on its own too, just to hold the mug in two cupped hands, and sip, and stay alive. Because, I promise you: it's worth it. But I think you know that by now.

Everything will be better if you learn how to make a good stock. Of course, it's okay to use stock cubes and stock pots, and nobody except you will even know – but they will notice the difference when you do use home-made stock.

The principal thing, here, is time: it's a sort of alchemy to take your peelings, scraps and bones and transfigure them into something golden, deep and gorgeous that transmits the flavour of all those elements into whatever you cook with your stock: soups, sauces and risottos. If you use bones, expect your stock (when they are really good bones) to set into a jelly as it cools.

When I'm organised, I make **chicken stock** with the carcass from a roast chicken; a couple of onions, skin on, rinsed and quartered; a celery stalk, rinsed and roughly chopped; a single carrot, ditto; and black pepper (but no salt, not until the end). Water to cover. And then I let it cook for 4–6 hours, on the lowest-possible heat, with the lid on (until I want to reduce it, to concentrate the flavour, when I bring the heat up and take the lid off).

Once the stock is ready, I usually strain the first jar's worth through a muslin-lined sieve to produce a clear stock. The rest I ladle out carefully, using a big spoon, to give me a stock with flecks of pepper and perfect morsels of tender meat suspended in the jelly. Both versions will keep for a few days in the fridge, or several months in the freezer.

I use the clear stock for clear soups, where the chicken flavour should be a subtle backdrop for everything else; and the other for risotto and pasta sauce, or anything where I want chicken to be a proper player. If I use this denser chicken stock for a risotto, say, then that's all the meat I need (this also makes me feel very thrifty).

For **vegetable stock**, I like to make a kind of onion base: half a dozen onions, quartered; 6 garlic cloves, left whole; 2 celery stalks, roughly chopped; 3 big leeks, ditto. I don't bother to peel any of these things, but I do rinse them pretty vigorously under the cold tap. (I also keep a big bag of well-rinsed vegetable peelings in my freezer and add those too, when I remember.) A big bundle of rosemary, bay and thyme, tied up with string. Water to cover. Give it about 2 hours of simmering over a low heat, with the lid on. Strain the stock through a muslin-lined sieve, then stash in the fridge for a few days, or in the freezer for several months.

You can make a very, very good **mushroom stock** by adding a generous handful of dried mushrooms to the vegetable stock above.

Acknowledgements

I used to think that acknowledgements in books were sort of tiresome (like an Oscars speech without having won anything) and then I wrote a book, and found that I had never been so grateful to so many people in my whole life. Anyway, you don't have to read it unless you're in it, but there's a heck of a brutal twist halfway down this page. (Sorry.)

The world of this book is a lost world now, in a lot of ways. I believe that it was truly magic. I don't know how we did any of it, but I am so glad we had that time, and I am so glad that I wrote it all down. Thank you for living in it with me, and for me – and for us. I miss it every day.

Thank you to my beloved and peerless agent, Daisy Parente. You could not possibly have foreseen how much trouble I would be. I am so, so glad to have you as an agent and my friend. (Also to Jane Finigan and everyone else at Lutyens & Rubinstein: I know in some ways looking after me has very much been a team effort.)

Thank you to everyone at Bloomsbury for your endless kindness, patience and willingness to move deadlines by several years. You *also* could not have foreseen how much trouble I would be! Thank you for sticking with it.

Thank you to Anita Mangan, who designed this book and pieced it all together so intuitively and precisely. You're a total marvel, and the book is beautiful, and also your hair is the best. Thank you, thank you, thank you.

Thank you to Elisa Cunningham, who drew the pictures. I don't know how you saw into my heart and drew everything you found there, but you did. You are an absolute joy. Thank you. (Also thank you for always understanding that meetings need snacks.)

Now here's where it gets harder to write.

You probably know – but maybe you don't – that John, the Tall Man, died just as I finished writing the last draft of this book. He got sick before I'd even started really writing the first. This book was written in hospital corridors and chapels and in the long, lonely nights watching to see if he was still breathing – and I wrote it at least in part to keep our world alive if he couldn't be. You don't write anything under these conditions without a great deal of help.

So thank you to the staff at Barts: you gave us so much more time. You gave him time to read this book, and to write his own, and you gave us birthdays by the sea and Christmases full of roses, and you gave us years we would never have had without you. You gave us time to say everything that needed saying. Thank you.

Thank you to everyone who supported us for so long. Thank you to everyone who joined the stem cell register; thank you to everyone who

donated money or marrow or blood in our names. Thank you to Twitter.
Amber: I wish you'd been able to come for dinner.

Thank you to everyone who kept us afloat emotionally, practically
and financially. Thank you to all my editors. Thank you particularly
to Sam Baker, who took me on out of nowhere and let me write until
I could write no more – and to Nicole Cliffe, for all the love and all the
bad-taste jokes.

Thank you to my family: all of you everywhere. I have tried to
be truthful. Thank you for all the stories. Especial thanks to my
extraordinary grandparents Beth and Andy Maslen, my wonderful
parents Nikki and David Risbridger; my brilliant, hilarious, astonishing
sisters Cia, Bee and Floss Risbridger. You all make me laugh so much.
I love you all. Thanks for everything – especially that cookbook the
year I left home. Would any of this have happened without it?

Thanks also to the Owens – to Todd, Meg, Kim and Joe – for
the truly mad bits of our childhood. Sometimes I think I must have
dreamed the dumper truck.

Thank you to everyone who came to dinner, in those golden evenings
in that cramped little house. Too many of you to thank by name, but you
know who you are. Thank you for the wine and the singing. I'm glad
you were there. I'm glad you remember, too.

To everyone I invited for dinner and then never got round to
organising it: I'm sorry, it's been A Time. I wish you'd been there.
Thank you for being our friends regardless. The invite stands.

Thank you to the Difficult Aunts for their profound support for
this book, and for everything I do. There is an alternate universe where
this book is called *Midnight Chicken: Brahms On Accordion*. Thank
you, Anna Scott-Piano, Phelpsie, Eley Williams, Sarah Gulick, Isabella
Streffen, Emma Nuclear Southon, Marika Prokosh, Xtin, Alice Tarbuck
(witch); Olivia Potts (and her culinary wisdom); Sarah Perry, foulest-
weather friend and kindred spirit; Kate Young, the kind of person who
brought me all the ingredients for Midnight Chicken when I was at a
low ebb; Fiona Zublin, who gave me so many recipes and never for one
moment let up with the puns (and love to Joe, Smitten and Blue too.
Thank 'er? I hardly even knew 'er, etc.).

Thank you to Cornelia Prior: my Fitzy sibling. Thanks for Paris.
Thanks for always being able to pick up exactly where we left off.

Thank you, Potkin-Daunts, for bed and board, baths, dinners,
dresses, Zuri 'Danger' Daunt, and my fairy goddaughter Leila.

Thank you to Leila 'The Kid' Abley for being the kind of joyful,
dedicated writer I always try to be. I'm sorry this book is lacking in aliens
and dolphins and horses and hip hop. I cannot wait to read all of yours.

Thank you to Josie Porridge, the kindest person I have ever met, for making everyone see the world the way you see it: beautiful and new and alive.

Thank you to Felix Hagan & The Family for teaching us to box-step, and for every dazzling evening over the years. Thanks for the houseful of glitter. Thank you, Hounds. Thank you, Ellie and Mike and Alice and my oldest friend Lettie – for being such easy company in the worst few months. Dancing soon?

Thank you, Best For Film (dead now, of course). Truly, you yielded a bumper crop.

And above all, thank you to the gang. What an inadequate phrase that is for what you are and what I owe you. I could not have written a word of this without you. You are my family: my weird, beautiful, twisted little London family. There is nobody I would rather have walked through this fire with. Remember before we were older than the moon? This is a love letter to who we used to be, but I'm so proud of who we all are now.

To Caroline O'Donoghue, my chaste wife; my sister-in-arms; my smartest pig and promising young woman: what would I do without you? Thank you for everything. Thank you for *never* letting me forget myself.

To Gavin J. Day: thank you for being the most sound person in the world. I would call you to rescue me at four in the morning. Thank you for being around so unflinchingly, and making the awful things so much fun, and thank you for never, ever minding that I am always in your house.

To Sylv: I know you can't read, but you hate being left out. Thank you for giving us all a reason to get outside.

To Harry Harris: *imagine* if you hadn't been early for dinner that time. You will note there is no recipe for poaching an egg in this book. Thank you for everything (esp. the last three things), but particularly thank you for the music, the songs we're singing. Thanks for all the joy they're bringing. (Sorry.)

To Tash Hodgson (husband, government and high priestess), without whom none of this fiasco would ever have started – and without whom this book would never have been finished. Fingers never stood a chance, frankly. Miracle, miracle, miracle. Thank you.

And in memory of John Underwood: the Tall Man. I loved you more than anything in the world. I think I probably always will. Thank you for Eating With My Fingers. Thank you for teaching me to cook. Thank you for reading every word I wrote. Thank you for my life.

You ate everything in this book first; and you read every single draft except this very last one. (I'm sorry about all the overworked metaphors: you weren't here to take them out.)

You were my best editor, my best sous-chef and my best friend. This book is – as it has always been and always will be – for you. ATW.

—Ella Risbridger, London, June 2018

Bibliography

I am indebted to an enormous number of books, cooks, writers and thinkers, some of them explicitly, some implicitly. This is absolutely not an exhaustive list, and if you aren't on here and you think you probably should be, I am so sorry. Please consider this both a heartfelt acknowledgement and an expression of my gratitude for making me the person I am, for teaching me to cook, for teaching me to think, and for teaching me to think about food.

Joan Aiken, *The Cuckoo Tree*, Doubleday, 1971
Isabella Beeton, *Mrs Beeton's Book of Household Management*,
    S. O. Beeton, 1861
John Burningham, *Avocado Baby*, Jonathan Cape, 1982
Jane Brocket, *Cherry Cake and Ginger Beer*, Hodder & Stoughton, 2008
Dora Charles, *A Real Southern Cook*, Houghton Mifflin, 2015
Laurie Colwin, *Home Cooking*, Knopf Doubleday, 1988
Roald Dahl, *Danny the Champion of the World*, Jonathan Cape, 1975
Elizabeth Goudge, *The Runaways,* Hodder & Stoughton, 1964
Tim Hayward, *Food DIY*, Fig Tree, 2013
Marcella Hazan, *The Second Classic Italian Cookbook*, Macmillan, 1987
Diana Henry, *A Change of Appetite*, Mitchell Beazley, 2014
Diana Henry, *Simple*, Mitchell Beazley, 2016
Olia Hercules, *Mamushka*, Mitchell Beazley, 2015
Shirley Jackson, *We Have Always Lived in the Castle*, Viking Press, 1962
Barbara Kingsolver, *Animal, Vegetable, Miracle*, HarperCollins, 2007
Sophie Kinsella, *The Undomestic Goddess*, Black Swan, 2006
Judith Kerr, *The Tiger Who Came to Tea*, Harper, 1968
Nigella Lawson, *Feast*, Chatto & Windus, 2004
Nigella Lawson, *How To Eat*, Chatto & Windus, 1998
Laurie Lee, *Cider with Rosie*, Chatto & Windus, 1959
Laurie Lee, *I Can't Stay Long*, André Deutsch, 1975
Rebecca Lindenberg, *Love, an Index*, McSweeney's, 2012
Helen Macdonald, *H is for Hawk*, Jonathan Cape, 2014
Harold McGee, *McGee on Food & Cooking*, Hodder & Stoughton, 2004
E. Nesbit, *The Railway Children*, Wells Gardner, 1906
Sarah Perry, *The Essex Serpent*, Serpent's Tail, 2016
Dorothy L. Sayers, *Busman's Honeymoon*, Gollancz, 1937
Niki Segnit, *The Flavour Thesaurus*, Bloomsbury, 2010
Dodie Smith, *I Capture the Castle*, William Heinemann, 1948
Nigel Slater, *Appetite*, Fourth Estate, 2000
Nigel Slater, *Toast*, Fourth Estate, 2003
Helen Stevenson, *Love Like Salt*, Virago, 2016
Noel Streatfeild, *Apple Bough*, Collins, 1962
Alice B. Toklas, *The Alice B. Toklas Cookbook*, Harper, 1954
Martin Waddell, *Owl Babies*, Walker Books, 1992
Louise Walker, *The Traditional AGA Cookery Book*, Absolute Press, 1994
Valentine Warner, *The Good Table*, Mitchell Beazley, 2011
Alice Waters, *Recipes and Lessons from a Delicious Cooking Revolution*,
    Penguin, 2011

Index

BLOOMSBURY PUBLISHING
Bloomsbury Publishing Plc
50 Bedford Square, London, WC1B 3DP, UK

BLOOMSBURY, BLOOMSBURY PUBLISHING and the Diana logo are trademarks
of Bloomsbury Publishing Plc

First published in Great Britain 2019

Text © Ella Risbridger, 2019
Illustrations © Elisa Cunningham, 2019

A catalogue record for this book is available from the British Library

ISBN: HB: 978-1-4088-6776-1

2 4 6 8 10 9 7 5 3 1

Project Editor: Alison Cowan
Designer: Anita Mangan, anitamangan.co.uk
Illustrations: Elisa Cunningham, elisacunningham.com
Indexer: Vanessa Bird

Printed and bound in China by C&C Offset Printing Co., Ltd

Bloomsbury Publishing Plc makes every effort to ensure that the papers used in the
manufacture of our books are natural, recyclable products made from wood grown in
well-managed forests. Our manufacturing processes conform to the environmental
regulations of the country of origin.

To find out more about our authors and books visit www.bloomsbury.com and sign up
for our newsletters